MW01293604

Washington State Constitution

Table of Contents

PREAMBLE

We, the people of the State of Washington, grateful to the Supreme Ruler of the universe for our liberties, do ordain this constitution.

ARTICLE I DECLARATION OF RIGHTS

SECTION 1 POLITICAL POWER. All political power is inherent in the people, and governments derive their just powers from the consent of the governed, and are established to protect and maintain individual rights.

SECTION 2 SUPREME LAW OF THE LAND. The Constitution of the United States is the supreme law of the land.

SECTION 3 PERSONAL RIGHTS. No person shall be deprived of life, liberty, or property, without due process of law.

SECTION 4 RIGHT OF PETITION AND ASSEMBLAGE. The right of petition and of the people peaceably to assemble for the common good shall never be abridged.

SECTION 5 FREEDOM OF SPEECH. Every person may freely speak, write and publish on all subjects, being responsible for the abuse of that right.

SECTION 6 OATHS - MODE OF ADMINISTERING. The mode of administering an oath, or affirmation, shall be such as may be most consistent with and binding upon the conscience of the person to whom such oath, or affirmation, may be administered.

SECTION 7 INVASION OF PRIVATE AFFAIRS OR HOME PROHIBITED. No person shall be disturbed in his private affairs, or his home invaded, without authority of law.

SECTION 8 IRREVOCABLE PRIVILEGE, FRANCHISE OR IMMUNITY PROHIBITED. No law granting irrevocably any privilege, franchise or immunity, shall be passed by the legislature.

SECTION 9 RIGHTS OF ACCUSED PERSONS. No person shall be compelled in any criminal case to give evidence against himself, or be twice put in jeopardy for the same offense.

SECTION 10 ADMINISTRATION OF JUSTICE. Justice in all cases shall be administered openly, and without unnecessary delay.

SECTION 11 RELIGIOUS FREEDOM. Absolute freedom of conscience in all matters of religious sentiment, belief and worship, shall be guaranteed to every individual, and no one shall be molested or disturbed in person or property on account of religion; but the liberty of conscience hereby secured shall not be so construed as to excuse acts of licentiousness or justify practices inconsistent with the peace and safety of the state. No public money or property shall be appropriated for or applied to any religious worship, exercise or instruction, or the support of any religious establishment: PROVIDED, HOWEVER, That this article shall not be so construed as to forbid the employment by the state of a chaplain for such of the state custodial, correctional, and mental institutions, or by a county's or public hospital district's hospital, health care facility, or hospice, as in the discretion of the legislature may seem justified. No religious qualification shall be required for any public office or employment, nor shall any person be incompetent as a witness or juror, in consequence of his opinion on matters of religion, nor be questioned in any court of justice touching his religious belief to affect the weight of his testimony. [**AMENDMENT 88,** 1993 House Joint Resolution No. 4200, p 3062. Approved November 2, 1993.]

Amendment 34 (1957) — Art. 1 Section 11 RELIGIOUS FREEDOM — Absolute freedom of conscience in all matters of religious sentiment, belief and worship, shall be guaranteed to every individual, and no one shall be molested or disturbed in person or property on account of religion; but the liberty of conscience hereby secured shall not be so construed as to excuse acts of licentiousness or justify practices inconsistent with the peace and safety of the state. No public money or property shall be appropriated for or applied to any religious worship, exercise or instruction, or the support of any religious establishment: Provided, however, That this article shall not be so construed as to forbid the employment by the state of a chaplain for such of the state custodial, correctional and mental institutions as in the discretion of the legislature may seem justified. No religious qualification shall be required for any public office or employment, nor shall any person be incompetent as a witness or juror, in consequence of his opinion on matters of religion, nor be questioned in any court of justice touching his religious belief to affect the weight of his testimony. [AMENDMENT 34, 1957 Senate Joint Resolution No. 14, p 1299. Approved November 4, 1958.]

Amendment 4 (1904) — Art. 1 Section 11 RELIGIOUS FREEDOM — Absolute freedom of conscience in all matters of religious sentiment, belief and worship, shall be guaranteed to every individual, and no one shall be molested or disturbed in person or property on account of religion; but the liberty of conscience hereby secured shall not be so construed as to excuse acts of licentiousness or justify practices inconsistent with the peace and safety of the state. No public money or property shall be appropriated for or applied to any religious worship, exercise or instruction, or the support of any religious establishment. Provided, however, That this article shall not be so construed as to forbid the employment by the state of a chaplain for the state penitentiary, and for such of the state reformatories as in the discretion of the legislature may seem justified. No religious qualification shall be required for any public office or employment, nor shall any person be incompetent as a witness or juror, in consequence of his opinion on matters of religion, nor be questioned in any court of justice touching his religious belief to affect the weight of his testimony. [AMENDMENT 4, 1903 p 283 Section 1. Approved November, 1904.]

Original text — Art. 1 Section 11 RELIGIOUS FREEDOM — Absolute freedom of conscience in all matters of religious sentiment, belief, and worship, shall be guaranteed to every individual, and no one shall be molested or disturbed in person, or property, on account of religion; but the liberty of conscience hereby secured shall not be so construed as to excuse acts of licentiousness, or justify practices inconsistent with the peace and safety of the state. No public money or property shall be appropriated for, or applied to any religious worship, exercise or instruction, or the support of any religious establishment. No religious qualification shall be required for any public office, or employment, nor shall any person be incompetent as a witness, or juror, in consequence of his opinion on matters of religion, nor be questioned in any court of justice touching his religious belief to affect the weight of his testimony.

SECTION 12 SPECIAL PRIVILEGES AND IMMUNITIES PROHIBITED. No law shall be passed granting to any citizen, class of citizens, or corporation other than municipal, privileges or immunities which upon the same terms shall not equally belong to all citizens, or corporations.

SECTION 13 HABEAS CORPUS. The privilege of the writ of habeas corpus shall not be suspended, unless in case of rebellion or invasion the public safety requires it.

SECTION 14 EXCESSIVE BAIL, FINES AND PUNISHMENTS. Excessive bail shall not be required, excessive fines imposed, nor cruel punishment inflicted.

SECTION 15 CONVICTIONS, EFFECT OF. No conviction shall work corruption of blood, nor forfeiture of estate.

SECTION 16 EMINENT DOMAIN. Private property shall not be taken for private use, except for private ways of necessity, and for drains, flumes, or ditches on or across the lands of others for agricultural, domestic, or sanitary purposes. No private property shall be taken or damaged for public or private use without just compensation having been first made, or paid into court for the owner, and no right-of-way shall be appropriated to the use of any corporation other than municipal until full compensation therefor be first made in money, or ascertained and paid into court for the owner, irrespective of any benefit from any improvement proposed by such corporation, which compensation shall be ascertained by a jury, unless a jury be waived, as in other civil cases in courts of record, in the manner prescribed by law. Whenever an attempt is made to take private property for a use alleged to be public, the question whether the contemplated use be really public shall be a judicial question, and determined as such, without regard to any legislative assertion that the use is public: Provided, That the taking of private property by the state for land reclamation and settlement purposes is hereby declared to be for public use. [**AMENDMENT 9,** 1919 p 385 Section 1. Approved November, 1920.]

Original text — Art. 1 Section 16 EMINENT DOMAIN — Private property shall not be taken for private use, except for private ways of necessity, and for drains, flumes or ditches on or across the lands of others for agricultural, domestic or sanitary purposes. No private property shall be taken or damaged for public or private use without just compensation having first been made, or paid into court for the owner, and no right of way shall be appropriated to the use of any corporation other than municipal, until full compensation therefor be first made in money, or ascertained and paid into the court for the owner, irrespective of any benefit from any improvement proposed by such corporation, which compensation shall be ascertained by a jury, unless a jury be waived as in other civil cases in courts of record, in the manner prescribed by law. Whenever an attempt is made to take private property for a use alleged to be public, the question whether the contemplated use be really public shall be a judicial question, and determined as such without regard to any legislative assertion that the use is public.

SECTION 17 IMPRISONMENT FOR DEBT. There shall be no imprisonment for debt, except in cases of absconding debtors.

SECTION 18 MILITARY POWER, LIMITATION OF. The military shall be in strict subordination to the civil power.

SECTION 19 FREEDOM OF ELECTIONS. All Elections shall be free and equal, and no power, civil or military, shall at any time interfere to prevent the free exercise of the right of suffrage.

SECTION 20 BAIL, WHEN AUTHORIZED. All persons charged with crime shall be bailable by sufficient sureties, except for capital offenses when the proof is evident, or the presumption great. Bail may be denied for offenses punishable by the possibility of life in prison upon a showing by clear and convincing evidence of a propensity for violence that creates a substantial likelihood of danger to the community or any persons, subject to such limitations as shall be determined by the legislature. [**AMENDMENT 104,** 2010 Engrossed Substitute House Joint Resolution No. 4220, p 3129. Approved November 2, 2010.]

Original text — Art. 1 Section 20 BAIL, WHEN AUTHORIZED — All persons charged with crime shall be bailable by sufficient sureties, except for capital offenses when the proof is evident, or the presumption great.

SECTION 21 TRIAL BY JURY. The right of trial by jury shall remain inviolate, but the legislature may provide for a jury of any number less than twelve in courts not of record, and for a verdict by nine or more jurors in civil cases in any court of record, and for waiving of the jury in civil cases where the consent of the parties interested is given thereto.

SECTION 22 RIGHTS OF THE ACCUSED. In criminal prosecutions the accused shall have the right to appear and defend in person, or by counsel, to demand the nature and cause of the accusation against him, to have a copy thereof, to testify in his own behalf, to meet the witnesses against him face to face, to have compulsory process to compel the attendance of witnesses in his own behalf, to have a speedy public trial by an impartial jury of the county in which the offense is charged to have been committed and the right to appeal in all cases: Provided, The route traversed by any railway coach, train or public conveyance, and the water traversed by any boat shall be criminal districts; and the jurisdiction of all public offenses committed on any such railway car, coach, train, boat or other public conveyance, or at any station or depot upon such route, shall be in any county through which the said car, coach, train, boat or other public conveyance may pass during the trip or voyage, or in which the trip or voyage may begin or terminate. In no instance shall any accused person before final judgment be compelled to advance money or fees to secure the rights herein guaranteed. [**AMENDMENT 10,** 1921 p 79 Section 1. Approved November, 1922.]

Original text — Art. 1 Section 22 RIGHTS OF ACCUSED PERSONS — In criminal prosecution, the accused shall have the right to appear and defend in person, and by counsel, to demand the nature and cause of the accusation against him, to have a copy thereof, to testify in his own behalf, to meet the witnesses against him face to face, to have compulsory process to compel the attendance of witnesses in his own behalf, to have a speedy public trial by an impartial jury of the county in which the offense is alleged to have been committed, and the right to appeal in all cases; and, in no instance, shall any accused person before final judgment be compelled to advance money or fees to secure the rights herein guaranteed.

SECTION 23 BILL OF ATTAINDER, EX POST FACTO LAW, ETC. No bill of attainder, ex post facto law, or law impairing the obligations of contracts shall ever be passed.

SECTION 24 RIGHT TO BEAR ARMS. The right of the individual citizen to bear arms in defense of himself, or the state, shall not be impaired, but nothing in this section shall be construed as authorizing individuals or corporations to organize, maintain or employ an armed body of men.

SECTION 25 PROSECUTION BY INFORMATION. Offenses heretofore required to be prosecuted by indictment may be prosecuted by information, or by indictment, as shall be prescribed by law.

SECTION 26 GRAND JURY. No grand jury shall be drawn or summoned in any county, except the superior judge thereof shall so order.

SECTION 27 TREASON, DEFINED, ETC. Treason against the state shall consist only in levying war against the state, or adhering to its enemies, or in giving them aid and comfort. No person shall be convicted of treason unless on the testimony of two witnesses to the same overt act, or confession in open court.

SECTION 28 HEREDITARY PRIVILEGES ABOLISHED. No hereditary emoluments, privileges, or powers, shall be granted or conferred in this state.

SECTION 29 CONSTITUTION MANDATORY. The provisions of this Constitution are mandatory, unless by express words they are declared to be otherwise.

SECTION 30 RIGHTS RESERVED. The enumeration in this Constitution of certain rights shall not be construed to deny others retained by the people.

SECTION 31 STANDING ARMY. No standing army shall be kept up by this state in time of peace, and no soldier shall in time of peace be quartered in any house without the consent of its owner, nor in time of war except in the manner prescribed by law.

SECTION 32 FUNDAMENTAL PRINCIPLES. A frequent recurrence to fundamental principles is essential to the security of individual right and the perpetuity of free government.

SECTION 33 RECALL OF ELECTIVE OFFICERS. Every elective public officer of the state of Washington expect [except] judges of courts of record is subject to recall and discharge by the legal voters of the state, or of the political subdivision of the state, from which he was elected whenever a petition demanding his recall, reciting that such officer has committed some act or acts of malfeasance or misfeasance while in office, or who has violated his oath of office, stating the matters complained of, signed by the percentages of the qualified electors thereof, hereinafter provided, the percentage required to be computed from the total number of votes cast for all candidates for his said office to which he was elected at the preceding election, is filed with the officer with whom a petition for nomination, or certificate for nomination, to such office must be filed under the laws of this state, and the same officer shall call a special election as provided by the general election laws of this state, and the result determined as therein provided. [**AMENDMENT 8,**1911 p 504 Section 1. Approved November, 1912.]

SECTION 34 SAME. The legislature shall pass the necessary laws to carry out the provisions of section thirty-three (33) of this article, and to facilitate its operation and effect without delay: Provided, That the authority hereby conferred upon the legislature shall not be construed to grant to the legislature any exclusive power of lawmaking nor in any way limit the initiative and referendum powers reserved by the people. The percentages required shall be, state officers, other than judges, senators and representatives, city officers of cities of the first class, school district boards in cities of the first class; county officers of counties of the first, second and third classes, twenty-five per cent. Officers of all other political subdivisions, cities, towns, townships, precincts and school districts not herein mentioned, and state senators and representatives, thirty-five per cent. [**AMENDMENT 8,** 1911 p 504 Section 1. Approved November, 1912.]

SECTION 35 VICTIMS OF CRIMES — RIGHTS. Effective law enforcement depends on cooperation from victims of crime. To ensure victims a meaningful role in the criminal justice system and to accord them due dignity and respect, victims of crime are hereby granted the following basic and fundamental rights.

Upon notifying the prosecuting attorney, a victim of a crime charged as a felony shall have the right to be informed of and, subject to the discretion of the individual presiding over the trial or court proceedings, attend trial and all other court proceedings the defendant has the right to attend, and to make a statement at sentencing and at any proceeding where the defendant's release is considered, subject to the same rules of procedure which govern the defendant's rights. In the event the victim is deceased, incompetent, a minor, or otherwise unavailable, the prosecuting attorney may identify a representative to appear to exercise the victim's rights. This provision shall not constitute a basis for error in favor of a defendant in a criminal proceeding nor a basis for providing a victim or the victim's representative with court appointed counsel. [**AMENDMENT 84,** 1989 Senate Joint Resolution No. 8200, p 2999. Approved November 7, 1989.]

ARTICLE II LEGISLATIVE DEPARTMENT

SECTION 1 LEGISLATIVE POWERS, WHERE VESTED. The legislative authority of the state of Washington shall be vested in the legislature, consisting of a senate and house of representatives, which shall be called the legislature of the state of Washington, but the people reserve to themselves the power to propose bills, laws, and to enact or reject the same at the polls, independent of the legislature, and also reserve power, at their own option, to approve or reject at the polls any act, item, section, or part of any bill, act, or law passed by the legislature.

(a) Initiative: The first power reserved by the people is the initiative. Every such petition shall include the full text of the measure so proposed. In the case of initiatives to the legislature and initiatives to the people, the number of valid signatures of legal voters required shall be equal to eight percent of the votes cast for the office of governor at the last gubernatorial election preceding the initial filing of the text of the initiative measure with the secretary of state.

Initiative petitions shall be filed with the secretary of state not less than four months before the election at which they are to be voted upon, or not less than ten days before any regular session of the legislature. If filed at least four months before the election at which they are to be voted upon, he shall submit the same to the vote of the people at the said election. If such petitions are filed not less than ten days before any regular session of the legislature, he shall certify the results within forty days of the filing. If certification is not complete by the date that the legislature convenes, he shall provisionally certify the measure pending final certification of the measure. Such initiative measures, whether certified or provisionally certified, shall take precedence over all other measures in the legislature except appropriation bills and shall be either enacted or rejected without change or amendment by the legislature before the end of such regular session. If any such initiative measures shall be enacted by the legislature it shall be subject to the referendum petition, or it may be enacted and referred by the legislature to the people for approval or rejection at the next regular election. If it is rejected or if no action is taken upon it by the legislature before the end of such regular session, the secretary of state shall submit it to the people for approval or rejection at the next ensuing regular general election. The legislature may reject any measure so proposed by initiative petition and propose a different one dealing with the same subject, and in such event both measures shall be submitted by the secretary of state to the people for approval or rejection at the next ensuing regular general election. When conflicting measures are submitted to the people the ballots shall be so printed that a voter can express separately by making one cross (X) for each, two preferences, first, as between either measure and neither, and secondly, as between one and the other. If the majority of those voting on the first issue is for neither, both fail, but in that case the votes on the second issue shall nevertheless be carefully counted and made public. If a majority voting on the first issue is for either, then the measure receiving a majority of the votes on the second issue shall be law.

(b) Referendum. The second power reserved by the people is the referendum, and it may be ordered on any act, bill, law, or any part thereof passed by the legislature, except such laws as may be necessary for the immediate preservation of the public peace, health or safety, support of the state government and its existing public institutions, either by petition signed by the required percentage of the legal voters, or by the legislature as other bills are enacted: Provided, That the legislature may not order a referendum on any initiative measure enacted by the legislature under the foregoing subsection (a). The number of valid signatures of registered voters required on a petition for referendum of an act of the legislature or any part thereof, shall be equal to or exceeding four percent of the votes cast for the office of governor at the last gubernatorial election preceding the filing of the text of the referendum measure with the secretary of state.

(c) No act, law, or bill subject to referendum shall take effect until ninety days after the adjournment of the session at which it was enacted. No act, law, or bill approved by a majority of the electors voting thereon shall be amended or repealed by the legislature within a period of two years following such enactment: Provided, That any such act, law, or bill may be amended within two years after such enactment at any regular or special session of the legislature by a vote of two-thirds of all the members elected to each house with full compliance with section 12, Article III, of the Washington Constitution, and no amendatory law adopted in accordance with this provision shall be subject to referendum. But such enactment may be amended or repealed at any general regular or special election by direct vote of the people thereon.

(d) The filing of a referendum petition against one or more items, sections, or parts of any act, law, or bill shall not delay the remainder of the measure from becoming operative. Referendum petitions against measures passed by the legislature shall be filed with the secretary of state not later than ninety days after the final adjournment of the session of the legislature which passed the measure on which the referendum is demanded. The veto power of the governor shall not extend to measures initiated by or referred to the people. All elections on measures referred to the people of the state shall be had at the next succeeding regular general election following the filing of the measure with the secretary of state, except when the legislature shall order a special election. Any measure initiated by the people or referred to the people as herein provided shall take effect and become the law if it is approved by a majority of the votes cast thereon: Provided, That the vote cast upon such question or measure shall equal one-third of the total votes cast at such election and not otherwise. Such measure shall be in operation on and after the thirtieth day after the election at which it is approved. The style of all bills proposed by initiative petition shall be: "Be it enacted by the people of the State of Washington." This section shall not be construed to deprive any member of the legislature of the right to introduce any measure. All such petitions shall be filed with the secretary of state, who shall be guided by the general laws in submitting the same to the people until additional legislation shall especially provide therefor. This section is self-executing, but legislation may be enacted especially to facilitate its operation.

(e) The legislature shall provide methods of publicity of all laws or parts of laws, and amendments to the Constitution referred to the people with arguments for and against the laws and amendments so referred. The secretary of state shall send one copy of the publication to each individual place of residence in the state and shall make such additional distribution as he shall determine necessary to reasonably assure that each voter will have an opportunity to study the measures prior to election. [**AMENDMENT 72,** 1981 Substitute Senate Joint Resolution No. 133, p 1796. Approved November 3, 1981.]

Referendum procedures regarding salaries: Art. 28 Section 1.
Amendment 7 (1911) — Art. 2 Section 1 Legislative Powers, Where Vested — The legislative authority of the state of Washington shall be vested in the legislature, consisting of a

senate and house of representatives, which shall be called the legislature of the state of Washington, but the people reserve to themselves the power to propose bills, laws, and to enact or reject the same at the polls, independent of the legislature, and also reserve power, at their own option, to approve or reject at the polls any act, item, section or part of any bill, act or law passed by the legislature.

(a) Initiative: The first power reserved by the people is the initiative. Ten per centum, but in no case more than fifty thousand, of the legal voters shall be required to propose any measure by such petition, and every such petition shall include the full text of the measure so proposed. [Note: Signature requirements were superseded by Art. 2 Sec. 1(a), AMENDMENT 30.] Initiative petitions shall be filed with the secretary of state not less than four months before the election at which they are to be voted upon, or not less than ten days before any regular session of the legislature. If filed at least four months before the election at which they are to be voted upon, he shall submit the same to the vote of the people at the said election. If such petitions are filed not less than ten days before any regular session of the legislature, he shall transmit the same to the legislature as soon as it convenes and organizes. Such initiative measure shall take precedence over all other measures in the legislature except appropriation bills and shall be either enacted or rejected without change or amendment by the legislature before the end of such regular session. If any such initiative measures shall be enacted by the legislature it shall be subject to the referendum petition, or it may be enacted and referred by the legislature to the people for approval or rejection at the next regular election. If it is rejected or if no action is taken upon it by the legislature before the end of such regular session, the secretary of state shall submit it to the people for approval or rejection at the next ensuing regular general election. The legislature may reject any measure so proposed by initiative petition and propose a different one dealing with the same subject, and in such event both measures shall be submitted by the secretary of state to the people for approval or rejection at the next ensuing regular general election. When conflicting measures are submitted to the people the ballots shall be so printed that a voter can express separately by making one cross (X) for each, two preferences, first, as between either measure and neither, and secondly, as between one and the other. If the majority of those voting on the first issue is for neither, both fail, but in that case the votes on the second issue shall nevertheless be carefully counted and made public. If a majority voting on the first issue is for either, then the measure receiving a majority of the votes on the second issue shall be law.

(b) Referendum. The second power reserved by the people is the referendum, and it may be ordered on any act, bill, law, or any part thereof passed by the legislature, except such laws as may be necessary for the immediate preservation of the public peace, health or safety, support of the state government and its existing public institutions, either by petition signed by the required percentage of the legal voters, or by the legislature as other bills are enacted. Six per centum, but in no case more than thirty thousand, of the legal voters shall be required to sign and make a valid referendum petition. [Note: Signature requirements were superseded by Art. 2 Sec. 1(a), AMENDMENT 30.]

(c) No act, law, or bill subject to referendum shall take effect until ninety days after the adjournment of the session at which it was enacted. No act, law, or bill approved by a majority of the electors voting thereon shall be amended or repealed by the legislature within a period of two years following such enactment. But such enactment may be amended or repealed at any general regular or special election by direct vote of the people thereon. [Note: Subsection (c) was expressly superseded by Art. 2 Sec. 41, AMENDMENT 26.]

(d) The filing of a referendum petition against one or more items, sections or parts of any act, law or bill shall not delay the remainder of the measure from becoming operative. Referendum petitions against measures passed by the legislature shall be filed with the secretary of state not later than ninety days after the final adjournment of the session of the legislature which passed the measure on which the referendum is demanded. The veto power of the governor shall not extend to measures initiated by or referred to the people. All elections on measures referred to the people of the state shall be had at the biennial regular elections, except when the legislature shall order a special election. Any measure initiated by the people or referred to the people as herein provided shall take effect and become the law if it is approved by a majority of the votes cast thereon: Provided, That the vote cast upon such question or measure shall equal one-third of the total votes cast at such election and not otherwise. Such measure shall be in operation on and after the thirtieth day after the election at which it is approved. The style of all bills proposed by initiative petition shall be: "Be it enacted by the people of the State of Washington." This section shall not be construed to deprive any member of the legislature of the right to introduce any measure. The whole number of electors who voted for governor at the regular gubernatorial election last preceding the filing of any petition for the initiative or for the referendum shall be the basis on which the number of legal voters necessary to sign such petition shall be counted. [Note: Cf. Art. 2 Sec. 1(a), AMENDMENT 30.] All such petitions shall be filed with the secretary of state, who shall be guided by the general laws in submitting the same to the people until additional legislation shall especially provide therefor. This section is self-executing, but legislation may be enacted especially to facilitate its operation.

The legislature shall provide methods of publicity of all laws or parts of laws, and amendments to the Constitution referred to the people with arguments for and against the laws and amendments so referred, so that each voter of the state shall receive the publication at least fifty days before the election at which they are to be voted upon. [Note: This paragraph was expressly superseded by subsection (e) of this section, which was added by AMENDMENT 36.]

(e) The legislature shall provide methods of publicity of all laws or parts of laws, and amendments to the Constitution referred to the people with arguments for and against the laws and amendments so referred. The secretary of state shall send one copy of the publication to each individual place of residence in the state and shall make such additional distribution as he shall determine necessary to reasonably assure that each voter will have an opportunity to study the measures prior to election. These provisions supersede the provisions set forth in the last paragraph of section 1 of this article as amended by the seventh amendment to the Constitution of this state. [AMENDMENT 7, 1911 House Bill No. 153 p 136. Approved November, 1912; Subsection (e) added by AMENDMENT 36, 1961 Senate Joint Resolution No. 9, p 2751. Approved November, 1962.]

Original text — Art. 2 Section 1 LEGISLATIVE POWERS, WHERE VESTED — The legislative powers shall be vested in a senate and house of representatives, which shall be called the legislature of the State of Washington.

Note: Art. 2 Sec. 31 was also stricken by AMENDMENT 7.
SECTION 1(a) INITIATIVE AND REFERENDUM, SIGNATURES REQUIRED.[Stricken by AMENDMENT 72, 1981 Substitute Senate Joint Resolution No. 133, p 1796. Approved November 3, 1981.]

Amendment 30 (1956) — Art. 2 Section 1(a) INITIATIVE AND REFERENDUM, SIGNATURES REQUIRED — Hereafter, the number of valid signatures of legal voters required upon a petition for an initiative measure shall be equal to eight per centum of the number of voters registered and voting for the office of governor at the last preceding regular gubernatorial election. Hereafter, the number of valid signatures of legal voters required upon a petition for a referendum of an act of the legislature or any part thereof, shall be equal to four per centum of the number of voters registered and voting for the office of governor at the last preceding regular gubernatorial election. These provisions supersede the requirements specified in section 1 of this article as amended by the seventh amendment to the Constitution of this state. [AMENDMENT 30, 1955 Senate Joint Resolution No. 4, p 1860. Approved November 6, 1956.]

SECTION 2 HOUSE OF REPRESENTATIVES AND SENATE. The house of representatives shall be composed of not less than sixty-three nor more than ninety-nine members. The number of senators shall not be more than one-half nor less than one-third of the number of members of the house of representatives. The first legislature shall be composed of seventy members of the house of representatives, and thirty-five senators.

SECTION 3 THE CENSUS. [Repealed by AMENDMENT 74, 1983 Substitute Senate Joint Resolution No. 103, p 2202. Approved November 8, 1983.]

Original text — Art. 2 Section 3 THE CENSUS — The legislature shall provide by law for an enumeration of the inhabitants of the state in the year one thousand eight hundred and ninety-five and every ten years thereafter; and at the first session after such enumeration, and also after each enumeration made by the authority of the United States, the legislature shall apportion and district anew the members of the senate and house of representatives, according to the number of inhabitants, excluding Indians not taxed, soldiers, sailors and officers of the United States army and navy in active service.

SECTION 4 ELECTION OF REPRESENTATIVES AND TERM OF OFFICE. Members of the house of representatives shall be elected in the year eighteen hundred and eighty-nine at the time and in the manner provided by this Constitution, and shall hold their offices for the term of one year and until their successors shall be elected.

SECTION 5 ELECTIONS, WHEN TO BE HELD. The next election of the members of the house of representatives after the adoption of this Constitution shall be on the first Tuesday after the first Monday of November, eighteen hundred and ninety, and thereafter, members of the house of representatives shall be elected biennially and their term of office shall be two years; and each election shall be on the first Tuesday after the first Monday in November, unless otherwise changed by law.

SECTION 6 ELECTION AND TERM OF OFFICE OF SENATORS. After the first election the senators shall be elected by single districts of convenient and contiguous territory, at the same time and in the same manner as members of the house of representatives are required to be elected; and no representative district shall be divided in the formation of a senatorial district. They shall be elected for the term of four years, one-half of their number retiring every two years. The senatorial districts shall be numbered consecutively, and the senators chosen at the first election had by virtue of this Constitution, in odd numbered districts, shall go out of office at the end of the first year; and the senators, elected in the even numbered districts, shall go out of office at the end of the third year.

SECTION 7 QUALIFICATIONS OF LEGISLATORS. No person shall be eligible to the legislature who shall not be a citizen of the United States and a qualified voter in the district for which he is chosen.

SECTION 8 JUDGES OF THEIR OWN ELECTION AND QUALIFICATION - QUORUM. Each house shall be the judge of the election, returns and qualifications of its own members, and a majority of each house shall constitute a quorum to do business; but a smaller number may adjourn from day to day and may compel the attendance of absent members, in such manner and under such penalties as each house may provide.

Governmental continuity during emergency periods: Art. 2 Section 42.

SECTION 9 RULES OF PROCEDURE. Each house may determine the rules of its own proceedings, punish for contempt and disorderly behavior, and, with the concurrence of two-thirds of all the members elected, expel a member, but no member shall be expelled a second time for the same offense.

SECTION 10 ELECTION OF OFFICERS. Each house shall elect its own officers; and when the lieutenant governor shall not attend as president, or shall act as governor, the senate shall choose a temporary president. When presiding, the lieutenant governor shall have the deciding vote in case of an equal division of the senate.

SECTION 11 JOURNAL, PUBLICITY OF MEETINGS - ADJOURNMENTS. Each house shall keep a journal of its proceedings and publish the same, except such parts as require secrecy. The doors of each house shall be kept open, except when the public welfare shall require secrecy. Neither house shall adjourn for more than three days, nor to any place other than that in which they may be sitting, without the consent of the other.

SECTION 12 SESSIONS, WHEN — DURATION. (1) Regular Sessions. A regular session of the legislature shall be convened each year. Regular sessions shall convene on such day and at such time as the legislature shall determine by statute. During each odd-numbered year, the regular session shall not be more than one hundred five consecutive days. During each even-numbered year, the regular session shall not be more than sixty consecutive days.

(2) Special Legislative Sessions. Special legislative sessions may be convened for a period of not more than thirty consecutive days by proclamation of the governor pursuant to Article III, section 7 of this Constitution. Special legislative sessions may also be convened for a period of not more than thirty consecutive days by resolution of the legislature upon the affirmative vote in each house of two-thirds of the members elected or appointed thereto, which vote may be taken and resolution executed either while the legislature is in session or during any interim between sessions in accordance with such procedures as the legislature may provide by law or resolution. The resolution convening the legislature shall specify a purpose or purposes for the convening of a special session, and any special session convened by the resolution shall consider only measures germane to the purpose or purposes expressed in the resolution, unless by resolution adopted during the session upon the affirmative vote in each house of two-thirds of the members elected or appointed thereto, an additional purpose or purposes are expressed. The specification of purpose by the governor pursuant to Article III, section 7 of this Constitution shall be considered by the legislature but shall not be mandatory.

(3) Committees of the Legislature. Standing and special committees of the legislature shall meet and conduct official business pursuant to such rules as the legislature may adopt.
[**AMENDMENT 68,** 1979 Substitute Senate Joint Resolution No. 110, p 2286. Approved November 6, 1979.]

Extraordinary sessions to reconsider vetoes: Art. 3 Section 12.
Sessions to convene on the second Monday in January: RCW 44.04.010.

Original text — Art. 2 Section 12 SESSIONS, WHEN — DURATION — The first legislature shall meet on the first Wednesday after the first Monday in November, A. D., 1889. The second legislature shall meet on the first Wednesday after the first Monday in January, A. D., 1891, and sessions of the legislature shall be held biennially thereafter, unless specially convened by the governor, but the times of meeting of subsequent sessions may be changed by the legislature. After the first legislature the sessions shall not be more than sixty days.

SECTION 13 LIMITATION ON MEMBERS HOLDING OFFICE IN THE STATE. No member of the legislature, during the term for which he is elected, shall be appointed or elected to any civil office in the state, which shall have been created during the term for which he was elected. Any member of the legislature who is appointed or elected to any civil office in the state, the emoluments of which have been increased during his legislative term of office, shall be compensated for the initial term of the civil office at the level designated prior to the increase in emoluments. [**AMENDMENT 69,** 1979 Senate Joint Resolution No. 112, p 2287. Approved November 6, 1979.]

Original text — Art 2 Section 13 LIMITATION ON MEMBERS HOLDING OFFICE IN THE STATE — No member of the legislature, during the term for which he is elected, shall be appointed or elected to any civil office in the state, which shall have been created, or the emoluments of which shall have been increased, during the term for which he was elected.

SECTION 14 SAME, FEDERAL OR OTHER OFFICE. No person, being a member of congress, or holding any civil or military office under the United States or any other power, shall be eligible to be a member of the legislature; and if any person after his election as a member of the legislature, shall be elected to congress or be appointed to any other office, civil or military, under the government of the United States, or any other power, his acceptance thereof shall vacate his seat, provided, that officers in the militia of the state who receive no annual salary, local officers and postmasters, whose compensation does not exceed three hundred dollars per annum, shall not be ineligible.

SECTION 15 VACANCIES IN LEGISLATURE AND IN PARTISAN COUNTY ELECTIVE OFFICE. Such vacancies as may occur in either house of the legislature or in any partisan county elective office shall be filled by appointment by the county legislative authority of the county in which the vacancy occurs: Provided, That the person appointed to fill the vacancy must be from the same legislative district, county, or county commissioner or council district and the same political party as the legislator or partisan county elective officer whose office has been vacated, and shall be one of three persons who shall be nominated by the county central committee of that party, and in case a majority of the members of the county legislative authority do not agree upon the appointment within sixty days after the vacancy occurs, the governor shall within thirty days thereafter, and from the list of nominees provided for herein, appoint a person who shall be from the same legislative district, county, or county commissioner or council district and of the same political party as the legislator or partisan county elective officer whose office has been vacated, and the person so appointed shall hold office until his or her successor is elected at the next general election, and has qualified: Provided, That in case of a vacancy occurring after the general election in a year that the office appears on the ballot and before the start of the next term, the term of the successor who is of the same party as the incumbent may commence once he or she has qualified and shall continue through the term for which he or she was elected: Provided, That in case of a vacancy occurring in the office of joint senator, or joint representative, the vacancy shall be filled from a list of three nominees selected by the state central committee, by appointment by the joint action of the boards of county legislative authorities of the counties composing the joint senatorial or joint representative district, the person appointed to fill the vacancy must be from the same legislative district and of the same political party as the legislator whose office has been vacated, and in case a majority of the members of the county legislative authority do not agree upon the appointment within sixty days after the vacancy occurs, the governor shall within thirty days thereafter, and from the list of nominees provided for herein, appoint a person who shall be from the same legislative district and of the same political party as the legislator whose office has been vacated. [**AMENDMENT 96,** 2003 House Joint Resolution No. 4206, p 2819. Approved November 4, 2003.]

Governmental continuity during emergency periods: Art. 2 Section 42.
Vacancies in county, etc., offices, how filled: Art. 11 Section 6.
Amendment 52, part (1967) — Art. 2 Section 15 VACANCIES IN LEGISLATURE AND IN PARTISAN COUNTY ELECTIVE OFFICE — Such vacancies as may occur in either

house of the legislature or in any partisan county elective office shall be filled by appointment by the board of county commissioners of the county in which the vacancy occurs: Provided, That the person appointed to fill the vacancy must be from the same legislative district, county or county commissioner district and the same political party as the legislator or partisan county elective officer whose office has been vacated, and shall be one of three persons who shall be nominated by the county central committee of that party, and in case a majority of said county commissioners do not agree upon the appointment within sixty days after the vacancy occurs, the governor shall within thirty days thereafter, and from the list of nominees provided for herein, appoint a person who shall be from the same legislative district, county or county commissioner district and of the same political party as the legislator or partisan county elective officer whose office has been vacated, and the person so appointed shall hold office until his successor is elected at the next general election, and shall have qualified: Provided, That in case of a vacancy occurring in the office of joint senator, or joint representative, the vacancy shall be filled from a list of three nominees selected by the state central committee, by appointment by the joint action of the boards of county commissioners of the counties composing the joint senatorial or joint representative district, the person appointed to fill the vacancy must be from the same legislative district and of the same political party as the legislator whose office has been vacated, and in case a majority of said county commissioners do not agree upon the appointment within sixty days after the vacancy occurs, the governor shall within thirty days thereafter, and from the list of nominees provided for herein, appoint a person who shall be from the same legislative district and of the same political party as the legislator whose office has been vacated. [AMENDMENT 52, part, 1967 Senate Joint Resolution No. 24, part; see 1969 p 2976. Approved November 5, 1968.]

Amendment 32 (1956) — Art. 2 Section 15 VACANCIES IN LEGISLATURE AND IN PARTISAN COUNTY ELECTIVE OFFICE —Such vacancies as may occur in either house of the legislature or in any partisan county elective office shall be filled by appointment by the board of county commissioners of the county in which the vacancy occurs: Provided, That the person appointed to fill the vacancy must be from the same legislative district and the same political party as the legislator whose office has been vacated, and shall be one of three persons who shall be nominated by the county central committee of that party, and the person so appointed shall hold office until his successor is elected at the next general election, and shall have qualified: Provided, That in case of a vacancy occurring in the office of joint senator, or joint representative, the vacancy shall be filled from a list of three nominees selected by the state central committee, by appointment by the joint action of the boards of county commissioners of the counties composing the joint senatorial or joint representative district, the person appointed to fill the vacancy must be from the same legislative district and of the same political party as the legislator whose office has been vacated, and in case a majority of said county commissioners do not agree upon the appointment within sixty days after the vacancy occurs, the governor shall within thirty days thereafter, and from the list of nominees provided for herein, appoint a person who shall be from the same legislative district and of the same political party as the legislator whose office has been vacated. [AMENDMENT 32, 1955 Senate Joint Resolution No. 14, p 1862. Approved November 6, 1956.]

Amendment 13 (1930) — Art. 2 Section 15 VACANCIES IN LEGISLATURE — Such vacancies as may occur in either house of the legislature shall be filled by appointment by the board of county commissioners of the county in which the vacancy occurs, and the person so appointed shall hold office until his successor is elected at the next general election, and shall have qualified: Provided, That in case of a vacancy occurring in the office of joint senator, the vacancy shall be filled by appointment by the joint action of the boards of county commissioners of the counties composing the joint senatorial district. [AMENDMENT 13, 1929 p 690. Approved November, 1930.]

Original text — Art. 2 Section 15 WRITS OF ELECTION TO FILL VACANCIES — The governor shall issue writs of election to fill such vacancies as may occur in either house of the legislature.

SECTION 16 PRIVILEGES FROM ARREST. Members of the legislature shall be privileged from arrest in all cases except treason, felony and breach of the peace; they shall not be subject to any civil process during the session of the legislature, nor for fifteen days next before the commencement of each session.

SECTION 17 FREEDOM OF DEBATE. No member of the legislature shall be liable in any civil action or criminal prosecution whatever, for words spoken in debate.

SECTION 18 STYLE OF LAWS. The style of the laws of the state shall be: "Be it enacted by the Legislature of the State of Washington." And no laws shall be enacted except by bill.

SECTION 19 BILL TO CONTAIN ONE SUBJECT. No bill shall embrace more than one subject, and that shall be expressed in the title.

SECTION 20 ORIGIN AND AMENDMENT OF BILLS. Any bill may originate in either house of the legislature, and a bill passed by one house may be amended in the other.

SECTION 21 YEAS AND NAYS. The yeas and nays of the members of either house shall be entered on the journal, on the demand of one-sixth of the members present.

SECTION 22 PASSAGE OF BILLS. No bill shall become a law unless on its final passage the vote be taken by yeas and nays, the names of the members voting for and against the same be entered on the journal of each house, and a majority of the members elected to each house be recorded thereon as voting in its favor.

Governmental continuity during emergency periods: Art. 2 Section 42.

SECTION 23 COMPENSATION OF MEMBERS. Each member of the legislature shall receive for his services five dollars for each day's attendance during the session, and ten cents for every mile he shall travel in going to and returning from the place of meeting of the legislature, on the most usual route.

Compensation of legislators, elected state officials, and judges: Art. 28 Section 1, Art. 30.

SECTION 24 LOTTERIES AND DIVORCE. The legislature shall never grant any divorce. Lotteries shall be prohibited except as specifically authorized upon the affirmative vote of sixty percent of the members of each house of the legislature or, notwithstanding any other provision of this Constitution, by referendum or initiative approved by a sixty percent affirmative vote of the electors voting thereon. [**AMENDMENT 56,** 1971 Senate Joint Resolution No. 5, p 1828. Approved November 7, 1972.]

Original text — Art. 2 Section 24 LOTTERIES AND DIVORCE — The legislature shall never authorize any lottery or grant any divorce.

SECTION 25 EXTRA COMPENSATION PROHIBITED. The legislature shall never grant any extra compensation to any public officer, agent, employee, servant, or contractor, after the services shall have been rendered, or the contract entered into, nor shall the compensation of any public officer be increased or diminished during his term of office. Nothing in this section shall be deemed to prevent increases in pensions after such pensions shall have been granted. [**AMENDMENT 35,** 1957 Senate Joint Resolution No. 18, p 1301. Approved November 4, 1958.]

Compensation of legislators, elected state officials, and judges: Art. 28 Section 1.

Increase during term of certain officers, authorized: Art. 30 Section 1.
Increase or diminution of compensation during term of office prohibited.
county, city, town or municipal officers: Art. 11 Section 8.
judicial officers: Art. 4 Section 13.
state officers: Art. 3 Section 25.

Original text — Art. 2 Section 25 EXTRA COMPENSATION, PROHIBITED — The legislature shall never grant any extra compensation to any public officer, agent, servant, or contractor, after the services shall have been rendered, or the contract entered into, nor shall the compensation of any public officer be increased or diminished during his term of office.

SECTION 26 SUITS AGAINST THE STATE. The legislature shall direct by law, in what manner, and in what courts, suits may be brought against the state.

SECTION 27 ELECTIONS — VIVA VOCE VOTE. In all elections by the legislature the members shall vote viva voce, and their votes shall be entered on the journal.

SECTION 28 SPECIAL LEGISLATION. The legislature is prohibited from enacting any private or special laws in the following cases:

1. For changing the names of persons, or constituting one person the heir at law of another.

2. For laying out, opening or altering highways, except in cases of state roads extending into more than one county, and military roads to aid in the construction of which lands shall have been or may be granted by congress.

3. For authorizing persons to keep ferries wholly within this state.

4. For authorizing the sale or mortgage of real or personal property of minors, or others under disability.

5. For assessment or collection of taxes, or for extending the time for collection thereof.

6. For granting corporate powers or privileges.

7. For authorizing the apportionment of any part of the school fund.

8. For incorporating any town or village or to amend the charter thereof.

9. From giving effect to invalid deeds, wills or other instruments.

10. Releasing or extinguishing in whole or in part, the indebtedness, liability or other obligation, of any person, or corporation to this state, or to any municipal corporation therein.

11. Declaring any person of age or authorizing any minor to sell, lease, or encumber his or her property.

12. Legalizing, except as against the state, the unauthorized or invalid act of any officer.

13. Regulating the rates of interest on money.

14. Remitting fines, penalties or forfeitures.

15. Providing for the management of common schools.

16. Authorizing the adoption of children.

17. For limitation of civil or criminal actions.

18. Changing county lines, locating or changing county seats, provided, this shall not be construed to apply to the creation of new counties.

Corporations for municipal purposes shall not be created by special laws: Art. 11 Section 10.

SECTION 29 CONVICT LABOR. The labor of inmates of this state shall not be let out by contract to any person, copartnership, company, or corporation, except as provided by statute, and the legislature shall by law provide for the working of inmates for the benefit of the state, including the working of inmates in state-run inmate labor programs. Inmate labor programs provided by statute that are operated and managed, in total or in part, by any profit or nonprofit entities shall be operated so that the programs do not unfairly compete with Washington businesses as determined by law. [**AMENDMENT 100,** 2007 Senate Joint Resolution No. 8212, p 3143. Approved November 6, 2007.]

Original text — Art. 2 Section 29 CONVICT LABOR — After the first day of January eighteen hundred and ninety the labor of convicts of this state shall not be let out by contract to any person, copartnership, company or corporation, and the legislature shall by law provide for the working of convicts for the benefit of the state.

SECTION 30 BRIBERY OR CORRUPT SOLICITATION. The offense of corrupt solicitation of members of the legislature, or of public officers of the state or any municipal division thereof, and any occupation or practice of solicitation of such members or officers to influence their official action, shall be defined by law, and shall be punished by fine and imprisonment. Any person may be compelled to testify in any lawful investigation or judicial proceeding against any person who may be charged with having committed the offense of bribery or corrupt solicitation, or practice of solicitation, and shall not be permitted to withhold his testimony on the ground that it may criminate himself or subject him to public infamy, but such testimony shall not afterwards be used against him in any judicial proceeding - except for perjury in giving such testimony - and any person convicted of either of the offenses aforesaid, shall as part of the punishment therefor, be disqualified from ever holding any position of honor, trust or profit in this state. A member who has a private interest in any bill or measure proposed or pending before the legislature, shall disclose the fact to the house of which he is a member, and shall not vote thereon.

SECTION 31 LAWS, WHEN TO TAKE EFFECT. [This section stricken by AMENDMENT 7, 1911 House Bill No. 153, p 136. Approved November, 1912.]

Original text — Art. 2 Section 31 LAWS, WHEN TO TAKE EFFECT — No law, except appropriation bills, shall take effect until ninety days after the adjournment of the session at which it was enacted, unless in case of an emergency (which emergency must be expressed in the preamble or in the body of the act) the legislature shall otherwise direct by a vote of two-thirds of all the members elected to each house; said vote to be taken by yeas and nays and entered on the journals.

Effective dates of laws: Art. 2 Sections 1 and 41.

SECTION 32 LAWS, HOW SIGNED. No bill shall become a law until the same shall have been signed by the presiding officer of each of the two houses in open session, and under such rules as the legislature shall prescribe.

SECTION 33 ALIEN OWNERSHIP. [Repealed by AMENDMENT 42, 1965 ex.s. Senate Joint Resolution No. 20, p 2816. Approved November 8, 1966.]

Amendment 29 (1954) — Art. 2 Section 33 ALIEN OWNERSHIP — The ownership of lands by aliens, other than those who in good faith have declared their intention to become citizens of the United States, is prohibited in this state, except where acquired by inheritance, under mortgage or in good faith in the ordinary course of justice in the collection of debts; and all conveyances of lands hereafter made to any alien directly, or in trust for such alien, shall be void: Provided, That the provisions of this section shall not apply to lands containing valuable deposits of minerals, metals, iron, coal, or fire clay, and the necessary land for mills and machinery to be used in the development thereof and the manufacture of the products therefrom: And provided further, That the provisions of this section shall not apply to the citizens of such of the Provinces of the Dominion of Canada as do not expressly or by implication prohibit ownership of provincial lands by citizens of this state. [AMENDMENT 29, 1953 House Joint Resolution No. 16, p 853. Approved November 2, 1954.]

Amendment 24 (1950) — Art. 2 Section 33 ALIEN OWNERSHIP — The ownership of lands by aliens, other than those who in good faith have declared their intention to become citizens of the United States, is prohibited in this state, except where acquired by inheritance, under mortgage or in good faith in the ordinary course of justice in the collection of debts; and all conveyances of lands hereafter made to any alien directly, or in trust for such alien, shall be void: Provided, That the provisions of this section shall not apply to lands containing valuable deposits of minerals, metals, iron, coal, or fire clay, and the necessary land for mills and machinery to be used in the development thereof and the manufacture of the products therefrom: And provided further, That the provisions of this section shall not apply to the citizens of such of the Provinces of the Dominion of Canada as do not expressly or by implication prohibit ownership of provincial lands by citizens of this state. Every corporation, the majority of the capital stock of which is owned by aliens, shall be considered an alien for the purposes of this prohibition. [AMENDMENT 24, 1949 Senate Joint Resolution No. 9, p 999. Approved November, 1950.]

Original text — Art. 2 Section 33 OWNERSHIP OF LANDS BY ALIENS, PROHIBITED — Exceptions — The ownership of lands by aliens, other than those who in good faith have declared their intention to become citizens of the United States, is prohibited in this state, except where acquired by inheritance, under mortgage or in good faith in the ordinary course of justice in the collection of debts; and all conveyances of lands hereafter made to any alien directly or in trust for such alien shall be void: Provided, That the provisions of this section shall not apply to lands containing valuable deposits of minerals, metals, iron, coal, or fire-clay, and the necessary land for mills and machinery to be used in the development thereof and the manufacture of the products therefrom. Every corporation, the majority of the capital stock of which is owned by aliens, shall be considered on alien for the purposes of this prohibition.

SECTION 34 BUREAU OF STATISTICS, AGRICULTURE AND IMMIGRATION. There shall be established in the office of the secretary of state, a bureau of statistics, agriculture and immigration, under such regulations as the legislature may provide.

SECTION 35 PROTECTION OF EMPLOYEES. The legislature shall pass necessary laws for the protection of persons working in mines, factories and other employments dangerous to life or deleterious to health; and fix pains and penalties for the enforcement of the same.

SECTION 36 WHEN BILLS MUST BE INTRODUCED. No bill shall be considered in either house unless the time of its introduction shall have been at least ten days before the final adjournment of the legislature, unless the legislature shall otherwise direct by a vote of two-thirds of all the members elected to each house, said vote to be taken by yeas and nays and entered upon the journal, or unless the same be at a special session.

SECTION 37 REVISION OR AMENDMENT. No act shall ever be revised or amended by mere reference to its title, but the act revised or the section amended shall be set forth at full length.

SECTION 38 LIMITATION ON AMENDMENTS. No amendment to any bill shall be allowed which shall change the scope and object of the bill.

SECTION 39 FREE TRANSPORTATION TO PUBLIC OFFICER PROHIBITED. It shall not be lawful for any person holding public office in this state to accept or use a pass or to purchase transportation from any railroad or other corporation, other than as the same may be purchased by the general public, and the legislature shall pass laws to enforce this provision.

SECTION 40 HIGHWAY FUNDS. All fees collected by the State of Washington as license fees for motor vehicles and all excise taxes collected by the State of Washington on the sale, distribution or use of motor vehicle fuel and all other state revenue intended to be used for highway purposes, shall be paid into the state treasury and placed in a special fund to be used exclusively for highway purposes. Such highway purposes shall be construed to include the following:

(a) The necessary operating, engineering and legal expenses connected with the administration of public highways, county roads and city streets;

(b) The construction, reconstruction, maintenance, repair, and betterment of public highways, county roads, bridges and city streets; including the cost and expense of (1) acquisition of rights-of-way, (2) installing, maintaining and operating traffic signs and signal lights, (3) policing by the state of public highways, (4) operation of movable span bridges, (5) operation of ferries which are a part of any public highway, county road, or city street;

(c) The payment or refunding of any obligation of the State of Washington, or any political subdivision thereof, for which any of the revenues described in section 1 may have been legally pledged prior to the effective date of this act;

(d) Refunds authorized by law for taxes paid on motor vehicle fuels;

(e) The cost of collection of any revenues described in this section:

Provided, That this section shall not be construed to include revenue from general or special taxes or excises not levied primarily for highway purposes, or apply to vehicle operator's license fees or any excise tax imposed on motor vehicles or the use thereof in lieu of a property tax thereon, or fees for certificates of ownership of motor vehicles. [**AMENDMENT 18,** 1943 House Joint Resolution No. 4, p 938. Approved November, 1944.]

SECTION 41 LAWS, EFFECTIVE DATE, INITIATIVE, REFERENDUM —AMENDMENT OR REPEAL. No act, law, or bill subject to referendum shall take effect until ninety days after the adjournment of the session at which it was enacted. No act, law or bill approved by a majority of the electors voting thereon shall be amended or repealed by the legislature within a period of two years following such enactment: Provided, That any such act, law or bill may be amended within two years after such enactment at any regular or special session of the legislature by a vote of two-thirds of all the members elected to each house with full compliance with section 12, Article III, of the Washington Constitution, and no amendatory law adopted in accordance with this provision shall be subject to referendum. But such enactment may be amended or repealed at any general regular or special election by direct vote of the people thereon. These provisions supersede the provisions of subsection (c) of section 1 of this article as amended by the seventh amendment to the Constitution of this state. [**AMENDMENT 26,** 1951 Substitute Senate Joint Resolution No. 7, p 959. Approved November 4, 1952.]

Reviser's note: (1) In third sentence, comma between "general" and "regular" omitted in conformity with enrolled resolution.

(2) Subsection (c) of section 1 of this article was amended by Amendment 72, approved November 3, 1981.

SECTION 42 GOVERNMENTAL CONTINUITY DURING EMERGENCY PERIODS. The legislature, in order to insure continuity of state and local governmental operations in periods of emergency resulting from enemy attack, shall have the power and the duty, immediately upon and after adoption of this amendment, to enact legislation providing for prompt and temporary succession to the powers and duties of public offices of whatever nature and whether filled by election or appointment, the incumbents and legal successors of which may become unavailable for carrying on the powers and duties of such offices; the legislature shall likewise enact such other measures as may be necessary and proper for insuring the continuity of governmental operations during such emergencies. Legislation enacted under the powers conferred by this amendment shall in all respects conform to the remainder of the Constitution: Provided, That if, in the judgment of the legislature at the time of disaster, conformance to the provisions of the Constitution would be impracticable or would admit of undue delay, such legislation may depart during the period of emergency caused by enemy attack only, from the following sections of the Constitution:

Article 14, Sections 1 and 2, Seat of Government;

Article 2, Sections 8, 15 (Amendments 13 and 32), and 22, Membership, Quorum of Legislature and Passage of Bills;

Article 3, Section 10 (Amendment 6), Succession to Governorship: Provided, That the legislature shall not depart from Section 10, Article III, as amended by Amendment 6, of the state Constitution relating to the Governor's office so long as any successor therein named is available and capable of assuming the powers and duties of such office as therein prescribed;

Article 3, Section 13, Vacancies in State Offices;

Article 11, Section 6, Vacancies in County Offices;

Article 11, Section 2, Seat of County Government;

Article 3, Section 24, State Records. [**AMENDMENT 39,** 1961 House Joint Resolution No. 9, p 2758. Approved November, 1962.]

Continuity of government act: Chapter 42.14 RCW.

SECTION 43 REDISTRICTING. (1) In January of each year ending in one, a commission shall be established to provide for the redistricting of state legislative and congressional districts.

(2) The commission shall be composed of five members to be selected as follows: The legislative leader of the two largest political parties in each house of the legislature shall appoint one voting member to the commission by January 15th of each year ending in one. By January 31st of each year ending in one, the four appointed members, by an affirmative vote of at least three, shall appoint the remaining member. The fifth member of the commission, who shall be nonvoting, shall act as its chairperson. If any appointing authority fails to make the required appointment by the date established by this subsection, within five days after that date the supreme court shall make the required appointment.

(3) No elected official and no person elected to legislative district, county, or state political party office may serve on the commission. A commission member shall not have been an elected official and shall not have been an elected legislative district, county, or state political party officer within two years of his or her appointment to the commission. The provisions of this subsection do not apply to the office of precinct committee person.

(4) The legislature shall enact laws providing for the implementation of this section, to include additional qualifications for commissioners and additional standards to govern the commission. The legislature shall appropriate funds to enable the commission to carry out its duties.

(5) Each district shall contain a population, excluding nonresident military personnel, as nearly equal as practicable to the population of any other district. To the extent reasonable, each district shall contain contiguous territory, shall be compact and convenient, and shall be separated from adjoining districts by natural geographic barriers, artificial barriers, or political subdivision boundaries. The commission's plan shall not provide for a number of legislative districts different than that established by the legislature. The commission's plan shall not be drawn purposely to favor or discriminate against any political party or group.

(6) The commission shall complete redistricting as soon as possible following the federal decennial census, but no later than November 15th of each year ending in one. At least three of the voting members shall approve such a redistricting plan. If three of the voting members of the commission fail to approve a plan within the time limitations provided in this subsection, the supreme court shall adopt a plan by April 30th of the year ending in two in conformance with the standards set forth in subsection (5) of this section.

(7) The legislature may amend the redistricting plan but must do so by a two-thirds vote of the legislators elected or appointed to each house of the legislature. Any amendment must have passed both houses by the end of the thirtieth day of the first session convened after the commission has submitted its plan to the legislature. After that day, the plan, with any legislative amendments, constitutes the state districting law.

(8) The legislature shall enact laws providing for the reconvening of a commission for the purpose of modifying a districting law adopted under this section. Such reconvening requires a two-thirds vote of the legislators elected or appointed to each house of the legislature. The commission shall conform to the standards prescribed under subsection (5) of this section and any other standards or procedures that the legislature may provide by law. At least three of the voting members shall approve such a modification. Any modification adopted by the commission may be amended by a two-thirds vote of the legislators elected and appointed to each house of the legislature. The state districting law shall include the modifications with amendments, if any.

(9) The legislature shall prescribe by law the terms of commission members and the method of filling vacancies on the commission.

(10) The supreme court has original jurisdiction to hear and decide all cases involving congressional and legislative redistricting.

(11) Legislative and congressional districts may not be changed or established except pursuant to this section. A districting plan and any legislative amendments to the plan are not subject to Article III, section 12 of this Constitution. [**AMENDMENT 108,** 2016 Senate Joint Resolution No. 8210. Approved November 8, 2016.]

Amendment 74 (1983) — Art. 2 Section 43 REDISTRICTING — (1) In January of each year ending in one, a commission shall be established to provide for the redistricting of state legislative and congressional districts.

(2) The commission shall be composed of five members to be selected as follows: The legislative leader of the two largest political parties in each house of the legislature shall appoint one voting member to the commission by January 15th of each year ending in one. By January 31st of each year ending in one, the four appointed members, by an affirmative vote of at least three, shall appoint the remaining member. The fifth member of the commission, who shall be nonvoting, shall act as its chairperson. If any appointing authority fails to make the required appointment by the date established by this subsection, within five days after that date the supreme court shall make the required appointment.

(3) No elected official and no person elected to legislative district, county, or state political party office may serve on the commission. A commission member shall not have been an elected official and shall not have been an elected legislative district, county, or state political party officer within two years of his or her appointment to the commission. The provisions of this subsection do not apply to the office of precinct committee person.

(4) The legislature shall enact laws providing for the implementation of this section, to include additional qualifications for commissioners and additional standards to govern the commission. The legislature shall appropriate funds to enable the commission to carry out its duties.

(5) Each district shall contain a population, excluding nonresident military personnel, as nearly equal as practicable to the population of any other district. To the extent reasonable, each district shall contain contiguous territory, shall be compact and convenient, and shall be separated from adjoining districts by natural geographic barriers, artificial barriers, or political subdivision boundaries. The commission's plan shall not provide for a number of legislative districts different than that established by the legislature. The commission's plan shall not be drawn purposely to favor or discriminate against any political party or group.

(6) The commission shall complete redistricting as soon as possible following the federal decennial census, but no later than January 1st of each year ending in two. At least three of the voting members shall approve such a redistricting plan. If three of the voting members of the commission fail to approve a plan within the time limitations provided in this subsection, the supreme court shall adopt a plan by April 30th of the year ending in two in conformance with the standards set forth in subsection (5) of this section.

(7) The legislature may amend the redistricting plan but must do so by a two-thirds vote of the legislators elected or appointed to each house of the legislature. Any amendment must have passed both houses by the end of the thirtieth day of the first session convened after the commission has submitted its plan to the legislature. After that day, the plan, with any legislative amendments, constitutes the state districting law.

(8) The legislature shall enact laws providing for the reconvening of a commission for the purpose of modifying a districting law adopted under this section. Such reconvening requires a two-thirds vote of the legislators elected or appointed to each house of the legislature. The commission shall conform to the standards prescribed under subsection (5) of this section and any other standards or procedures that the legislature may provide by law. At least three of the voting members shall approve such a modification. Any modification adopted by the commission may be amended by a two-thirds vote of the legislators elected and appointed to each house of the legislature. The state districting law shall include the modifications with amendments, if any.

(9) The legislature shall prescribe by law the terms of commission members and the method of filling vacancies on the commission.

(10) The supreme court has original jurisdiction to hear and decide all cases involving congressional and legislative redistricting.

(11) Legislative and congressional districts may not be changed or established except pursuant to this section. A districting plan and any legislative amendments to the plan are not subject to Article III, section 12 of this Constitution. [AMENDMENT 74, 1983 Substitute Senate Joint Resolution No. 103, p 2202. Approved November 8, 1983.]

ARTICLE III
THE EXECUTIVE

SECTION 1 EXECUTIVE DEPARTMENT. The executive department shall consist of a governor, lieutenant governor, secretary of state, treasurer, auditor, attorney general, superintendent of public instruction, and a commissioner of public lands, who shall be severally chosen by the qualified electors of the state at the same time and place of voting as for the members of the legislature.

SECTION 2 GOVERNOR, TERM OF OFFICE. The supreme executive power of this state shall be vested in a governor, who shall hold his office for a term of four years, and until his successor is elected and qualified.

SECTION 3 OTHER EXECUTIVE OFFICERS, TERMS OF OFFICE. The lieutenant governor, secretary of state, treasurer, auditor, attorney general, superintendent of public instruction, and commissioner of public lands, shall hold their offices for four years respectively, and until their successors are elected and qualified.

SECTION 4 RETURNS OF ELECTIONS, CANVASS, ETC. The returns of every election for the officers named in the first section of this article shall be sealed up and transmitted to the seat of government by the returning officers, directed to the secretary of state, who shall deliver the same to the speaker of the house of representatives at the first meeting of the house thereafter, who shall open, publish and declare the result thereof in the presence of a majority of the members of both houses. The person having the highest number of votes shall be declared duly elected, and a certificate thereof shall be given to such person, signed by the presiding officers of both houses; but if any two or more shall be highest and equal in votes for the same office, one of them shall be chosen by the joint vote of both houses. Contested elections for such officers shall be decided by the legislature in such manner as shall be determined by law. The terms of all officers named in section one of this article shall commence on the second Monday in January after their election until otherwise provided by law.

SECTION 5 GENERAL DUTIES OF GOVERNOR. The governor may require information in writing from the officers of the state upon any subject relating to the duties of their respective offices, and shall see that the laws are faithfully executed.

SECTION 6 MESSAGES. He shall communicate at every session by message to the legislature the condition of the affairs of the state, and recommend such measures as he shall deem expedient for their action.

SECTION 7 EXTRA LEGISLATIVE SESSIONS. He may, on extraordinary occasions, convene the legislature by proclamation, in which shall be stated the purposes for which the legislature is convened.

Extraordinary sessions to reconsider vetoes: Art. 3 Section 12.

SECTION 8 COMMANDER-IN-CHIEF. He shall be commander-in-chief of the military in the state except when they shall be called into the service of the United States.

SECTION 9 PARDONING POWER. The pardoning power shall be vested in the governor under such regulations and restrictions as may be prescribed by law.

SECTION 10 VACANCY IN OFFICE OF GOVERNOR. In case of the removal, resignation, death or disability of the governor, the duties of the office shall devolve upon the lieutenant governor; and in case of a vacancy in both the offices of governor and lieutenant governor, the duties of the governor shall devolve upon the secretary of state. In addition to the line of succession to the office and duties of governor as hereinabove indicated, if the necessity shall arise, in order to fill the vacancy in the office of governor, the following state officers shall succeed to the duties of governor and in the order named, viz.: Treasurer, auditor, attorney general, superintendent of public instruction and commissioner of public lands. In case of the death, disability, failure or refusal of the person regularly elected to the office of governor to qualify at the time provided by law, the duties of the office shall devolve upon the person regularly elected to and qualified for the office of lieutenant governor, who shall act as governor until the disability be removed, or a governor be elected; and in case of the death, disability, failure or refusal of both the governor and the lieutenant governor elect to qualify, the duties of the governor shall devolve upon the secretary of state; and in addition to the line of succession to the office and duties of governor as hereinabove indicated, if there shall be the failure or refusal of any officer named above to qualify, and if the necessity shall arise by reason thereof, then in that event in order to fill the vacancy in the office of governor, the following state officers shall succeed to the duties of governor in the order named, viz: Treasurer, auditor, attorney general, superintendent of public instruction and commissioner of public lands. Any person succeeding to the office of governor as in this section provided, shall perform the duties of such office only until the disability be removed, or a governor be elected and qualified; and if a vacancy occur more than thirty days before the next general election occurring within two years after the commencement of the term, a person shall be elected at such election to fill the office of governor for the remainder of the unexpired term. [**AMENDMENT 6,** 1909 p 642 Section 1. Approved November, 1910.]

Governmental continuity during emergency periods: Art. 2 Section 42.

Original text — Art. 3 Section 10 VACANCY IN — In case of the removal, resignation, death, or disability of the governor, the duties of the office shall devolve upon the lieutenant governor, and in case of a vacancy in both the offices of governor and lieutenant governor, the duties of governor shall devolve upon the secretary of state, who shall act as governor until the disability be removed or a governor elected.

SECTION 11 REMISSION OF FINES AND FORFEITURES. The governor shall have power to remit fines and forfeitures, under such regulations as may be prescribed by law, and shall report to the legislature at its next meeting each case of reprieve, commutation or pardon granted, and the reasons for granting the same, and also the names of all persons in whose favor remission of fines and forfeitures shall have been made, and the several amounts remitted and the reasons for the remission.

SECTION 12 VETO POWERS. Every act which shall have passed the legislature shall be, before it becomes a law, presented to the governor. If he approves, he shall sign it; but if not, he shall return it, with his objections, to that house in which it shall have originated, which house shall enter the objections at large upon the journal and proceed to reconsider. If, after such reconsideration, two-thirds of the members present shall agree to pass the bill it shall be sent, together with the objections, to the other house, by which it shall likewise be reconsidered, and if approved by two-thirds of the members present, it shall become a law; but in all such cases the vote of both houses shall be determined by the yeas and nays, and the names of the members voting for or against the bill shall be entered upon the journal of each house respectively. If any bill shall not be returned by the governor within five days, Sundays excepted, after it shall be presented to him, it shall become a law without his signature, unless the general adjournment shall prevent its return, in which case it shall become a law unless the governor, within twenty days next after the adjournment, Sundays excepted, shall file such bill with his objections thereto, in the office of secretary of state, who shall lay the same before the legislature at its next session in like manner as if it had been returned by the governor: Provided, That within forty-five days next after the adjournment, Sundays excepted, the legislature may, upon petition by a two-thirds majority or more of the membership of each house, reconvene in extraordinary session, not to exceed five days duration, solely to reconsider any bills vetoed. If any bill presented to the governor contain several sections or appropriation items, he may object to one or more sections or appropriation items while approving other portions of the bill: Provided,That he may not object to less than an entire section, except that if the section contain one or more appropriation items he may object to any such appropriation item or items. In case of objection he shall append to the bill, at the time of signing it, a statement of the section or sections, appropriation item or items to which he objects and the reasons therefor; and the section or sections, appropriation item or items so objected to shall not take effect unless passed over the governor's objection, as hereinbefore provided. The provisions of Article II, section 12 insofar as they are inconsistent herewith are hereby repealed. [**AMENDMENT 62,** 1974 Senate Joint Resolution No. 140, p 806. Approved November 5, 1974.]

Veto power withheld from initiated and referred measures: Art. 2 Section 1.

Original text — Art. 3 Section 12 VETO POWER — Every act which shall have passed the legislature shall be, before it becomes a law, presented to the governor. If he approves, he shall sign it; but if not, he shall return it, with his objections, to that house in which it shall have originated, which house shall enter the objections at large upon the journal and proceed to reconsider. If, after such reconsideration, two-thirds of the members present shall agree to pass the bill it shall be sent, together with the objections, to the other house, by which it shall likewise be reconsidered, and if approved by two-thirds of the members present, it shall become a law; but in all cases the vote of both houses shall be determined by the yeas and nays, and the names of the members voting for or against the bill shall be entered upon the journal of each house respectively. If any bill shall not be returned by the governor within five days, Sundays excepted, after it shall be presented to him, it shall become a law without his signature, unless the general adjournment shall prevent its return, in which case it shall become a law unless the governor, within ten days next after the adjournment, Sundays excepted, shall file such bill with his objections thereto, in the office of secretary of state, who shall lay the same before the legislature at its next session in like manner as if it had been returned by the governor. If any bill presented to the governor contain several sections or items, he may object to one or more sections or items while approving other portions of the bill. In such case he shall append to the bill, at the time of signing it, a statement of the section, or sections; item or items to which he objects and the reasons therefor, and the section or sections, item or items so objected to, shall not take effect unless passed over the governor's objection, as hereinbefore provided.

Veto power does not extend to initiated or referred measures: Art. 2 Section 1(d).

SECTION 13 VACANCY IN APPOINTIVE OFFICE. When, during a recess of the legislature, a vacancy shall happen in any office, the appointment to which is vested in the legislature, or when at any time a vacancy shall have occurred in any other state office, for the filling of which vacancy no provision is made elsewhere in this Constitution, the governor shall fill such vacancy by appointment, which shall expire when a successor shall have been elected and qualified.

Appointment of governing boards of educational, reformatory and penal institutions: Art. 13 Section 1.
Governmental continuity during emergency periods: Art. 2 Section 42.

SECTION 14 SALARY. The governor shall receive an annual salary of four thousand dollars, which may be increased by law, but shall never exceed six thousand dollars per annum.

Compensation of legislators, elected state officials, and judges: Art. 28 Section 1, Art. 30.

SECTION 15 COMMISSIONS, HOW ISSUED. All commissions shall issue in the name of the state, shall be signed by the governor, sealed with the seal of the state, and attested by the secretary of state.

SECTION 16 LIEUTENANT GOVERNOR, DUTIES AND SALARY. The lieutenant governor shall be presiding officer of the state senate, and shall discharge such other duties as may be prescribed by law. He shall receive an annual salary of one thousand dollars, which may be increased by the legislature, but shall never exceed three thousand dollars per annum.

Compensation of legislators, elected state officials, and judges: Art. 28 Section 1, Art. 30.

SECTION 17 SECRETARY OF STATE, DUTIES AND SALARY. The secretary of state shall keep a record of the official acts of the legislature, and executive department of the state, and shall, when required, lay the same, and all matters relative thereto, before either branch of the legislature, and shall perform such other duties as shall be assigned him by law. He shall receive an annual salary of twenty-five hundred dollars, which may be increased by the legislature, but shall never exceed three thousand dollars per annum.

Compensation of legislators, elected state officials, and judges: Art. 28 Section 1, Art. 30.

SECTION 18 SEAL. There shall be a seal of the state kept by the secretary of state for official purposes, which shall be called, "The Seal of the State of Washington."

Design of the Seal: Art. 18 Section 1.
State seal: RCW 1.20.080.

SECTION 19 STATE TREASURER, DUTIES AND SALARY. The treasurer shall perform such duties as shall be prescribed by law. He shall receive an annual salary of two thousand dollars, which may be increased by the legislature, but shall never exceed four thousand dollars per annum.

Compensation of legislators, elected state officials, and judges: Art. 28 Section 1, Art. 30.

SECTION 20 STATE AUDITOR, DUTIES AND SALARY. The auditor shall be auditor of public accounts, and shall have such powers and perform such duties in connection therewith as may be prescribed by law. He shall receive an annual salary of two thousand dollars, which may be increased by the legislature, but shall never exceed three thousand dollars per annum.

Compensation of legislators, elected state officials, and judges: Art. 28 Section 1, Art. 30.

SECTION 21 ATTORNEY GENERAL, DUTIES AND SALARY. The attorney general shall be the legal adviser of the state officers, and shall perform such other duties as may be prescribed by law. He shall receive an annual salary of two thousand dollars, which may be increased by the legislature, but shall never exceed thirty-five hundred dollars per annum.

Compensation of legislators, elected state officials, and judges: Art. 28 Section 1, Art. 30.

SECTION 22 SUPERINTENDENT OF PUBLIC INSTRUCTION, DUTIES AND SALARY. The superintendent of public instruction shall have supervision over all matters pertaining to public schools, and shall perform such specific duties as may be prescribed by law. He shall receive an annual salary of twenty-five hundred dollars, which may be increased by law, but shall never exceed four thousand dollars per annum.

Compensation of legislators, elected state officials, and judges: Art. 28 Section 1, Art. 30.

SECTION 23 COMMISSIONER OF PUBLIC LANDS — COMPENSATION. The commissioner of public lands shall perform such duties and receive such compensation as the legislature may direct.

SECTION 24 RECORDS, WHERE KEPT, ETC. The governor, secretary of state, treasurer, auditor, superintendent of public instruction, commissioner of public lands and attorney general shall severally keep the public records, books and papers relating to their respective offices, at the seat of government, at which place also the governor, secretary of state, treasurer and auditor shall reside.

Governmental continuity during emergency periods: Art. 2 Section 42.

SECTION 25 QUALIFICATIONS, COMPENSATION, OFFICES WHICH MAY BE ABOLISHED. No person, except a citizen of the United States and a qualified elector of this state, shall be eligible to hold any state office. The compensation for state officers shall not be increased or diminished during the term for which they shall have been elected. The legislature may in its discretion abolish the offices of the lieutenant governor, auditor and commissioner of public lands. [**AMENDMENT 31,** 1955 Senate Joint Resolution No. 6, p 1861. Approved November 6, 1956.]

Authorizing compensation increase during term: Art. 30 Section 1.
Increase or diminution of compensation during term of office prohibited.
county, city, town or municipal officers: Art. 11 Section 8.
judicial officers: Art. 4 Section 13.
public officers: Art. 2 Section 25.

Original text — Art. 3 Section 25 QUALIFICATIONS — No person, except a citizen of the United States and a qualified elector of this state, shall be eligible to hold any state office, and the state treasurer shall be ineligible for the term succeeding that for which he was elected. The compensation for state officers shall not be increased or diminished during the term for which they shall have been elected. The legislature may in its discretion abolish the offices of the lieutenant governor, auditor and commissioner of public lands.

ARTICLE IV THE JUDICIARY

SECTION 1 JUDICIAL POWER, WHERE VESTED. The judicial power of the state shall be vested in a supreme court, superior courts, justices of the peace, and such inferior courts as the legislature may provide.

Court of appeals: Art. 4 Section 30.

SECTION 2 SUPREME COURT. The supreme court shall consist of five judges, a majority of whom shall be necessary to form a quorum, and pronounce a decision. The said court shall always be open for the transaction of business except on nonjudicial days. In the determination of causes all decisions of the court shall be given in writing and the grounds of the decision shall be stated. The legislature may increase the number of judges of the supreme court from time to time and may provide for separate departments of said court.

SECTION 2(a) TEMPORARY PERFORMANCE OF JUDICIAL DUTIES. When necessary for the prompt and orderly administration of justice a majority of the Supreme Court is empowered to authorize judges or retired judges of courts of record of this state, to perform, temporarily, judicial duties in the Supreme Court, and to authorize any superior court judge to perform judicial duties in any superior court of this state. [**AMENDMENT 38,** 1961 House Joint Resolution No. 6, p 2757. Approved November, 1962.]

SECTION 3 ELECTION AND TERMS OF SUPREME COURT JUDGES. The judges of the supreme court shall be elected by the qualified electors of the state at large at the general state election at the times and places at which state officers are elected, unless some other time be provided by the legislature. The first election of judges of the supreme court shall be at the election which shall be held upon the adoption of this Constitution and the judges elected thereat shall be classified by lot, so that two shall hold their office for the term of three years, two for the term of five years, and one for the term of seven years. The lot shall be drawn by the judges who shall for that purpose assemble at the seat of government, and they shall cause the result thereof to be certified to the secretary of state, and filed in his office. The supreme court shall select a chief justice from its own membership to serve for a four-year term at the pleasure of a majority of the court as prescribed by supreme court rule. The chief justice shall preside at all sessions of the supreme court. In case of the absence of the chief justice, the majority of the remaining court shall select one of their members to serve as acting chief justice. After the first election the terms of judges elected shall be six years from and after the second Monday in January next succeeding their election. If a vacancy occur in the office of a judge of the supreme court the governor shall only appoint a person to ensure the number of judges as specified by the legislature, to hold the office until the election and qualification of a judge to fill the vacancy, which election shall take place at the next succeeding general election, and the judge so elected shall hold the office for the remainder of the unexpired term. The term of office of the judges of the supreme court, first elected, shall commence as soon as the state shall have been admitted into the Union, and continue for the term herein provided, and until their successors are elected and qualified. The sessions of the supreme court shall be held at the seat of government until otherwise provided by law. [**AMENDMENT 89,** 1995 Substitute Senate Joint Resolution No. 8210, p 2905. Approved November 7, 1995.]

Original text — Art. 4 Section 3 ELECTION AND TERMS OF SUPREME COURT JUDGES — The judges of the supreme court shall be elected by the qualified electors of the state at large at the general state election at the times and places at which state officers are elected, unless some other time be provided by the legislature. The first election of judges of the supreme court shall be at the election which shall be held upon the adoption of this Constitution and the judges elected thereat shall be classified by lot, so that two shall hold their office for the term of three years, two for the term of five years, and one for the term of seven years. The lot shall be drawn by the judges who shall for that purpose assemble at the seat of government, and they shall cause the result thereof to be certified to the secretary of state, and filed in his office. The judge having the shortest term to serve not holding his office by appointment or election to fill a vacancy, shall be the chief justice, and shall preside at all sessions of the supreme court, and in case there shall be two judges having in like manner the same short term, the other judges of the supreme court shall determine which of them shall be chief justice. In case of the absence of the chief justice, the judge having in like manner the shortest or next shortest term to serve shall preside. After the first election the terms of judges elected shall be six years from and after the second Monday in January next succeeding their election. If a vacancy occur in the office of a judge of the supreme court the governor shall appoint a person to hold the office until the election and qualification of a judge to fill the vacancy, which election shall take place at the next succeeding general election, and the judge so elected shall hold the office for the remainder of the unexpired term. The term of office of the judges of the supreme court, first elected, shall commence as soon as the state shall have been admitted into the Union, and continue for the term herein provided, and until their successors are elected and qualified. The sessions of the supreme court shall be held at the seat of government until otherwise provided by law.

SECTION 3(a) RETIREMENT OF SUPREME COURT AND SUPERIOR COURT JUDGES. A judge of the supreme court or the superior court shall retire from judicial office at the end of the calendar year in which he attains the age of seventy-five years. The legislature may, from time to time, fix a lesser age for mandatory retirement, not earlier than the end of the calendar year in which any such judge attains the age of seventy years, as the legislature deems proper. This provision shall not affect the term to which any such judge shall have been elected or appointed prior to, or at the time of, approval and ratification of this provision. Notwithstanding the limitations of this section, the legislature may by general law authorize or require the retirement of judges for physical or mental disability, or any cause rendering judges incapable of performing their judicial duties. [**AMENDMENT 25,** 1951 House Joint Resolution No. 6, p 960. Approved November 4, 1952.]

SECTION 4 JURISDICTION. The supreme court shall have original jurisdiction in habeas corpus, and quo warranto and mandamus as to all state officers, and appellate jurisdiction in all actions and proceedings, excepting that its appellate jurisdiction shall not extend to civil actions at law for the recovery of money or personal property when the original amount in controversy, or the value of the property does not exceed the sum of two hundred dollars ($200) unless the action involves the legality of a tax, impost, assessment, toll, municipal fine, or the validity of a statute. The supreme court shall also have power to issue writs of mandamus, review, prohibition, habeas corpus, certiorari and all other writs necessary and proper to the complete exercise of its appellate and revisory jurisdiction. Each of the judges shall have power to issue writs of habeas corpus to any part of the state upon petition by or on behalf of any person held in actual custody, and may make such writs returnable before himself, or before the supreme court, or before any superior court of the state or any judge thereof.

SECTION 5 SUPERIOR COURT — ELECTION OF JUDGES, TERMS OF, ETC. There shall be in each of the organized counties of this state a superior court for which at least one judge shall be elected by the qualified electors of the county at the general state election: **Provided,** That until otherwise directed by the legislature one judge only shall be elected for the counties of Spokane and Stevens; one judge for the county of Whitman; one judge for the counties of Lincoln, Okanogan, Douglas and Adams; one judge for the counties of Walla Walla and Franklin; one judge for the counties of Columbia, Garfield and Asotin; one judge for the counties of Kittitas, Yakima and Klickitat; one judge for the counties of Clarke, Skamania, Pacific, Cowlitz and Wahkiakum; one judge for the counties of Thurston, Chehalis, Mason and Lewis; one judge for the county of Pierce; one judge for the county of King; one judge for the counties of Jefferson, Island, Kitsap, San Juan and Clallam; and one judge for the counties of Whatcom, Skagit and Snohomish. In any county where there shall be more than one superior judge, there may be as many sessions of the superior court at the same time as there are judges thereof, and whenever the governor shall direct a superior judge to hold court in any county other than that for which he has been elected, there may be as many sessions of the superior court in said county at the same time as there are judges therein or assigned to duty therein by the governor, and the business of the court shall be so distributed and assigned by law or in the absence of legislation therefor, by such rules and orders of court as shall best promote and secure the convenient and expeditious transaction thereof. The judgments, decrees, orders and proceedings of any session of the superior court held by any one or more of the judges of such court shall be equally effectual as if all the judges of said court presided at such session. The first superior judges elected under this Constitution shall hold their offices for the period of three years, and until their successors shall be elected and qualified, and thereafter the term of office of all superior judges in this state shall be for four years from the second Monday in January next succeeding their election and until their successors are elected and qualified. The first election of judges of the superior court shall be at the election held for the adoption of this Constitution. If a vacancy occurs in the office of judge of the superior court, the governor shall appoint a person to hold the office until the election and qualification of a judge to fill the vacancy, which election shall be at the next succeeding general election, and the judge so elected shall hold office for the remainder of the unexpired term.

Supreme court may authorize superior court judge to perform judicial duties in any superior court: Art. 4 Section 2(a).

SECTION 6 JURISDICTION OF SUPERIOR COURTS. Superior courts and district courts have concurrent jurisdiction in cases in equity. The superior court shall have original jurisdiction in all cases at law which involve the title or possession of real property, or the legality of any tax, impost, assessment, toll, or municipal fine, and in all other cases in which the demand or the value of the property in controversy amounts to three thousand dollars or as otherwise determined by law, or a lesser sum in excess of the jurisdiction granted to justices of the peace and other inferior courts, and in all criminal cases amounting to felony, and in all cases of misdemeanor not otherwise provided for by law; of actions of forcible entry and detainer; of proceedings in insolvency; of actions to prevent or abate a nuisance; of all matters of probate, of divorce, and for annulment of marriage; and for such special cases and proceedings as are not otherwise provided for. The superior court shall also have original jurisdiction in all cases and of all proceedings in which jurisdiction shall not have been by law vested exclusively in some other court; and said court shall have the power of naturalization and to issue papers therefor. They shall have such appellate jurisdiction in cases arising in justices' and other inferior courts in their respective counties as may be prescribed by law. They shall always be open, except on nonjudicial days, and their process shall extend to all parts of the state. Said courts and their judges shall have power to issue writs of mandamus, quo warranto, review, certiorari, prohibition, and writs of habeas corpus, on petition by or on behalf of any person in actual custody in their respective counties. Injunctions and writs of prohibition and of habeas corpus may be issued and served on legal holidays and nonjudicial days.
[**AMENDMENT 87,** 1993 House Joint Resolution No. 4201, p 3063. Approved November 2, 1993.]

Amendment 65, part (1977) — Art. 4 Section 6 Jurisdiction of Superior Courts —
The superior court shall have original jurisdiction in all cases in equity and in all cases at law which involve the title or possession of real property, or the legality of any tax, impost, assessment, toll, or municipal fine, and in all other cases in which the demand or the value of

the property in controversy amounts to three thousand dollars or as otherwise determined by law, or a lesser sum in excess of the jurisdiction granted to justices of the peace and other inferior courts, and in all criminal cases amounting to felony, and in all cases of misdemeanor not otherwise provided for by law; of actions of forcible entry and detainer; of proceedings in insolvency; of actions to prevent or abate a nuisance; of all matters of probate, of divorce, and for annulment of marriage; and for such special cases and proceedings as are not otherwise provided for. The superior court shall also have original jurisdiction in all cases and of all proceedings in which jurisdiction shall not have been by law vested exclusively in some other court; and said court shall have the power of naturalization and to issue papers therefor. They shall have such appellate jurisdiction in cases arising in justices' and other inferior courts in their respective counties as may be prescribed by law. They shall always be open, except on nonjudicial days, and their process shall extend to all parts of the state. Said courts and their judges shall have power to issue writs of mandamus, quo warranto, review, certiorari, prohibition, and writs of habeas corpus, on petition by or on behalf of any person in actual custody in their respective counties. Injunctions and writs of prohibition and of habeas corpus may be issued and served on legal holidays and nonjudicial days. [**AMENDMENT 65**, part, 1977 Senate Joint Resolution No. 113, p 1714. Approved November 8, 1977.]

Amendment 65 also amended Art. 4 Section 10.

Amendment 28, part (1952) — Art. 4 Section 6 JURISDICTION OF SUPERIOR COURTS — The superior court shall have original jurisdiction in all cases in equity and in all cases at law which involve the title or possession of real property, or the legality of any tax, impost, assessment, toll, or municipal fine, and in all other cases in which the demand or the value of the property in controversy amounts to one thousand dollars, or a lesser sum in excess of the jurisdiction granted to justices of the peace and other inferior courts, and in all criminal cases amounting to felony, and in all cases of misdemeanor not otherwise provided for by law; of actions of forcible entry and detainer; of proceedings in insolvency; of actions to prevent or abate a nuisance; of all matters of probate, of divorce, and for annulment of marriage; and for such special cases and proceedings as are not otherwise provided for. The superior court shall also have original jurisdiction in all cases and of all proceedings in which jurisdiction shall not have been by law vested exclusively in some other court; and said court shall have the power of naturalization and to issue papers therefor. They shall have such appellate jurisdiction in cases arising in justices' and other inferior courts in their respective counties as may be prescribed by law. They shall always be open, except on nonjudicial days, and their process shall extend to all parts of the state. Said courts and their judges shall have power to issue writs of mandamus, quo warranto, review, certiorari, prohibition, and writs of habeas corpus, on petition by or on behalf of any person in actual custody in their respective counties. Injunctions and writs of prohibition and of habeas corpus may be issued and served on legal holidays and nonjudicial days. [AMENDMENT 28, part, 1951 Substitute House Joint Resolution No. 13, p 962. Approved November 4, 1952.]

Note: Amendment 28 also amended Art. 4 Section 10.

ORIGINAL TEXT — ART. 4 Section 6 JURISDICTION OF SUPERIOR COURTS —
The superior court shall have original jurisdiction in all cases in equity, and in all cases at law which involve the title or possession of real property, or the legality of any tax, impost, assessment, toll or municipal fine, and in all other cases in which the demand, or the value of the property in controversy amounts to one hundred dollars, and in all criminal cases amounting to felony, and in all cases of misdemeanor not otherwise provided for by law; of actions of forcible entry and detainer; of proceedings in insolvency; of actions to prevent or abate a

nuisance; of all matters of probate, of divorce, and for annulment of marriage; and for such special cases and proceedings as are not otherwise provided for. The superior court shall also have original jurisdiction in all cases and of all proceedings in which jurisdiction shall not have been by law vested exclusively in some other court; and said court shall have the power of naturalization, and to issue papers therefor. They shall have such appellate jurisdiction in cases arising in justice's and other inferior courts in their respective counties as may be prescribed by law. They shall be always open except on non-judicial days, and their process shall extend to all parts of the state. Said courts and their judges shall have power to issue writs of mandamus, quo warranto, review, certiorari, prohibition, and writs of habeas corpus on petition by or on behalf of any person in actual custody in their respective counties. Injunctions and writs of prohibition and of habeas corpus may be issued and served on legal holidays and non-judicial days.

SECTION 7 EXCHANGE OF JUDGES — JUDGE PRO TEMPORE. The judge of any superior court may hold a superior court in any county at the request of the judge of the superior court thereof, and upon the request of the governor it shall be his or her duty to do so. A case in the superior court may be tried by a judge pro tempore either with the agreement of the parties if the judge pro tempore is a member of the bar, is agreed upon in writing by the parties litigant or their attorneys of record, and is approved by the court and sworn to try the case; or without the agreement of the parties if the judge pro tempore is a sitting elected judge and is acting as a judge pro tempore pursuant to supreme court rule. The supreme court rule must require assignments of judges pro tempore based on the judges' experience and must provide for the right, exercisable once during a case, to a change of judge pro tempore. Such right shall be in addition to any other right provided by law. However, if a previously elected judge of the superior court retires leaving a pending case in which the judge has made discretionary rulings, the judge is entitled to hear the pending case as a judge pro tempore without any written agreement. [**AMENDMENT 94**, 2001 Engrossed Senate Joint Resolution No. 8208, p 2327. Approved November 6, 2001.

Amendment 80 — Art. 4 Section 7 EXCHANGE OF JUDGES — JUDGE PRO TEMPORE — The judge of any superior court may hold a superior court in any county at the request of the judge of the superior court thereof, and upon the request of the governor it shall be his duty to do so. A case in the superior court may be tried by a judge, pro tempore, who must be a member of the bar, agreed upon in writing by the parties litigant, or their attorneys of record, approved by the court and sworn to try the case. However, if a previously elected judge of the superior court retires leaving a pending case in which the judge has made discretionary rulings, the judge is entitled to hear the pending case as a judge pro tempore without any written agreement.[Amendment 80, 1987 Senate Joint Resolution No. 8207, p 2815. Approved November 3, 1987.]

ORIGINAL TEXT — Art. 4 Section 7 EXCHANGE OF JUDGES — JUDGE PRO TEMPORE — The judge of any superior court may hold a superior court in any county at the request of the judge of the superior court thereof, and upon the request of the governor it shall be his duty to do so. A case in the superior court may be tried by a judge, pro tempore, who must be a member of the bar, agreed upon in writing by the parties litigant, or their attorneys of record, approved by the court and sworn to try the case.

SECTION 8 ABSENCE OF JUDICIAL OFFICER. Any judicial officer who shall absent himself from the state for more than sixty consecutive days shall be deemed to have forfeited his office: Provided, That in cases of extreme necessity the governor may extend the leave of absence such time as the necessity therefor shall exist.

SECTION 9 REMOVAL OF JUDGES, ATTORNEY GENERAL, ETC. Any judge of any court of record, the attorney general, or any prosecuting attorney may be removed from office by joint resolution of the legislature, in which three-fourths of the members elected to each house shall concur, for incompetency, corruption, malfeasance, or delinquency in office, or other sufficient cause stated in such resolution. But no removal shall be made unless the officer complained of shall have been served with a copy of the charges against him as the ground of removal, and shall have an opportunity of being heard in his defense. Such resolution shall be entered at length on the journal of both houses and on the question of removal the ayes and nays shall also be entered on the journal.

Removal, censure, suspension, or retirement of judges or justices: Art. 4 Section 31.

SECTION 10 JUSTICES OF THE PEACE. The legislature shall determine the number of justices of the peace to be elected and shall prescribe by law the powers, duties and jurisdiction of justices of the peace: Provided, That such jurisdiction granted by the legislature shall not trench upon the jurisdiction of superior or other courts of record, except that justices of the peace may be made police justices of incorporated cities and towns. Justices of the peace shall have original jurisdiction in cases where the demand or value of the property in controversy is less than three hundred dollars or such greater sum, not to exceed three thousand dollars or as otherwise determined by law, as shall be prescribed by the legislature. In incorporated cities or towns having more than five thousand inhabitants, the justices of the peace shall receive such salary as may be provided by law, and shall receive no fees for their own use. [**AMENDMENT 65,** part, 1977 Senate Joint Resolution No. 113, p 1714. Approved November 8, 1977.]

Amendment 65 also amended Art. 4 Section 6.

Amendment 28, part (1952) — Art. 4 Section 10 JUSTICES OF THE PEACE — The legislature shall determine the number of justices of the peace to be elected and shall prescribe by law the powers, duties and jurisdiction of justices of the peace: Provided, That such jurisdiction granted by the legislature shall not trench upon the jurisdiction of superior or other courts of record, except that justices of the peace may be made police justices of incorporated cities and towns. Justices of the peace shall have original jurisdiction in cases where the demand or value of the property in controversy is less than three hundred dollars or such greater sum, not to exceed one thousand dollars, as shall be prescribed by the legislature. In incorporated cities or towns having more than five thousand inhabitants, the justices of the peace shall receive such salary as may be provided by law, and shall receive no fees for their own use.[AMENDMENT 28, part, 1951 Substitute House Joint Resolution No. 13, p 962. Approved November 4, 1952.]

Note: Amendment 28 also amended Art. 4 Section 6.

Original text — Art. 4 Section 10 JUSTICES OF THE PEACE — The legislature shall determine the number of justices of the peace to be elected in incorporated cities or towns and in precincts, and shall prescribe by law the powers, duties and jurisdiction of justices of the peace; Provided, That such jurisdiction granted by the legislature shall not trench upon the jurisdiction of superior or other courts of record, except that justices of the peace may be made police justices of incorporated cities and towns. In incorporated cities or towns having more than five thousand inhabitants the justices of the peace shall receive such salary as may be provided by law, and shall receive no fees for their own use.

SECTION 11 COURTS OF RECORD. The supreme court and the superior courts shall be courts of record, and the legislature shall have power to provide that any of the courts of this state, excepting justices of the peace, shall be courts of record.

SECTION 12 INFERIOR COURTS. The legislature shall prescribe by law the jurisdiction and powers of any of the inferior courts which may be established in pursuance of this Constitution.

SECTION 13 SALARIES OF JUDICIAL OFFICERS — HOW PAID, ETC. No judicial officer, except court commissioners and unsalaried justices of the peace, shall receive to his own use any fees or perquisites of office. The judges of the supreme court and judges of the superior courts shall severally at stated times, during their continuance in office, receive for their services the salaries prescribed by law therefor, which shall not be increased after their election, nor during the term for which they shall have been elected. The salaries of the judges of the supreme court shall be paid by the state. One-half of the salary of each of the superior court judges shall be paid by the state, and the other one-half by the county or counties for which he is elected. In cases where a judge is provided for more than one county, that portion of his salary which is to be paid by the counties shall be apportioned between or among them according to the assessed value of their taxable property, to be determined by the assessment next preceding the time for which such salary is to be paid.

Authorizing compensation increase during term: Art. 30 Section 1.
Increase or diminution of compensation during term of office prohibited
county, city or municipal officers: Art. 11 Section 8.
public officers: Art. 2 Section 25.
state officers: Art. 3 Section 25.

SECTION 14 SALARIES OF SUPREME AND SUPERIOR COURT JUDGES. Each of the judges of the supreme court shall receive an annual salary of four thousand dollars ($4,000); each of the superior court judges shall receive an annual salary of three thousand dollars ($3,000), which said salaries shall be payable quarterly. The legislature may increase the salaries of judges herein provided.

Compensation of legislators, elected state officials, and judges: Art. 28 Section 1.

SECTION 15 INELIGIBILITY OF JUDGES. The judges of the supreme court and the judges of the superior court shall be ineligible to any other office or public employment than a judicial office, or employment, during the term for which they shall have been elected.

SECTION 16 CHARGING JURIES. Judges shall not charge juries with respect to matters of fact, nor comment thereon, but shall declare the law.

SECTION 17 ELIGIBILITY OF JUDGES. No person shall be eligible to the office of judge of the supreme court, or judge of a superior court, unless he shall have been admitted to practice in the courts of record of this state, or of the Territory of Washington.

SECTION 18 SUPREME COURT REPORTER. The judges of the supreme court shall appoint a reporter for the decisions of that court, who shall be removable at their pleasure. He shall receive such annual salary as shall be prescribed by law.

SECTION 19 JUDGES MAY NOT PRACTICE LAW. No judge of a court of record shall practice law in any court of this state during his continuance in office.

SECTION 20 DECISIONS, WHEN TO BE MADE. Every cause submitted to a judge of a superior court for his decision shall be decided by him within ninety days from the submission thereof; Provided, That if within said period of ninety days a rehearing shall have been ordered, then the period within which he is to decide shall commence at the time the cause is submitted upon such a hearing.

SECTION 21 PUBLICATION OF OPINIONS. The legislature shall provide for the speedy publication of opinions of the supreme court, and all opinions shall be free for publication by any person.

SECTION 22 CLERK OF THE SUPREME COURT. The judges of the supreme court shall appoint a clerk of that court who shall be removable at their pleasure, but the legislature may provide for the election of the clerk of the supreme court, and prescribe the term of his office. The clerk of the supreme court shall receive such compensation by salary only as shall be provided by law.

SECTION 23 COURT COMMISSIONERS. There may be appointed in each county, by the judge of the superior court having jurisdiction therein, one or more court commissioners, not exceeding three in number, who shall have authority to perform like duties as a judge of the superior court at chambers, subject to revision by such judge, to take depositions and to perform such other business connected with the administration of justice as may be prescribed by law.

SECTION 24 RULES FOR SUPERIOR COURTS. The judges of the superior courts, shall from time to time, establish uniform rules for the government of the superior courts.

SECTION 25 REPORTS OF SUPERIOR COURT JUDGES. Superior judges, shall on or before the first day of November in each year, report in writing to the judges of the supreme court such defects and omissions in the laws as their experience may suggest, and the judges of the supreme court shall on or before the first day of January in each year report in writing to the governor such defects and omissions in the laws as they may believe to exist.

SECTION 26 CLERK OF THE SUPERIOR COURT. The county clerk shall be by virtue of his office, clerk of the superior court.

SECTION 27 STYLE OF PROCESS. The style of all process shall be, "The State of Washington," and all prosecutions shall be conducted in its name and by its authority.

SECTION 28 OATH OF JUDGES. Every judge of the supreme court, and every judge of a superior court shall, before entering upon the duties of his office, take and subscribe an oath that he will support the Constitution of the United States and the Constitution of the State of Washington, and will faithfully and impartially discharge the duties of judge to the best of his ability, which oath shall be filed in the office of the secretary of state.

SECTION 29 ELECTION OF SUPERIOR COURT JUDGES. Notwithstanding any provision of this Constitution to the contrary, if, after the last day as provided by law for the withdrawal of declarations of candidacy has expired, only one candidate has filed for any single position of superior court judge in any county containing a population of one hundred thousand or more, no primary or election shall be held as to such position, and a certificate of election shall be issued to such candidate. If, after any contested primary for superior court judge in any county, only one candidate is entitled to have his name printed on the general election ballot for any single position, no election shall be held as to such position, and a certificate of election shall be issued to such candidate: Provided, That in the event that there is filed with the county auditor within ten days after the date of the primary, a petition indicating that a write in campaign will be conducted for such single position and signed by one hundred registered voters qualified to vote with respect of the office, then such single position shall be subject to the general election. Provisions for the contingency of the death or disqualification of a sole candidate between the last date for withdrawal and the time when the election would be held but for the provisions of this section, and such other provisions as may be deemed necessary to implement the provisions of this section, may be enacted by the legislature. [**AMENDMENT 41,** 1965 ex.s. Substitute Senate Joint Resolution No. 6, p 2815. Approved November 8, 1966.]

SECTION 30 COURT OF APPEALS. (1) Authorization. In addition to the courts authorized in section 1 of this article, judicial power is vested in a court of appeals, which shall be established by statute.

(2) Jurisdiction. The jurisdiction of the court of appeals shall be as provided by statute or by rules authorized by statute.

(3) Review of Superior Court. Superior court actions may be reviewed by the court of appeals or by the supreme court as provided by statute or by rule authorized by statute.

(4) Judges. The number, manner of election, compensation, terms of office, removal and retirement of judges of the court of appeals shall be as provided by statute.

(5) Administration and Procedure. The administration and procedures of the court of appeals shall be as provided by rules issued by the supreme court.

(6) Conflicts. The provisions of this section shall supersede any conflicting provisions in prior sections of this article. [**AMENDMENT 50,** 1967 Senate Joint Resolution No. 6; see 1969 p 2975. Approved November 5, 1968.]

Reviser's note: This section which was adopted as Sec. 29 is herein renumbered Sec. 30 to avoid confusion with Sec. 29, supra.

SECTION 31 COMMISSION ON JUDICIAL CONDUCT. (1) There shall be a commission on judicial conduct, existing as an independent agency of the judicial branch, and consisting of a judge selected by and from the court of appeals judges, a judge selected by and from the superior court judges, a judge selected by and from the limited jurisdiction court judges, two persons admitted to the practice of law in this state selected by the state bar association, and six persons who are not attorneys appointed by the governor.

(2) Whenever the commission receives a complaint against a judge or justice, or otherwise has reason to believe that a judge or justice should be admonished, reprimanded, censured, suspended, removed, or retired, the commission shall first investigate the complaint or belief and then conduct initial proceedings for the purpose of determining whether probable cause exists for conducting a public hearing or hearings to deal with the complaint or belief. The investigation and initial proceedings shall be confidential. Upon beginning an initial proceeding, the commission shall notify the judge or justice of the existence of and basis for the initial proceeding.

(3) Whenever the commission concludes, based on an initial proceeding, that there is probable cause to believe that a judge or justice has violated a rule of judicial conduct or that the judge or justice suffers from a disability which is permanent or likely to become permanent and which seriously interferes with the performance of judicial duties, the commission shall conduct a public hearing or hearings and shall make public all those records of the initial proceeding that provide the basis for its conclusion. If the commission concludes that there is not probable cause, it shall notify the judge or justice of its conclusion.

(4) Upon the completion of the hearing or hearings, the commission in open session shall either dismiss the case, or shall admonish, reprimand, or censure the judge or justice, or shall censure the judge or justice and recommend to the supreme court the suspension or removal of the judge or justice, or shall recommend to the supreme court the retirement of the judge or justice. The commission may not recommend suspension or removal unless it censures the judge or justice for the violation serving as the basis for the recommendation. The commission may recommend retirement of a judge or justice for a disability which is permanent or likely to become permanent and which seriously interferes with the performance of judicial duties.

(5) Upon the recommendation of the commission, the supreme court may suspend, remove, or retire a judge or justice. The office of a judge or justice retired or removed by the supreme court becomes vacant, and that person is ineligible for judicial office until eligibility is reinstated by the supreme court. The salary of a removed judge or justice shall cease. The supreme court shall specify the effect upon salary when it suspends a judge or justice. The supreme court may not suspend, remove, or retire a judge or justice until the commission, after

notice and hearing, recommends that action be taken, and the supreme court conducts a hearing, after notice, to review commission proceedings and findings against the judge or justice.

(6) Within thirty days after the commission admonishes, reprimands, or censures a judge or justice, the judge or justice shall have a right of appeal de novo to the supreme court.

(7) Any matter before the commission or supreme court may be disposed of by a stipulation entered into in a public proceeding. The stipulation shall be signed by the judge or justice and the commission or court. The stipulation may impose any terms and conditions deemed appropriate by the commission or court. A stipulation shall set forth all material facts relating to the proceeding and the conduct of the judge or justice.

(8) Whenever the commission adopts a recommendation that a judge or justice be removed, the judge or justice shall be suspended immediately, with salary, from his or her judicial position until a final determination is made by the supreme court.

(9) The legislature shall provide for commissioners' terms of office and compensation. The commission shall employ one or more investigative officers with appropriate professional training and experience. The investigative officers of the commission shall report directly to the commission. The commission shall also employ such administrative or other staff as are necessary to manage the affairs of the commission.

(10) The commission shall, to the extent that compliance does not conflict with this section, comply with laws of general applicability to state agencies with respect to rule-making procedures, and with respect to public notice of and attendance at commission proceedings other than initial proceedings. The commission shall establish rules of procedure for commission proceedings including due process and confidentiality of proceedings. [**AMENDMENT 97,** 2005 Senate Joint Resolution No. 8207, pp 2799, 2800. Approved November 8, 2005.]

Removal by legislature: Art. 4 Section 9.

Amendment 85 (1989) — Art. 4 Section 31 COMMISSION ON JUDICIAL CONDUCT — (1) There shall be a commission on judicial conduct, existing as an independent agency of the judicial branch, and consisting of a judge selected by and from the court of appeals judges, a judge selected by and from the superior court judges, a judge selected by and from the district court judges, two persons admitted to the practice of law in this state selected by the state bar association, and six persons who are not attorneys appointed by the governor.

(2) Whenever the commission receives a complaint against a judge or justice, or otherwise has reason to believe that a judge or justice should be admonished, reprimanded, censured, suspended, removed, or retired, the commission shall first investigate the complaint or belief and then conduct initial proceedings for the purpose of determining whether probable cause exists for conducting a public hearing or hearings to deal with the complaint or belief. The investigation and initial proceedings shall be confidential. Upon beginning an initial proceeding, the commission shall notify the judge or justice of the existence of and basis for the initial proceeding.

(3) Whenever the commission concludes, based on an initial proceeding, that there is probable cause to believe that a judge or justice has violated a rule of judicial conduct or that the judge or justice suffers from a disability which is permanent or likely to become permanent and which seriously interferes with the performance of judicial duties, the commission shall conduct a public hearing or hearings and shall make public all those records of the initial proceeding that provide the basis for its conclusion. If the commission concludes that there is not probable cause, it shall notify the judge or justice of its conclusion.

(4) Upon the completion of the hearing or hearings, the commission in open session shall either dismiss the case, or shall admonish, reprimand, or censure the judge or justice, or shall censure the judge or justice and recommend to the supreme court the suspension or removal of the judge or justice, or shall recommend to the supreme court the retirement of the

judge or justice. The commission may not recommend suspension or removal unless it censures the judge or justice for the violation serving as the basis for the recommendation. The commission may recommend retirement of a judge or justice for a disability which is permanent or likely to become permanent and which seriously interferes with the performance of judicial duties.

(5) Upon the recommendation of the commission, the supreme court may suspend, remove, or retire a judge or justice. The office of a judge or justice retired or removed by the supreme court becomes vacant, and that person is ineligible for judicial office until eligibility is reinstated by the supreme court. The salary of a removed judge or justice shall cease. The supreme court shall specify the effect upon salary when it suspends a judge or justice. The supreme court may not suspend, remove, or retire a judge or justice until the commission, after notice and hearing, recommends that action be taken, and the supreme court conducts a hearing, after notice, to review commission proceedings and findings against the judge or justice.

(6) Within thirty days after the commission admonishes, reprimands, or censures a judge or justice, the judge or justice shall have a right of appeal de novo to the supreme court.

(7) Any matter before the commission or supreme court may be disposed of by a stipulation entered into in a public proceeding. The stipulation shall be signed by the judge or justice and the commission or court. The stipulation may impose any terms and conditions deemed appropriate by the commission or court. A stipulation shall set forth all material facts relating to the proceeding and the conduct of the judge or justice.

(8) Whenever the commission adopts a recommendation that a judge or justice be removed, the judge or justice shall be suspended immediately, with salary, from his or her judicial position until a final determination is made by the supreme court.

(9) The legislature shall provide for commissioners' terms of office and compensation. The commission shall employ one or more investigative officers with appropriate professional training and experience. The investigative officers of the commission shall report directly to the commission. The commission shall also employ such administrative or other staff as are necessary to manage the affairs of the commission.

(10) The commission shall, to the extent that compliance does not conflict with this section, comply with laws of general applicability to state agencies with respect to rule-making procedures, and with respect to public notice of and attendance at commission proceedings other than initial proceedings. The commission shall establish rules of procedure for commission proceedings including due process and confidentiality of proceedings. [AMENDMENT 85, 1989 Substitute Senate Joint Resolution No. 8202, p 3000. Approved November 7, 1989.]

Amendment 77 (1986) — Art. 4 Section 31 COMMISSION ON JUDICIAL CONDUCT — REMOVAL, CENSURE, SUSPENSION, OR RETIREMENT OF JUDGES OR JUSTICES — PROCEEDINGS — There shall be a commission on judicial conduct consisting of a judge selected by and from the court of appeals judges, a judge selected by and from the superior court judges, a judge selected by and from the district court judges, two persons admitted to the practice of law in this state selected by the state bar association, and four persons who are not attorneys appointed by the governor and confirmed by the senate.

The supreme court may censure, suspend, or remove a judge or justice for violating a rule of judicial conduct and may retire a judge or justice for disability which is permanent or is likely to become permanent and which seriously interferes with the performance of judicial duties. The office of a judge or justice retired or removed by the supreme court becomes vacant, and that person is ineligible for judicial office until eligibility is reinstated by the supreme court. The salary of a removed judge or justice shall cease.

The supreme court shall specify the effect upon salary when disciplinary action other than removal is taken. The supreme court may not discipline or retire a judge or justice until the commission on judicial conduct recommends after notice and hearing that action be taken and the supreme court conducts a hearing, after notice, to review commission proceedings and findings against a judge or justice.

Whenever the commission receives a complaint against a judge or justice, it shall first conduct proceedings for the purpose of determining whether sufficient reason exists for conducting a hearing or hearings to deal with the accusations. These initial proceedings shall be confidential, unless confidentiality is waived by the judge or justice, but all subsequent hearings conducted by the commission shall be open to members of the public.

Whenever the commission adopts a recommendation that a judge or justice be removed, the judge or justice shall be suspended immediately, with salary, from his or her judicial position until a final determination is made by the supreme court.

The legislature shall provide for commissioners' terms of office and compensation. The commission shall establish rules of procedure for commission proceedings including due process and confidentiality of proceedings. [AMENDMENT 77, 1986 Senate Joint Resolution No. 136, p 1532. Approved November 4, 1986.]

Amendment 71 (1980) — Art. 4 Section 31 JUDICIAL QUALIFICATIONS COMMISSION — REMOVAL, CENSURE, SUSPENSION, OR RETIREMENT OF JUDGES OR JUSTICES — There shall be a judicial qualifications commission consisting of a judge selected by and from the court of appeals judges, a judge selected by and from the superior court judges, a judge selected by and from the district court judges, two persons admitted to the practice of law in this state selected by the state bar association, and two persons who are not attorneys appointed by the governor and confirmed by the senate.

The supreme court may censure, suspend, or remove a judge or justice for violating a rule of judicial conduct and may retire a judge or justice for disability which is permanent or is likely to become permanent and which seriously interferes with the performance of judicial duties. The office of a judge or justice retired or removed by the supreme court becomes vacant, and that person is ineligible for judicial office until eligibility is reinstated by the supreme court. The salary of a removed judge or justice shall cease.

The supreme court shall specify the effect upon salary when disciplinary action other than removal is taken. The supreme court may not discipline or retire a judge or justice until the judicial qualifications commission recommends after notice and hearing that action be taken and the supreme court conducts a hearing, after notice, to review commission proceedings and findings against a judge or justice.

The legislature shall provide for commissioners' terms of office and compensation. The commission shall establish rules of procedure for commission proceedings including due process and confidentiality of proceedings. [AMENDMENT 71, 1980 Substitute House Joint Resolution No. 37, p 652. Approved November 4, 1980.]

ARTICLE V IMPEACHMENT

SECTION 1 IMPEACHMENT - POWER OF AND PROCEDURE. The house of representatives shall have the sole power of impeachment. The concurrence of a majority of all the members shall be necessary to an impeachment. All impeachments shall be tried by the senate, and, when sitting for that purpose, the senators shall be upon oath or affirmation to do justice according to law and evidence. When the governor or lieutenant governor is on trial, the chief justice of the supreme court shall preside. No person shall be convicted without a concurrence of two-thirds of the senators elected.

SECTION 2 OFFICERS LIABLE TO. The governor and other state and judicial officers, except judges and justices of courts not of record, shall be liable to impeachment for high crimes or misdemeanors, or malfeasance in office, but judgment in such cases shall extend only to removal from office and disqualification to hold any office of honor, trust or profit, in the state. The party, whether convicted or acquitted, shall, nevertheless, be liable to prosecution, trial, judgment and punishment according to law.

SECTION 3 REMOVAL FROM OFFICE. All officers not liable to impeachment shall be subject to removal for misconduct or malfeasance in office, in such manner as may be provided by law.

ARTICLE VI ELECTIONS AND ELECTIVE RIGHTS

SECTION 1 QUALIFICATIONS OF ELECTORS. All persons of the age of eighteen years or over who are citizens of the United States and who have lived in the state, county, and precinct thirty days immediately preceding the election at which they offer to vote, except those disqualified by Article VI, section 3 of this Constitution, shall be entitled to vote at all elections. [**AMENDMENT 63,** 1974 Senate Joint Resolution No. 143, p 807. Approved November 5, 1974.]

Amendment 5 (1910) — Art. 6 Section 1 QUALIFICATIONS OF ELECTORS — All persons of the age of twenty-one years or over, possessing the following qualifications, shall be entitled to vote at all elections: They shall be citizens of the United States; they shall have lived in the state one year, and in the county ninety days, and in the city, town, ward or precinct thirty days immediately preceding the election at which they offer to vote; they shall be able to read and speak the English language: Provided, That Indians not taxed shall never be allowed the elective franchise: And further provided, That this amendment shall not affect the rights of franchise of any person who is now a qualified elector of this state. The legislative authority shall enact laws defining the manner of ascertaining the qualifications of voters as to their ability to read and speak the English language, and providing for punishment of persons voting or registering in violation of the provision of this section. There shall be no denial of the elective franchise at any election on account of sex. [AMENDMENT 5, 1909 p 26 Section 1. Approved November, 1910.]

Amendment 2 (1896) — Art. 6 Section 1 QUALIFICATIONS OF VOTERS — All male persons of the age of twenty-one years or over, possessing the following qualifications, shall be entitled to vote at all elections: They shall be citizens of the United States; they shall have lived in the state one year, and in the county ninety days, and in the city, town, ward or precinct thirty days immediately preceding the election at which they offer to vote; they shall be able to read and speak the English language: Provided, That Indians not taxed shall never be allowed the elective franchise: And further provided, That this amendment shall not effect [affect] the right of franchise of any person who is now a qualified elector of this state. The legislature shall enact laws defining the manner of ascertaining the qualifications of voters as to their ability to read and speak the English language, and providing for punishment of persons voting or registering in violation of the provisions of this section. [AMENDMENT 2, 1895 p 60 Section 1. Approved November, 1896.]

Original text — Art. 6 Section 1 QUALIFICATIONS OF ELECTORS — All male persons of the age of twenty-one years or over, possessing the following qualifications, shall be entitled to vote at all elections: They shall be citizens of the United States; They shall have lived in the state one year, and in the county ninety days, and in the city, town, ward or precinct thirty days immediately preceding the election at which they offer to vote; Provided, that Indians not taxed shall never be allowed the elective franchise; Provided, further; that all male persons who at the time of the adoption of this Constitution are qualified electors of the Territory, shall be electors.

SECTION 1A VOTER QUALIFICATIONS FOR PRESIDENTIAL ELECTIONS. [Repealed by AMENDMENT 105, 2011 Senate Joint Resolution No. 8205, p 4281. Approved November 8, 2011.]

Original text — Art. 6 Section 1A VOTER QUALIFICATIONS FOR PRESIDENTIAL ELECTIONS — In consideration of those citizens of the United States who become residents of the state of Washington during the year of a presidential election with the intention of making this state their permanent residence, this section is for the purpose of authorizing such persons who can meet all qualifications for voting as set forth in section 1 of this article, except for residence, to vote for presidential electors or for the office of President and Vice-President of the United States, as the case may be, but no other: Provided, That such persons have resided in the state at least sixty days immediately preceding the presidential election concerned.

The legislature shall establish the time, manner and place for such persons to cast such presidential ballots.

SECTION 2 SCHOOL ELECTIONS — FRANCHISE, HOW EXTENDED. [This section stricken by AMENDMENT 5, see Art. 6 Section 1.]

Original text — Art. 6 Section 2 SCHOOL ELECTIONS — FRANCHISE, HOW EXTENDED — The legislature may provide that there shall be no denial of the elective franchise at any school election on account of sex.

SECTION 3 WHO DISQUALIFIED. All persons convicted of infamous crime unless restored to their civil rights and all persons while they are judicially declared mentally incompetent are excluded from the elective franchise. [**AMENDMENT 83,** 1988 House Joint Resolution No. 4231, p 1553. Approved November 8, 1988.]

Original text — Art. 6 Section 3 WHO DISQUALIFIED — All idiots, insane persons, and persons convicted of infamous crime unless restored to their civil rights are excluded from the elective franchise.

SECTION 4 RESIDENCE, CONTINGENCIES AFFECTING. For the purpose of voting and eligibility to office no person shall be deemed to have gained a residence by reason of his presence or lost it by reason of his absence, while in the civil or military service of the state or of the United States, nor while a student at any institution of learning, nor while kept at public expense at any poor-house or other asylum, nor while confined in public prison, nor while engaged in the navigation of the waters of this state or of the United States, or of the high seas.

SECTION 5 VOTER — WHEN PRIVILEGED FROM ARREST. Voters shall in all cases except treason, felony, and breach of the peace be privileged from arrest during their attendance at elections and in going to, and returning therefrom. No elector shall be required to do military duty on the day of any election except in time of war or public danger.

SECTION 6 BALLOT. All elections shall be by ballot. The legislature shall provide for such method of voting as will secure to every elector absolute secrecy in preparing and depositing his ballot.

SECTION 7 REGISTRATION. The legislature shall enact a registration law, and shall require a compliance with such law before any elector shall be allowed to vote; Provided, that this provision is not compulsory upon the legislature except as to cities and towns having a population of over five hundred inhabitants. In all other cases the legislature may or may not require registration as a pre-requisite to the right to vote, and the same system of registration need not be adopted for both classes.

SECTION 8 ELECTIONS, TIME OF HOLDING. The first election of county and district officers not otherwise provided for in this Constitution shall be on the Tuesday next after the first Monday in November 1890, and thereafter all elections for such officers shall be held bi-ennially on the Tuesday next succeeding the first Monday in November. The first election of all state officers not otherwise provided for in this Constitution, after the election held for the adoption of this Constitution, shall be on the Tuesday next after the first Monday in November, 1892, and the elections for such state officers shall be held in every fourth year thereafter on the Tuesday succeeding the first Monday in November.

Cf. Art. 27 Section 14.

ARTICLE VII REVENUE AND TAXATION

SECTION 1 TAXATION. The power of taxation shall never be suspended, surrendered or contracted away. All taxes shall be uniform upon the same class of property within the territorial limits of the authority levying the tax and shall be levied and collected for public purposes only. The word "property" as used herein shall mean and include everything, whether tangible or intangible, subject to ownership. All real estate shall constitute one class: Provided, That the legislature may tax mines and mineral resources and lands devoted to reforestation by either a yield tax or an ad valorem tax at such rate as it may fix, or by both. Such property as the legislature may by general laws provide shall be exempt from taxation. Property of the United States and of the state, counties, school districts and other municipal corporations, and credits secured by property actually taxed in this state, not exceeding in value the value of such property, shall be exempt from taxation. The legislature shall have power, by appropriate legislation, to exempt personal property to the amount of fifteen thousand ($15,000.00) dollars for each head of a family liable to assessment and taxation under the provisions of the laws of this state of which the individual is the actual bona fide owner. [**AMENDMENT 98**, 2006 House Joint Resolution No. 4223, p 2117. Approved November 7, 2006.]

Amendment 81 (1988) — Art. 7 Section 1 TAXATION —The power of taxation shall never be suspended, surrendered or contracted away. All taxes shall be uniform upon the same class of property within the territorial limits of the authority levying the tax and shall be levied and collected for public purposes only. The word "property" as used herein shall mean and include everything, whether tangible or intangible, subject to ownership. All real estate shall constitute one class: Provided, That the legislature may tax mines and mineral resources and lands devoted to reforestation by either a yield tax or an ad valorem tax at such rate as it may fix, or by both. Such property as the legislature may by general laws provide shall be exempt from taxation. Property of the United States and of the state, counties, school districts and other municipal corporations, and credits secured by property actually taxed in this state, not exceeding in value the value of such property, shall be exempt from taxation. The legislature shall have power, by appropriate legislation, to exempt personal property to the amount of three thousand ($3,000.00) dollars for each head of a family liable to assessment and taxation under the provisions of the laws of this state of which the individual is the actual bona fide owner.[AMENDMENT 81, 1988 House Joint Resolution No. 4222, p 1551. Approved November 8, 1988.]

Amendment 14 (1930) — Art. 7 Section 1 TAXATION — The power of taxation shall never be suspended, surrendered or contracted away. All taxes shall be uniform upon the same class of property within the territorial limits of the authority levying the tax and shall be levied and collected for public purposes only. The word "property" as used herein shall mean and include everything, whether tangible or intangible, subject to ownership. All real estate shall constitute one class: Provided, That the legislature may tax mines and mineral resources and lands devoted to reforestation by either a yield tax or an ad valorem tax at such rate as it may fix, or by both. Such property as the legislature may by general laws provide shall be exempt from taxation. Property of the United States and of the state, counties, school districts and other municipal corporations, and credits secured by property actually taxed in this state, not exceeding in value the value of such property, shall be exempt from taxation. The legislature shall have power, by appropriate legislation, to exempt personal property to the amount of three hundred ($300.00) dollars for each head of a family liable to assessment and taxation under the provisions of the laws of this state of which the individual is the actual bona fide owner. [AMENDMENT 14, 1929 p 499 Section 1. Approved November, 1930.]

Reviser's note: Amendment 14 amended Art. 7 by striking all of Sections 1, 2, 3 and 4. Subsequently, Amendment 17 added a new Section 2, and Amendment 19 added a new Section 3.

Original text — Art. 7 Section 1 ANNUAL STATE TAX — All property in the state, not exempt under the laws of the United States, or under this Constitution, shall be taxed in proportion to its value, to be ascertained as provided by law. The legislature shall provide by law for an annual tax sufficient, with other sources of revenue to defray the estimated ordinary expenses of the state for each fiscal year. And for the purpose of paying the state debt, if there be any, the legislature shall provide for levying a tax annually, sufficient to pay the annual interest and principal of such debt within twenty years from the final passage of the law creating the debt.

————

Amendment 3 (1900) — Art. 7 Section 2, was amended by adding the following proviso: "And provided further, That the legislature shall have power, by appropriate legislation, to exempt personal property to the amount of three hundred dollars ($300) for each head of a family liable to assessment and taxation under the provisions of the laws of this state of which the individual is the actual and bona fide owner." [AMENDMENT 3, 1899 p 121 Section 1. Approved November, 1900.]

Original text — Art. 7 Section 2 TAXATION — UNIFORMITY AND EQUALITY — EXEMPTION — The legislature shall provide by law a uniform and equal rate of assessment and taxation on all property in the state, according to its value in money, and shall prescribe such regulations by general law as shall secure a just valuation for taxation of all property, so that every person and corporation shall pay a tax in proportion to the value of his, her, or its property; Provided, that a deduction of debts from credits may be authorized: Provided, further, that the property of the United States and of the state, counties, school districts and other municipal corporations, and such other property as the legislature may by general laws provide, shall be exempt from taxation.

————

Original text — Art. 7 Section 3 ASSESSMENT OF CORPORATE PROPERTY — The legislature shall provide by general law for the assessing and levying of taxes on all corporation property as near as may be by the same methods as are provided for the assessing and levying of taxes on individual property.

————

Original text — Art. 7 Section 4 NO SURRENDER OF POWER OR SUSPENSION OF TAX ON CORPORATE PROPERTY — The power to tax corporations and corporate property shall not be surrendered or suspended by any contract or grant to which the state shall be a party.

SECTION 2 LIMITATION ON LEVIES. Except as hereinafter provided and notwithstanding any other provision of this Constitution, the aggregate of all tax levies upon real and personal property by the state and all taxing districts now existing or hereafter created, shall not in any year exceed one percent of the true and fair value of such property in money. Nothing herein shall prevent levies at the rates now provided by law by or for any port or public utility district. The term "taxing district" for the purposes of this section shall mean any political subdivision, municipal corporation, district, or other governmental agency authorized by law to levy, or have levied for it, ad valorem taxes on property, other than a port or public utility district. Such aggregate limitation or any specific limitation imposed by law in conformity therewith may be exceeded only as follows:

(a) By any taxing district when specifically authorized so to do by a majority of at least three-fifths of the voters of the taxing district voting on the proposition to levy such additional tax submitted not more than twelve months prior to the date on which the proposed initial levy is to be made and not oftener than twice in such twelve month period, either at a special election or at the regular election of such taxing district, at which election the number of voters voting "yes" on the proposition shall constitute three-fifths of a number equal to forty percent of the total number of voters voting in such taxing district at the last preceding general election when the number of voters voting on the proposition does not exceed forty percent of the total number of voters voting in such taxing district in the last preceding general election; or by a majority of at least three-fifths of the voters of the taxing district voting on the proposition to levy when the number of voters voting on the proposition exceeds forty percent of the number of voters voting in such taxing district in the last preceding general election. Notwithstanding any other provision of this Constitution, any proposition pursuant to this subsection to levy additional tax for the support of the common schools or fire protection districts may provide such support for a period of up to four years and any proposition to levy an additional tax to support the construction, modernization, or remodelling of school facilities or fire facilities may provide such support for a period not exceeding six years. Notwithstanding any other provision of this subsection, a proposition under this subsection to levy an additional tax for a school district shall be authorized by a majority of the voters voting on the proposition, regardless of the number of voters voting on the proposition;

(b) By any taxing district otherwise authorized by law to issue general obligation bonds for capital purposes, for the sole purpose of making the required payments of principal and interest on general obligation bonds issued solely for capital purposes, other than the replacement of equipment, when authorized so to do by majority of at least three-fifths of the voters of the taxing district voting on the proposition to issue such bonds and to pay the principal and interest thereon by annual tax levies in excess of the limitation herein provided during the term of such bonds, submitted not oftener than twice in any calendar year, at an election held in the manner provided by law for bond elections in such taxing district, at which election the total number of voters voting on the proposition shall constitute not less than forty percent of the total number of voters voting in such taxing district at the last preceding general election. Any such taxing district shall have the right by vote of its governing body to refund any general obligation bonds of said district issued for capital purposes only, and to provide for the interest thereon and amortization thereof by annual levies in excess of the tax limitation provided for herein. The provisions of this section shall also be subject to the limitations contained in Article VIII, Section 6, of this Constitution;

(c) By the state or any taxing district for the purpose of preventing the impairment of the obligation of a contract when ordered so to do by a court of last resort. [**AMENDMENT 101,** 2007 Engrossed House Joint Resolution No. 4204, pp 3143-3145. Approved November 6, 2007.]

Prior amendments of Art. 7 Section 2, see Amendments 17, 55, 59, 64, 79, and 90.

Amendment 95 (2002) — Art. 7 Section 2 LIMITATION ON LEVIES — Except as hereinafter provided and notwithstanding any other provision of this Constitution, the aggregate of all tax levies upon real and personal property by the state and all taxing districts now existing or hereafter created, shall not in any year exceed one percent of the true and fair value of such property in money: Provided, however, That nothing herein shall prevent levies at the rates now provided by law by or for any port or public utility district. The term "taxing district" for the purposes of this section shall mean any political subdivision, municipal corporation, district, or other governmental agency authorized by law to levy, or have levied for it, ad valorem taxes on property, other than a port or public utility district. Such aggregate limitation or any specific limitation imposed by law in conformity therewith may be exceeded only as follows:

(a) By any taxing district when specifically authorized so to do by a majority of at least three-fifths of the voters of the taxing district voting on the proposition to levy such additional tax submitted not more than twelve months prior to the date on which the proposed levy is to be made and not oftener than twice in such twelve month period, either at a special election or at the regular election of such taxing district, at which election the number of voters voting "yes" on the proposition shall constitute three-fifths of a number equal to forty percent of the total number of voters voting in such taxing district at the last preceding general election when the number of voters voting on the proposition does not exceed forty percent of the total number of voters voting in such taxing district in the last preceding general election; or by a majority of at least three-fifths of the voters of the taxing district voting on the proposition to levy when the number of voters voting on the proposition exceeds forty percent of the number of voters voting in such taxing district in the last preceding general election: Provided, That notwithstanding any other provision of this Constitution, any proposition pursuant to this subsection to levy additional tax for the support of the common schools or fire protection districts may provide such support for a period of up to four years and any proposition to levy an additional tax to support the construction, modernization, or remodelling of school facilities or fire facilities may provide such support for a period not exceeding six years;

(b) By any taxing district otherwise authorized by law to issue general obligation bonds for capital purposes, for the sole purpose of making the required payments of principal and interest on general obligation bonds issued solely for capital purposes, other than the replacement of equipment, when authorized so to do by majority of at least three-fifths of the voters of the taxing district voting on the proposition to issue such bonds and to pay the principal and interest thereon by annual tax levies in excess of the limitation herein provided during the term of such bonds, submitted not oftener than twice in any calendar year, at an election held in the manner provided by law for bond elections in such taxing district, at which election the total number of voters voting on the proposition shall constitute not less than forty percent of the total number of voters voting in such taxing district at the last preceding general election: Provided, That any such taxing district shall have the right by vote of its governing body to refund any general obligation bonds of said district issued for capital purposes only, and to provide for the interest thereon and amortization thereof by annual levies in excess of the tax limitation provided for herein, And provided further, That the provisions of this section shall also be subject to the limitations contained in Article VIII, Section 6, of this Constitution;

(c) By the state or any taxing district for the purpose of preventing the impairment of the obligation of a contract when ordered so to do by a court of last resort. [AMENDMENT 95, 2002 House Joint Resolution No. 4220, p 2203. Approved November 5, 2002.]

Amendment 90 (1997) — Art. 7 Section 2 LIMITATION ON LEVIES — Except as hereinafter provided and notwithstanding any other provision of this Constitution, the aggregate of all tax levies upon real and personal property by the state and all taxing districts now existing or hereafter created, shall not in any year exceed one per centum of the true and fair value of such property in money:Provided, however, That nothing herein shall prevent levies at the rates now provided by law by or for any port or public utility district. The term "taxing district" for the purposes of this section shall mean any political subdivision, municipal corporation, district, or other governmental agency authorized by law to levy, or have levied for it, ad valorem taxes on property, other than a port or public utility district. Such aggregate limitation or any specific limitation imposed by law in conformity therewith may be exceeded only

(a) By any taxing district when specifically authorized so to do by a majority of at least three-fifths of the electors thereof voting on the proposition to levy such additional tax submitted not more than twelve months prior to the date on which the proposed levy is to be made and not oftener than twice in such twelve month period, either at a special election or at the regular election of such taxing district, at which election the number of persons voting "yes" on the proposition shall constitute three-fifths of a number equal to forty per centum of the total votes cast in such taxing district at the last preceding general election when the number of electors voting on the proposition does not exceed forty per centum of the total votes cast in such taxing district in the last preceding general election; or by a majority of at least three-fifths of the electors thereof voting on the proposition to levy when the number of electors voting on the proposition exceeds forty percentum of the total votes cast in such taxing district in the last preceding general election: Provided, That notwithstanding any other provision of this Constitution, any proposition pursuant to this subsection to levy additional tax for the support of the common schools may provide such support for a two year period and any proposition to levy an additional tax to support the construction, modernization, or remodelling of school facilities may provide such support for a period not exceeding six years;

(b) By any taxing district otherwise authorized by law to issue general obligation bonds for capital purposes, for the sole purpose of making the required payments of principal and interest on general obligation bonds issued solely for capital purposes, other than the replacement of equipment, when authorized so to do by majority of at least three-fifths of the electors thereof voting on the proposition to issue such bonds and to pay the principal and interest thereon by an annual tax levy in excess of the limitation herein provided during the term of such bonds, submitted not oftener than twice in any calendar year, at an election held in the manner provided by law for bond elections in such taxing district, at which election the total number of persons voting on the proposition shall constitute not less than forty per centum of the total number of votes cast in such taxing district at the last preceding general election: Provided, That any such taxing district shall have the right by vote of its governing body to refund any general obligation bonds of said district issued for capital purposes only, and to provide for the interest thereon and amortization thereof by annual levies in excess of the tax limitation provided for herein, And provided further, That the provisions of this section shall also be subject to the limitations contained in Article VIII, Section 6, of this Constitution;

(c) By the state or any taxing district for the purpose of paying the principal or interest on general obligation bonds outstanding on December 6, 1934; or for the purpose of preventing the impairment of the obligation of a contract when ordered so to do by a court of last resort. [AMENDMENT 90, 1997 House Joint Resolution No. 4208, p 3063. Approved November 4, 1997.]

Amendment 79 (1986) — Art. 7 Section 2 LIMITATION ON LEVIES — Except as hereinafter provided and notwithstanding any other provision of this Constitution, the aggregate of all tax levies upon real and personal property by the state and all taxing districts now existing or hereafter created, shall not in any year exceed one per centum of the true and fair value of such property in money:Provided, however, That nothing herein shall prevent levies at the rates now provided by law by or for any port or public utility district. The term "taxing district" for the purposes of this section shall mean any political subdivision, municipal corporation, district, or other governmental agency authorized by law to levy, or have levied for it, ad valorem taxes on property, other than a port or public utility district. Such aggregate limitation or any specific limitation imposed by law in conformity therewith may be exceeded only

(a) By any taxing district when specifically authorized so to do by a majority of at least three-fifths of the electors thereof voting on the proposition to levy such additional tax submitted not more than twelve months prior to the date on which the proposed levy is to be made and not oftener than twice in such twelve month period, either at a special election or at the regular election of such taxing district, at which election the number of persons voting "yes" on the proposition shall constitute three-fifths of a number equal to forty per centum of the total votes cast in such taxing district at the last preceding general election when the number of electors voting on the proposition does not exceed forty per centum of the total votes cast in such taxing district in the last preceding general election; or by a majority of at least three-fifths of the electors thereof voting on the proposition to levy when the number of electors voting on the proposition exceeds forty percentum of the total votes cast in such taxing district in the last preceding general election: Provided, That notwithstanding any other provision of this Constitution, any proposition pursuant to this subsection to levy additional tax for the support of the common schools may provide such support for a two year period and any proposition to levy an additional tax to support the construction, modernization, or remodelling of school facilities may provide such support for a period not exceeding six years;

(b) By any taxing district otherwise authorized by law to issue general obligation bonds for capital purposes, for the sole purpose of making the required payments of principal and interest on general obligation bonds issued solely for capital purposes, other than the replacement of equipment, when authorized so to do by majority of at least three-fifths of the electors thereof voting on the proposition to issue such bonds and to pay the principal and interest thereon by an annual tax levy in excess of the limitation herein provided during the term of such bonds, submitted not oftener than twice in any calendar year, at an election held in the manner provided by law for bond elections in such taxing district, at which election the total number of persons voting on the proposition shall constitute not less than forty per centum of the total number of votes cast in such taxing district at the last preceding general election: Provided, That any such taxing district shall have the right by vote of its governing body to refund any general obligation bonds of said district issued for capital purposes only, and to provide for the interest thereon and amortization thereof by annual levies in excess of the tax limitation provided for herein, And provided further, That the provisions of this section shall also be subject to the limitations contained in Article VIII, Section 6, of this Constitution;

(c) By the state or any taxing district for the purpose of paying the principal or interest on general obligation bonds outstanding on December 6, 1934; or for the purpose of preventing the impairment of the obligation of a contract when ordered so to do by a court of last resort. [AMENDMENT 79, 1986 House Joint Resolution No. 55, p 1530. Approved November 4, 1986.]

Amendment 64 (1976) — Art. 7 Section 2 LIMITATION ON LEVIES — Except as hereinafter provided and notwithstanding any other provision of this Constitution, the aggregate of all tax levies upon real and personal property by the state and all taxing districts now existing or hereafter created, shall not in any year exceed one per centum of the true and fair value of such property in money:Provided, however, That nothing herein shall prevent levies at the rates now provided by law by or for any port or public utility district. The term "taxing district" for the purposes of this section shall mean any political subdivision, municipal corporation, district, or other governmental agency authorized by law to levy, or have levied for it, ad valorem taxes on property, other than a port or public utility district. Such aggregate limitation or any specific limitation imposed by law in conformity therewith may be exceeded only

(a) By any taxing district when specifically authorized so to do by a majority of at least three-fifths of the electors thereof voting on the proposition to levy such additional tax submitted not more than twelve months prior to the date on which the proposed levy is to be made and not oftener than twice in such twelve month period, either at a special election or at the regular election of such taxing district, at which election the number of persons voting "yes" on the proposition shall constitute three-fifths of a number equal to forty per centum of the total votes cast in such taxing district at the last preceding general election when the number of electors voting on the proposition does not exceed forty per centum of the total votes cast in such taxing district in the last preceding general election; or by a majority of at least three-fifths of the electors thereof voting on the proposition to levy when the number of electors voting on the proposition exceeds forty percentum of the total votes cast in such taxing district in the last preceding general election: Provided, That notwithstanding any other provision of this Constitution, any proposition pursuant to this subsection to levy additional tax for the support of the common schools may provide such support for a two year period;

(b) By any taxing district otherwise authorized by law to issue general obligation bonds for capital purposes, for the sole purpose of making the required payments of principal and interest on general obligation bonds issued solely for capital purposes, other than the replacement of equipment, when authorized so to do by majority of at least three-fifths of the electors thereof voting on the proposition to issue such bonds and to pay the principal and interest thereon by an annual tax levy in excess of the limitation herein provided during the term of such bonds, submitted not oftener than twice in any calendar year, at an election held in the manner provided by law for bond elections in such taxing district, at which election the total number of persons voting on the proposition shall constitute not less than forty per centum of the total number of votes cast in such taxing district at the last preceding general election: Provided, That any such taxing district shall have the right by vote of its governing body to refund any general obligation bonds of said district issued for capital purposes only, and to provide for the interest thereon and amortization thereof by annual levies in excess of the tax limitation provided for herein, And provided further, That the provisions of this section shall also be subject to the limitations contained in Article VIII, Section 6, of this Constitution;

(c) By the state or any taxing district for the purpose of paying the principal or interest on general obligation bonds outstanding on December 6, 1934; or for the purpose of preventing the impairment of the obligation of a contract when ordered so to do by a court of last resort. [AMENDMENT 64, 1975-'76 2nd ex.s. Senate Joint Resolution No. 137, p 518. Approved November 2, 1976.]

Amendment 59 (1972) and Amendment 55 (1972) — Art. 7 Section 2 LIMITATION ON LEVIES — Except as hereinafter provided and notwithstanding any other provision of this Constitution, the aggregate of all tax levies upon real and personal property by the state and all taxing districts now existing or hereafter created, shall not in any year exceed one per centum of the true and fair value of such property in money: Provided, however, That nothing herein shall prevent levies at the rates now provided by law by or for any port or public utility district. The term "taxing district" for the purposes of this section shall mean any political subdivision, municipal corporation, district, or other governmental agency authorized by law to levy, or have levied for it, ad valorem taxes on property, other than a port or public utility district. Such aggregate limitation or any specific limitation imposed by law in conformity therewith may be exceeded only

(a) By any taxing district when specifically authorized so to do by a majority of at least three-fifths of the electors thereof voting on the proposition to levy such additional tax submitted not more than twelve months prior to the date on which the proposed levy is to be made and not oftener than twice in such twelve month period, either at a special election or at the regular election of such taxing district, at which election the number of persons voting "yes" on the proposition shall constitute three-fifths of a number equal to forty per centum of the total votes cast in such taxing district at the last preceding general election when the number of electors voting on the proposition does not exceed forty per centum of the total votes cast in such taxing district in the last preceding general election; or by a majority of at least three-fifths of the electors thereof voting on the proposition to levy when the number of electors voting on the proposition exceeds forty percentum of the total votes cast in such taxing district in the last preceding general election;

     (b) By any taxing district otherwise authorized by law to issue general obligation bonds for capital purposes, for the sole purpose of making the required payments of principal and interest on general obligation bonds issued solely for capital purposes, other than the replacement of equipment, when authorized so to do by majority of at least three-fifths of the electors thereof voting on the proposition to issue such bonds and to pay the principal and interest thereon by an annual tax levy in excess of the limitation herein provided during the term of such bonds, submitted not oftener than twice in any calendar year, at an election held in the manner provided by law for bond elections in such taxing district, at which election the total number of persons voting on the proposition shall constitute not less than forty per centum of the total number of votes cast in such taxing district at the last preceding general election: Provided, That any such taxing district shall have the right by vote of its governing body to refund any general obligation bonds of said district issued for capital purposes only, and to provide for the interest thereon and amortization thereof by annual levies in excess of the tax limitation provided for herein, And provided further, That the provisions of this section shall also be subject to the limitations contained in Article VIII, Section 6, of this Constitution;

     (c) By the state or any taxing district for the purpose of paying the principal or interest on general obligation bonds outstanding on December 6, 1934; or for the purpose of preventing the impairment of the obligation of a contract when ordered so to do by a court of last resort. [(i) AMENDMENT 59, 1971 House Joint Resolution No. 47, p 1834. Approved November, 1972. (ii) AMENDMENT 55, 1971 Senate Joint Resolution No. 1, p 1827. Approved November, 1972.]

    Reviser's note: Article 7 Section 2 was twice amended in different respects at the November 1972 general election by the ratification of both S.J.R. No. 1. (AMENDMENT 55) and H.J.R. No. 47. (AMENDMENT 59.) 1971 HJR No. 47 contained the following paragraph:

    "Be It Further Resolved, That the foregoing amendment shall be submitted to the qualified electors of the state in such a manner that they may vote for or against it separately from the proposed amendment to Article VII, section 2, (Amendment 17) of the Constitution of the State of Washington contained in Senate Joint Resolution No. 1: Provided, That if both proposed amendments are approved and ratified, both shall become part of the Constitution" [1971 House Joint Resolution No. 47, part, p 1834]

    The section as printed above reflects the content of both amendments.

    Amendment 17 (1944) — Art. 7 Section 2 FORTY MILL LIMIT — Except as hereinafter provided and notwithstanding any other provision of this Constitution, the aggregate of all tax levies upon real and personal property by the state and all taxing districts now existing or hereafter created, shall not in any year exceed forty mills on the dollar of assessed valuation, which assessed valuation shall be fifty per centum of the true and fair value of such property in money: Provided, however, That nothing herein shall prevent levies at the rates now provided by law by or for any port or public utility district. The term "taxing district" for the purposes of this section shall mean any political subdivision, municipal corporation, district, or other governmental agency authorized by law to levy, or have levied for it, ad valorem taxes on property, other than a port or public utility district. Such aggregate limitation or any specific limitation imposed by law in conformity therewith may be exceeded only

(a) By any taxing district when specifically authorized so to do by a majority of at least three-fifths of the electors thereof voting on the proposition to levy such additional tax submitted not more than twelve months prior to the date on which the proposed levy is to be made and not oftener than twice in such twelve month period, either at a special election or at the regular election of such taxing district, at which election the number of persons voting on the proposition shall constitute not less than forty per centum of the total number of votes cast in such taxing district at the last preceding general election;

(b) By any taxing district otherwise authorized by law to issue general obligation bonds for capital purposes, for the sole purpose of making the required payments of principal and interest on general obligation bonds issued solely for capital purposes, other than the replacement of equipment, when authorized so to do by majority of at least three-fifths of the electors thereof voting on the proposition to issue such bonds and to pay the principal and interest thereon by an annual tax levy in excess of the limitation herein provided during the term of such bonds, submitted not oftener than twice in any calendar year, at an election held in the manner provided by law for bond elections in such taxing district, at which election the total number of persons voting on the proposition shall constitute not less than forty per centum of the total number of votes cast in such taxing district at the last preceding general election: Provided, That any such taxing district shall have the right by vote of its governing body to refund any general obligation bonds of said district issued for capital purposes only, and to provide for the interest thereon and amortization thereof by annual levies in excess of the tax limitation provided for herein, and Provided further, That the provisions of this section shall also be subject to the limitations contained in Article VIII, Section 6, of this Constitution;

(c) By the state or any taxing district for the purpose of paying the principal or interest on general obligation bonds outstanding on December 6, 1934; or for the purpose of preventing the impairment of the obligation of a contract when ordered so to do by a court of last resort. [AMENDMENT 17, 1943 House Joint Resolution No. 1, p 936. Approved November, 1944.]

Reviser's note: Original section 2, as amended by Amendment 3, was stricken by Amendment 14. The original section and Amendment 3, are set out following Art. 7, Section 1, above.

SECTION 3 TAXATION OF FEDERAL AGENCIES AND PROPERTY. The United States and its agencies and instrumentalities, and their property, may be taxed under any of the tax laws of this state, whenever and in such manner as such taxation may be authorized or permitted under the laws of the United States, notwithstanding anything to the contrary in the Constitution of this state. [**AMENDMENT 19,** 1945 House Joint Resolution No. 9, p 932. Approved November, 1946.]

Reviser's note: Original section 3 was stricken by Amendment 14. The original section is set out following Art. 7 Section 1, above.

SECTION 4 NO SURRENDER OF POWER OR SUSPENSION OF TAX ON CORPORATE PROPERTY.

Reviser's note: Original section 4 was stricken by Amendment 14. It is set out following Art. 7 Section 1, above.

SECTION 5 TAXES, HOW LEVIED. No tax shall be levied except in pursuance of law; and every law imposing a tax shall state distinctly the object of the same to which only it shall be applied.

SECTION 6 TAXES, HOW PAID. All taxes levied and collected for state purposes shall be paid in money only into the state treasury.

SECTION 7 ANNUAL STATEMENT. An accurate statement of the receipts and expenditures of the public moneys shall be published annually in such manner as the legislature may provide.

SECTION 8 TAX TO COVER DEFICIENCIES. Whenever the expenses of any fiscal year shall exceed the income, the legislature may provide for levying a tax for the ensuing fiscal year, sufficient, with other sources of income, to pay the deficiency, as well as the estimated expenses of the ensuing fiscal year.

SECTION 9 SPECIAL ASSESSMENTS OR TAXATION FOR LOCAL IMPROVEMENTS. The legislature may vest the corporate authorities of cities, towns and villages with power to make local improvements by special assessment, or by special taxation of property benefited. For all corporate purposes, all municipal corporations may be vested with authority to assess and collect taxes and such taxes shall be uniform in respect to persons and property within the jurisdiction of the body levying the same.

SECTION 10 RETIRED PERSONS PROPERTY TAX EXEMPTION. Notwithstanding the provisions of Article 7, section 1 (Amendment 14) and Article 7, section 2 (Amendment 17), the following tax exemption shall be allowed as to real property:

The legislature shall have the power, by appropriate legislation, to grant to retired property owners relief from the property tax on the real property occupied as a residence by those owners. The legislature may place such restrictions and conditions upon the granting of such relief as it shall deem proper. Such restrictions and conditions may include, but are not limited to, the limiting of the relief to those property owners below a specific level of income and those fulfilling certain minimum residential requirements. [**AMENDMENT 47,** 1965 ex.s. House Joint Resolution No. 7, p 2821. Approved November 8, 1966.]

SECTION 11 TAXATION BASED ON ACTUAL USE. Nothing in this Article VII as amended shall prevent the legislature from providing, subject to such conditions as it may enact, that the true and fair value in money (a) of farms, agricultural lands, standing timber and timberlands, and (b) of other open space lands which are used for recreation or for enjoyment of their scenic or natural beauty shall be based on the use to which such property is currently applied, and such values shall be used in computing the assessed valuation of such property in the same manner as the assessed valuation is computed for all property. [**AMENDMENT 53,** 1967 House Joint Resolution No. 1; see 1969 p 2976. Approved November 5, 1968.]

SECTION 12 BUDGET STABILIZATION ACCOUNT. (a) A budget stabilization account shall be established and maintained in the state treasury.

(b)(1) By June 30th of each fiscal year, an amount equal to one percent of the general state revenues for that fiscal year shall be transferred to the budget stabilization account. Nothing in this subsection (b) shall prevent the appropriation of additional amounts to the budget stabilization account.

(2) By June 30th of the second year of each fiscal biennium, three-quarters of any extraordinary revenue growth shall be transferred to the budget stabilization account. However, no transfer of extraordinary revenue growth under this subsection (b)(2) shall occur in a fiscal biennium following a fiscal biennium in which annual average state employment growth averaged less than one percent per fiscal year. "Extraordinary revenue growth" means the amount by which the growth in general state revenues for that fiscal biennium exceeds by one-third the average biennial percentage growth in general state revenues over the prior five fiscal biennia. In making this determination, the comparability of data shall be maintained by adjusting

historical general state revenues to reflect statutory changes to the dedication of state revenues. The transfer under this subsection shall be made only to the extent that it exceeds the total transfers under (1) of this subsection for that fiscal biennium.

(c) Each fiscal quarter, the state economic and revenue forecast council appointed and authorized as provided by statute, or successor entity, shall estimate state employment growth for the current and next two fiscal years.

(d) Moneys may be withdrawn and appropriated from the budget stabilization account as follows:

(i) If the governor declares a state of emergency resulting from a catastrophic event that necessitates government action to protect life or public safety, then for that fiscal year moneys may be withdrawn and appropriated from the budget stabilization account, via separate legislation setting forth the nature of the emergency and containing an appropriation limited to the above-authorized purposes as contained in the declaration, by a favorable vote of a majority of the members elected to each house of the legislature.

(ii) If the employment growth forecast for any fiscal year is estimated to be less than one percent, then for that fiscal year moneys may be withdrawn and appropriated from the budget stabilization account by the favorable vote of a majority of the members elected to each house of the legislature.

(iii) Any amount may be withdrawn and appropriated from the budget stabilization account at any time by the favorable vote of at least three-fifths of the members of each house of the legislature.

(e) Amounts in the budget stabilization account may be invested as provided by law and retained in that account. When the balance in the budget stabilization account, including investment earnings, equals more than ten percent of the estimated general state revenues in that fiscal year, the legislature by the favorable vote of a majority of the members elected to each house of the legislature may withdraw and appropriate the balance to the extent that the balance exceeds ten percent of the estimated general state revenues. Appropriations under this subsection (e) may be made solely for deposit to the education construction fund.

(f) As used in this section, "general state revenues" has the meaning set forth in Article VIII, section 1 of the Constitution. Forecasts and estimates shall be made by the state economic and revenue forecast council appointed and authorized as provided by statute, or successor entity.

(g) The legislature shall enact appropriate laws to carry out the purposes of this section.

(h) This section takes effect July 1, 2008. [**AMENDMENT 106,** 2011 Senate Joint Resolution No. 8206, p 4281-4283. Approved November 8, 2011.]

Amendment 99 (2007) — Art. 7 Section 12 BUDGET STABILIZATION ACCOUNT —
(a) A budget stabilization account shall be established and maintained in the state treasury.

(b) By June 30th of each fiscal year, an amount equal to one percent of the general state revenues for that fiscal year shall be transferred to the budget stabilization account. Nothing in this subsection (b) shall prevent the appropriation of additional amounts to the budget stabilization account.

(c) Each fiscal quarter, the state economic and revenue forecast council appointed and authorized as provided by statute, or successor entity, shall estimate state employment growth for the current and next two fiscal years.

(d) Moneys may be withdrawn and appropriated from the budget stabilization account as follows:

(i) If the governor declares a state of emergency resulting from a catastrophic event that necessitates government action to protect life or public safety, then for that fiscal year moneys may be withdrawn and appropriated from the budget stabilization account, via separate legislation setting forth the nature of the emergency and containing an appropriation limited to the above-authorized purposes as contained in the declaration, by a favorable vote of a majority of the members elected to each house of the legislature.

(ii) If the employment growth forecast for any fiscal year is estimated to be less than one percent, then for that fiscal year moneys may be withdrawn and appropriated from the budget stabilization account by the favorable vote of a majority of the members elected to each house of the legislature.

(iii) Any amount may be withdrawn and appropriated from the budget stabilization account at any time by the favorable vote of at least three-fifths of the members of each house of the legislature.

(e) Amounts in the budget stabilization account may be invested as provided by law and retained in that account. When the balance in the budget stabilization account, including investment earnings, equals more than ten percent of the estimated general state revenues in that fiscal year, the legislature by the favorable vote of a majority of the members elected to each house of the legislature may withdraw and appropriate the balance to the extent that the balance exceeds ten percent of the estimated general state revenues. Appropriations under this subsection (e) may be made solely for deposit to the education construction fund.

(f) As used in this section, "general state revenues" has the meaning set forth in Article VIII, section 1 of the Constitution. Forecasts and estimates shall be made by the state economic and revenue forecast council appointed and authorized as provided by statute, or successor entity.

(g) The legislature shall enact appropriate laws to carry out the purposes of this section.

(h) This section takes effect July 1, 2008. [AMENDMENT 99, 2007 Engrossed Substitute Senate Joint Resolution No. 8206, pp 3146, 3147. Approved November 6, 2007.]

ARTICLE VIII
STATE, COUNTY, AND
MUNICIPAL INDEBTEDNESS

SECTION 1 STATE DEBT. (a) The state may contract debt, the principal of which shall be paid and discharged within thirty years from the time of contracting thereof, in the manner set forth herein.

(b) The aggregate debt contracted by the state, as calculated by the treasurer at the time debt is contracted, shall not exceed that amount for which payments of principal and interest in any fiscal year would require the state to expend more than the applicable percentage limit of the arithmetic mean of its general state revenues for the six immediately preceding fiscal years as certified by the treasurer. The term "applicable percentage limit" means eight and one-half percent from July 1, 2014, through June 30, 2016; eight and one-quarter percent from July 1, 2016, through June 30, 2034; eight percent from July 1, 2034, and thereafter. The term "fiscal year" means that period of time commencing July 1 of any year and ending on June 30 of the following year.

(c) The term "general state revenues," when used in this section, shall include all state money received in the treasury from each and every source, including moneys received from ad valorem taxes levied by the state and deposited in the general fund in each fiscal year, but not including: (1) Fees and other revenues derived from the ownership or operation of any undertaking, facility, or project; (2) Moneys received as gifts, grants, donations, aid, or assistance or otherwise from the United States or any department, bureau, or corporation thereof, or any person, firm, or corporation, public or private, when the terms and conditions of such gift, grant, donation, aid, or assistance require the application and disbursement of such moneys otherwise than for the general purposes of the state of Washington; (3) Moneys to be paid into and received from retirement system funds, and performance bonds and deposits; (4) Moneys to be paid into and received from trust funds and the several permanent and irreducible funds of the state and the moneys derived therefrom but excluding bond redemption funds; (5) Moneys received from taxes levied for specific purposes and required to be deposited for those purposes into specified funds or accounts other than the general fund; and (6) Proceeds received from the sale of bonds or other evidences of indebtedness.

(d) In computing the amount required for payment of principal and interest on outstanding debt under this section, debt shall be construed to mean borrowed money represented by bonds, notes, or other evidences of indebtedness which are secured by the full faith and credit of the state or are required to be repaid, directly or indirectly, from general state revenues and which are incurred by the state, any department, authority, public corporation, or quasi public corporation of the state, any state university or college, or any other public agency created by the state but not by counties, cities, towns, school districts, or other municipal corporations, but shall not include obligations for the payment of current expenses of state government, nor shall it include debt hereafter incurred pursuant to section 3 of this article, obligations guaranteed as provided for in subsection (g) of this section, principal of bond anticipation notes or obligations issued to fund or refund the indebtedness of the Washington state building authority. In addition, for the purpose of computing the amount required for payment of interest on outstanding debt under subsection (b) of this section and this subsection, "interest" shall be reduced by subtracting the amount scheduled to be received by the state as payments from the federal government in each year in respect of bonds, notes, or other evidences of indebtedness subject to this section.

(e) The state may pledge the full faith, credit, and taxing power of the state to guarantee the voter approved general obligation debt of school districts in the manner authorized by the legislature. Any such guarantee does not remove the debt obligation of the school district and is not state debt.

(f) The state may, without limitation, fund or refund, at or prior to maturity, the whole or any part of any existing debt or of any debt hereafter contracted pursuant to section 1, section 2, or section 3 of this article, including any premium payable with respect thereto and interest thereon, or fund or refund, at or prior to maturity, the whole or any part of any indebtedness incurred or authorized prior to the effective date of this amendment by any entity of the type described in subsection (h) of this section, including any premium payable with respect thereto and any interest thereon. Such funding or refunding shall not be deemed to be contracting debt by the state.

(g) Notwithstanding the limitation contained in subsection (b) of this section, the state may pledge its full faith, credit, and taxing power to guarantee the payment of any obligation payable from revenues received from any of the following sources: (1) Fees collected by the state as license fees for motor vehicles; (2) Excise taxes collected by the state on the sale, distribution or use of motor vehicle fuel; and (3) Interest on the permanent common school fund: Provided, That the legislature shall, at all times, provide sufficient revenues from such sources to pay the principal and interest due on all obligations for which said source of revenue is pledged.

(h) No money shall be paid from funds in custody of the treasurer with respect to any debt contracted after the effective date of this amendment by the Washington state building authority, the capitol committee, or any similar entity existing or operating for similar purposes pursuant to which such entity undertakes to finance or provide a facility for use or occupancy by the state or any agency, department, or instrumentality thereof.

(i) The legislature shall prescribe all matters relating to the contracting, funding or refunding of debt pursuant to this section, including: The purposes for which debt may be contracted; by a favorable vote of three-fifths of the members elected to each house, the amount of debt which may be contracted for any class of such purposes; the kinds of notes, bonds, or other evidences of debt which may be issued by the state; and the manner by which the treasurer shall determine and advise the legislature, any appropriate agency, officer, or instrumentality of the state as to the available debt capacity within the limitation set forth in this section. The legislature may delegate to any state officer, agency, or instrumentality any of its powers relating to the contracting, funding or refunding of debt pursuant to this section except its power to determine the amount and purposes for which debt may be contracted.

(j) The full faith, credit, and taxing power of the state of Washington are pledged to the payment of the debt created on behalf of the state pursuant to this section and the legislature shall provide by appropriation for the payment of the interest upon and installments of principal of all such debt as the same falls due, but in any event, any court of record may compel such payment.

(k) Notwithstanding the limitations contained in subsection (b) of this section, the state may issue certificates of indebtedness in such sum or sums as may be necessary to meet temporary deficiencies of the treasury, to preserve the best interests of the state in the conduct of the various state institutions, departments, bureaus, and agencies during each fiscal year; such certificates may be issued only to provide for appropriations already made by the legislature and such certificates must be retired and the debt discharged other than by refunding within twelve months after the date of incurrence.

(l) Bonds, notes, or other obligations issued and sold by the state of Washington pursuant to and in conformity with this article shall not be invalid for any irregularity or defect in the proceedings of the issuance or sale thereof and shall be incontestable in the hands of a bona fide purchaser or holder thereof. [**AMENDMENT 107,** 2012 Engrossed Senate Joint Resolution No. 8221, p 2429-2432. Approved November 6, 2012.]

Amendment 103 (2010) — Art. 8 Section 1 STATE DEBT — (a) The state may contract debt, the principal of which shall be paid and discharged within thirty years from the time of contracting thereof, in the manner set forth herein.

(b) The aggregate debt contracted by the state shall not exceed that amount for which payments of principal and interest in any fiscal year would require the state to expend more than nine percent of the arithmetic mean of its general state revenues for the three immediately preceding fiscal years as certified by the treasurer. The term "fiscal year" means that period of time commencing July 1 of any year and ending on June 30 of the following year.

(c) The term "general state revenues" when used in this section, shall include all state money received in the treasury from each and every source whatsoever except: (1) Fees and revenues derived from the ownership or operation of any undertaking, facility, or project; (2) Moneys received as gifts, grants, donations, aid, or assistance or otherwise from the United States or any department, bureau, or corporation thereof, or any person, firm, or corporation, public or private, when the terms and conditions of such gift, grant, donation, aid, or assistance require the application and disbursement of such moneys otherwise than for the general purposes of the state of Washington; (3) Moneys to be paid into and received from retirement system funds, and performance bonds and deposits; (4) Moneys to be paid into and received from trust funds including but not limited to moneys received from taxes levied for specific purposes and the several permanent and irreducible funds of the state and the moneys derived therefrom but excluding bond redemption funds; (5) Proceeds received from the sale of bonds or other evidences of indebtedness.

(d) In computing the amount required for payment of principal and interest on outstanding debt under this section, debt shall be construed to mean borrowed money represented by bonds, notes, or other evidences of indebtedness which are secured by the full faith and credit of the state or are required to be repaid, directly or indirectly, from general state revenues and which are incurred by the state, any department, authority, public corporation, or quasi public corporation of the state, any state university or college, or any other public agency created by the state but not by counties, cities, towns, school districts, or other municipal corporations, but shall not include obligations for the payment of current expenses of state government, nor shall it include debt hereafter incurred pursuant to section 3 of this article, obligations guaranteed as provided for in subsection (g) of this section, principal of bond anticipation notes or obligations issued to fund or refund the indebtedness of the Washington state building authority. In addition, for the purpose of computing the amount required for payment of interest on outstanding debt under subsection (b) of this section and this subsection, "interest" shall be reduced by subtracting the amount scheduled to be received by the state as payments from the federal government in each year in respect of bonds, notes, or other evidences of indebtedness subject to this section.

(e) The state may pledge the full faith, credit, and taxing power of the state to guarantee the voter approved general obligation debt of school districts in the manner authorized by the legislature. Any such guarantee does not remove the debt obligation of the school district and is not state debt.

(f) The state may, without limitation, fund or refund, at or prior to maturity, the whole or any part of any existing debt or of any debt hereafter contracted pursuant to section 1, section 2, or section 3 of this article, including any premium payable with respect thereto and interest thereon, or fund or refund, at or prior to maturity, the whole or any part of any indebtedness incurred or authorized prior to the effective date of this amendment by any entity of the type described in subsection (h) of this section, including any premium payable with respect thereto and any interest thereon. Such funding or refunding shall not be deemed to be contracting debt by the state.

(g) Notwithstanding the limitation contained in subsection (b) of this section, the state may pledge its full faith, credit, and taxing power to guarantee the payment of any obligation payable from revenues received from any of the following sources: (1) Fees collected by the state as license fees for motor vehicles; (2) Excise taxes collected by the state on the sale, distribution or use of motor vehicle fuel; and (3) Interest on the permanent common school fund: Provided, That the legislature shall, at all times, provide sufficient revenues from such sources to pay the principal and interest due on all obligations for which said source of revenue is pledged.

(h) No money shall be paid from funds in custody of the treasurer with respect to any debt contracted after the effective date of this amendment by the Washington state building authority, the capitol committee, or any similar entity existing or operating for similar purposes pursuant to which such entity undertakes to finance or provide a facility for use or occupancy by the state or any agency, department, or instrumentality thereof.

(i) The legislature shall prescribe all matters relating to the contracting, funding or refunding of debt pursuant to this section, including: The purposes for which debt may be contracted; by a favorable vote of three-fifths of the members elected to each house, the amount of debt which may be contracted for any class of such purposes; the kinds of notes, bonds, or other evidences of debt which may be issued by the state; and the manner by which the treasurer shall determine and advise the legislature, any appropriate agency, officer, or instrumentality of the state as to the available debt capacity within the limitation set forth in this section. The legislature may delegate to any state officer, agency, or instrumentality any of its powers relating to the contracting, funding or refunding of debt pursuant to this section except its power to determine the amount and purposes for which debt may be contracted.

(j) The full faith, credit, and taxing power of the state of Washington are pledged to the payment of the debt created on behalf of the state pursuant to this section and the legislature shall provide by appropriation for the payment of the interest upon and installments of principal of all such debt as the same falls due, but in any event, any court of record may compel such payment.

(k) Notwithstanding the limitations contained in subsection (b) of this section, the state may issue certificates of indebtedness in such sum or sums as may be necessary to meet temporary deficiencies of the treasury, to preserve the best interests of the state in the conduct of the various state institutions, departments, bureaus, and agencies during each fiscal year; such certificates may be issued only to provide for appropriations already made by the legislature and such certificates must be retired and the debt discharged other than by refunding within twelve months after the date of incurrence.

(l) Bonds, notes, or other obligations issued and sold by the state of Washington pursuant to and in conformity with this article shall not be invalid for any irregularity or defect in the proceedings of the issuance or sale thereof and shall be incontestable in the hands of a bona fide purchaser or holder thereof. [AMENDMENT 103, 2010 Senate Joint Resolution No. 8225, p 3129-3132. Approved November 2, 2010.]

Amendment 92 (1999) — Art. 8 Section 1 STATE DEBT — (a) The state may contract debt, the principal of which shall be paid and discharged within thirty years from the time of contracting thereof, in the manner set forth herein.

(b) The aggregate debt contracted by the state shall not exceed that amount for which payments of principal and interest in any fiscal year would require the state to expend more than nine percent of the arithmetic mean of its general state revenues for the three immediately preceding fiscal years as certified by the treasurer. The term "fiscal year" means that period of time commencing July 1 of any year and ending on June 30 of the following year.

(c) The term "general state revenues" when used in this section, shall include all state money received in the treasury from each and every source whatsoever except: (1) Fees and revenues derived from the ownership or operation of any undertaking, facility, or project; (2) Moneys received as gifts, grants, donations, aid, or assistance or otherwise from the United States or any department, bureau, or corporation thereof, or any person, firm, or corporation, public or private, when the terms and conditions of such gift, grant, donation, aid, or assistance require the application and disbursement of such moneys otherwise than for the general purposes of the state of Washington; (3) Moneys to be paid into and received from retirement system funds, and performance bonds and deposits; (4) Moneys to be paid into and received from trust funds including but not limited to moneys received from taxes levied for specific purposes and the several permanent and irreducible funds of the state and the moneys derived therefrom but excluding bond redemption funds; (5) Proceeds received from the sale of bonds or other evidences of indebtedness.

(d) In computing the amount required for payment of principal and interest on outstanding debt under this section, debt shall be construed to mean borrowed money represented by bonds, notes, or other evidences of indebtedness which are secured by the full faith and credit of the state or are required to be repaid, directly or indirectly, from general state revenues and which are incurred by the state, any department, authority, public corporation, or quasi public corporation of the state, any state university or college, or any other public agency created by the state but not by counties, cities, towns, school districts, or other municipal corporations, but shall not include obligations for the payment of current expenses of state government, nor shall it include debt hereafter incurred pursuant to section 3 of this article, obligations guaranteed as provided for in subsection (g) of this section, principal of bond anticipation notes or obligations issued to fund or refund the indebtedness of the Washington state building authority.

(e) The state may pledge the full faith, credit, and taxing power of the state to guarantee the voter approved general obligation debt of school districts in the manner authorized by the legislature. Any such guarantee does not remove the debt obligation of the school district and is not state debt.

(f) The state may, without limitation, fund or refund, at or prior to maturity, the whole or any part of any existing debt or of any debt hereafter contracted pursuant to section 1, section 2, or section 3 of this article, including any premium payable with respect thereto and interest thereon, or fund or refund, at or prior to maturity, the whole or any part of any indebtedness incurred or authorized prior to the effective date of this amendment by any entity of the type described in subsection (h) of this section, including any premium payable with respect thereto and any interest thereon. Such funding or refunding shall not be deemed to be contracting debt by the state.

(g) Notwithstanding the limitation contained in subsection (b) of this section, the state may pledge its full faith, credit, and taxing power to guarantee the payment of any obligation payable from revenues received from any of the following sources: (1) Fees collected by the state as license fees for motor vehicles; (2) Excise taxes collected by the state on the sale, distribution or use of motor vehicle fuel; and (3) Interest on the permanent common school fund: Provided, That the legislature shall, at all times, provide sufficient revenues from such sources to pay the principal and interest due on all obligations for which said source of revenue is pledged.

(h) No money shall be paid from funds in custody of the treasurer with respect to any debt contracted after the effective date of this amendment by the Washington state building authority, the capitol committee, or any similar entity existing or operating for similar purposes pursuant to which such entity undertakes to finance or provide a facility for use or occupancy by the state or any agency, department, or instrumentality thereof.

(i) The legislature shall prescribe all matters relating to the contracting, funding or refunding of debt pursuant to this section, including: The purposes for which debt may be contracted; by a favorable vote of three-fifths of the members elected to each house, the amount of debt which may be contracted for any class of such purposes; the kinds of notes, bonds, or other evidences of debt which may be issued by the state; and the manner by which the treasurer shall determine and advise the legislature, any appropriate agency, officer, or instrumentality of the state as to the available debt capacity within the limitation set forth in this section. The legislature may delegate to any state officer, agency, or instrumentality any of its powers relating to the contracting, funding or refunding of debt pursuant to this section except its power to determine the amount and purposes for which debt may be contracted.

(j) The full faith, credit, and taxing power of the state of Washington are pledged to the payment of the debt created on behalf of the state pursuant to this section and the legislature shall provide by appropriation for the payment of the interest upon and installments of principal of all such debt as the same falls due, but in any event, any court of record may compel such payment.

(k) Notwithstanding the limitations contained in subsection (b) of this section, the state may issue certificates of indebtedness in such sum or sums as may be necessary to meet temporary deficiencies of the treasury, to preserve the best interests of the state in the conduct of the various state institutions, departments, bureaus, and agencies during each fiscal year; such certificates may be issued only to provide for appropriations already made by the legislature and such certificates must be retired and the debt discharged other than by refunding within twelve months after the date of incurrence.

(l) Bonds, notes, or other obligations issued and sold by the state of Washington pursuant to and in conformity with this article shall not be invalid for any irregularity or defect in the proceedings of the issuance or sale thereof and shall be incontestable in the hands of a bona fide purchaser or holder thereof. [AMENDMENT 92, 1999 Senate Joint Resolution No. 8206, p 2387. Approved November 2, 1999.]

Amendment 60, part, (1972) — Art. 8 Section 1 STATE DEBT — (a) The state may contract debt, the principal of which shall be paid and discharged within thirty years from the time of contracting thereof, in the manner set forth herein.

(b) The aggregate debt contracted by the state shall not exceed that amount for which payments of principal and interest in any fiscal year would require the state to expend more than nine percent of the arithmetic mean of its general state revenues for the three immediately preceding fiscal years as certified by the treasurer. The term "fiscal year" means that period of time commencing July 1 of any year and ending on June 30 of the following year.

(c) The term "general state revenues" when used in this section, shall include all state money received in the treasury from each and every source whatsoever except: (1) Fees and revenues derived from the ownership or operation of any undertaking, facility, or project; (2) Moneys received as gifts, grants, donations, aid, or assistance or otherwise from the United States or any department, bureau, or corporation thereof, or any person, firm, or corporation, public or private, when the terms and conditions of such gift, grant, donation, aid, or assistance require the application and disbursement of such moneys otherwise than for the general purposes of the state of Washington; (3) Moneys to be paid into and received from retirement system funds, and performance bonds and deposits; (4) Moneys to be paid into and received from trust funds including but not limited to moneys received from taxes levied for specific purposes and the several permanent and irreducible funds of the state and the moneys derived therefrom but excluding bond redemption funds; (5) Proceeds received from the sale of bonds or other evidences of indebtedness.

(d) In computing the amount required for payment of principal and interest on outstanding debt under this section, debt shall be construed to mean borrowed money represented by bonds, notes, or other evidences of indebtedness which are secured by the full faith and credit of the state or are required to be repaid, directly or indirectly, from general state revenues and which are incurred by the state, any department, authority, public corporation, or quasi public corporation of the state, any state university or college, or any other public agency created by the state but not by counties, cities, towns, school districts, or other municipal corporations, but shall not include obligations for the payment of current expenses of state government, nor shall it include debt hereafter incurred pursuant to section 3 of this article, obligations guaranteed as provided for in subsection (f) of this section, principal of bond anticipation notes or obligations issued to fund or refund the indebtedness of the Washington state building authority.

(e) The state may, without limitation, fund or refund, at or prior to maturity, the whole or any part of any existing debt or of any debt hereafter contracted pursuant to section 1, section 2, or section 3 of this article, including any premium payable with respect thereto and interest thereon, or fund or refund, at or prior to maturity, the whole or any part of any indebtedness incurred or authorized prior to the effective date of this amendment by any entity of the type described in subsection (g) of this section, including any premium payable with respect thereto and any interest thereon. Such funding or refunding shall not be deemed to be contracting debt by the state.

(f) Notwithstanding the limitation contained in subsection (b) of this section, the state may pledge its full faith, credit, and taxing power to guarantee the payment of any obligation payable from revenues received from any of the following sources: (1) Fees collected by the state as license fees for motor vehicles; (2) Excise taxes collected by the state on the sale, distribution or use of motor vehicle fuel; and (3) Interest on the permanent common school fund: Provided, That the legislature shall, at all times, provide sufficient revenues from such sources to pay the principal and interest due on all obligations for which said source of revenue is pledged.

(g) No money shall be paid from funds in custody of the treasurer with respect to any debt contracted after the effective date of this amendment by the Washington state building authority, the capitol committee, or any similar entity existing or operating for similar purposes pursuant to which such entity undertakes to finance or provide a facility for use or occupancy by the state or any agency, department, or instrumentality thereof.

(h) The legislature shall prescribe all matters relating to the contracting, funding or refunding of debt pursuant to this section, including: The purposes for which debt may be contracted; by a favorable vote of three-fifths of the members elected to each house, the amount of debt which may be contracted for any class of such purposes; the kinds of notes, bonds, or other evidences of debt which may be issued by the state; and the manner by which the treasurer shall determine and advise the legislature, any appropriate agency, officer, or instrumentality of the state as to the available debt capacity within the limitation set forth in this section. The legislature may delegate to any state officer, agency, or instrumentality any of its powers relating to the contracting, funding or refunding of debt pursuant to this section except its power to determine the amount and purposes for which debt may be contracted.

(i) The full faith, credit, and taxing power of the state of Washington are pledged to the payment of the debt created on behalf of the state pursuant to this section and the legislature shall provide by appropriation for the payment of the interest upon and installments of principal of all such debt as the same falls due, but in any event, any court of record may compel such payment.

(j) Notwithstanding the limitations contained in subsection (b) of this section, the state may issue certificates of indebtedness in such sum or sums as may be necessary to meet temporary deficiencies of the treasury, to preserve the best interests of the state in the conduct of the various state institutions, departments, bureaus, and agencies during each fiscal year; such certificates may be issued only to provide for appropriations already made by the legislature and such certificates must be retired and the debt discharged other than by refunding within twelve months after the date of incurrence.

(k) Bonds, notes, or other obligations issued and sold by the state of Washington pursuant to and in conformity with this article shall not be invalid for any irregularity or defect in the proceedings of the issuance or sale thereof and shall be incontestable in the hands of a bona fide purchaser or holder thereof. [AMENDMENT 60, part, 1971 House Joint Resolution No. 52, part, p 1836. Approved November, 1972.]

Original text — Art. 8 Section 1 LIMITATION OF STATE DEBT — The state may to meet casual deficits or failure in revenues, or for expenses not provided for, contract debts, but such debts, direct and contingent, singly or in the aggregate, shall not at any time exceed four hundred thousand dollars ($400,000), and the moneys arising from the loans creating such debts shall be applied to the purpose for which they were obtained or to repay the debts so contracted, and to no other purpose whatever.

SECTION 2 POWERS EXTENDED IN CERTAIN CASES. In addition to the above limited power to contract debts the state may contract debts to repel invasion, suppress insurrection, or to defend the state in war, but the money arising from the contracting of such debts shall be applied to the purpose for which it was raised and to no other purpose whatever.

SECTION 3 SPECIAL INDEBTEDNESS, HOW AUTHORIZED. Except the debt specified in sections one and two of this article, no debts shall hereafter be contracted by, or on behalf of this state, unless such debt shall be authorized by law for some single work or object to be distinctly specified therein. No such law shall take effect until it shall, at a general election, or a special election called for that purpose, have been submitted to the people and have received a majority of all the votes cast for and against it at such election. [**AMENDMENT 60,** part, 1971 House Joint Resolution No. 52, part, p 1836. Approved November, 1972.]

Amendment 48 (1966) — Art. 8 Section 3 SPECIAL INDEBTEDNESS, HOW AUTHORIZED — Except the debt specified in sections one and two of this article, no debts shall hereafter be contracted by, or on behalf of this state, unless such debt shall be authorized by law for some single work or object to be distinctly specified therein, which law shall provide ways and means, exclusive of loans, for the payment of the interest on such debt as it falls due, and also to pay and discharge the principal of such debt within twenty years from the time of the contracting thereof. No such law shall take effect until it shall, at a general election, have been submitted to the people and have received a majority of all the votes cast for and against it at such election, and all moneys raised by authority of such law shall be applied only to the specific object therein stated, or to the payment of the debt thereby created, and notice that such law will be submitted to the people shall be published at least four times during the four weeks next preceding the election in every legal newspaper in the state: Provided, That failure of any newspaper to publish this notice shall not be interpreted as affecting the outcome of the election. [AMENDMENT 48, 1965 ex.s. House Joint Resolution No. 39, p 2822. Approved November 8, 1966.]

Original text — Art. 8 Section 3 SPECIAL INDEBTEDNESS HOW AUTHORIZED — Except the debt specified in sections one and two of this article, no debts shall hereafter be contracted by, or on behalf of this state, unless such debt shall be authorized by law for some single work or object to be distinctly specified therein, which law shall provide ways and means, exclusive of loans, for the payment of the interest on such debt as it falls due, and also to pay and discharge the principal of such debt within twenty years from the time of the contracting thereof. No such law shall take effect until it shall, at a general election, have been submitted to the people and have received a majority of all the votes cast for and against it at such election, and all moneys raised by authority of such law shall be applied only to the specific object therein stated, or to the payment of the debt thereby created, and such law shall be published in at least one newspaper in each county, if one be published therein, throughout the state, for three months next preceding the election at which it is submitted to the people.

SECTION 4 MONEYS DISBURSED ONLY BY APPROPRIATIONS. No moneys shall ever be paid out of the treasury of this state, or any of its funds, or any of the funds under its management, except in pursuance of an appropriation by law; nor unless such payment be made within one calendar month after the end of the next ensuing fiscal biennium, and every such law making a new appropriation, or continuing or reviving an appropriation, shall distinctly specify the sum appropriated, and the object to which it is to be applied, and it shall not be sufficient for such law to refer to any other law to fix such sum. [**AMENDMENT 11,** 1921 p 80 Section 1. Approved November, 1922.]

Original text — Art. 8 Section 4 MONEYS DISBURSED ONLY BY APPROPRIATIONS — No moneys shall ever be paid out of the treasury of this state, or any of its funds, or any of the funds under its management, except in pursuance of an appropriation by law; nor unless such payment be made within two years from the first day of May next after the passage of such appropriation act, and every such law making a new appropriation, or continuing or reviving an appropriation, shall distinctly specify the sum appropriated, and the object to which it is to be applied, and it shall not be sufficient for such law to refer to any other law to fix such sum.

SECTION 5 CREDIT NOT TO BE LOANED. The credit of the state shall not, in any manner be given or loaned to, or in aid of, any individual, association, company or corporation.

SECTION 6 LIMITATIONS UPON MUNICIPAL INDEBTEDNESS. No county, city, town, school district, or other municipal corporation shall for any purpose become indebted in any manner to an amount exceeding one and one-half per centum of the taxable property in such county, city, town, school district, or other municipal corporation, without the assent of three-fifths of the voters therein voting at an election to be held for that purpose, nor in cases requiring such assent shall the total indebtedness at any time exceed five per centum on the value of the taxable property therein, to be ascertained by the last assessment for state and county purposes previous to the incurring of such indebtedness, except that in incorporated cities the assessment shall be taken from the last assessment for city purposes: Provided, That no part of the indebtedness allowed in this section shall be incurred for any purpose other than strictly county, city, town, school district, or other municipal purposes: Provided further, That (a) any city or town, with such assent, may be allowed to become indebted to a larger amount, but not exceeding five per centum additional for supplying such city or town with water, artificial light, and sewers, when the works for supplying such water, light, and sewers shall be owned and controlled by the municipality and (b) any school district with such assent, may be allowed to become indebted to a larger amount but not exceeding five per centum additional for capital outlays. [**AMENDMENT 27,** 1951 House Joint Resolution No. 8, p 961. Approved November 4, 1952.]

Provisions of Art. 7 Section 2 (Limitation on Levies) also subject to limitations contained in Art. 8 Section 6: Art. 7 Section 2 (b).

Original text — Art. 8 Section 6 LIMITATIONS UPON MUNICIPAL INDEBTEDNESS — No county, city, town, school district or other municipal corporation, shall for any purpose become indebted in any manner to an amount exceeding one and one-half percentum of the taxable property in such county, city, town, school district or other municipal corporation, without the assent of three-fifths of the voters therein, voting at an election to be held for that purpose, nor in cases requiring such assent shall the total indebtedness at any time exceed five per centum on the value of the taxable property therein, to be ascertained by the last assessment for state, and county purposes previous to the incurring of such indebtedness; except that in incorporated cities the assessment shall be taken from the last assessment for city purposes; Provided, That no part of the indebtedness allowed in this section, shall be incurred for any purpose other than strictly county, city, town, school district, or other municipal purposes. Provided further; that any city or town, with such assent may be allowed to become indebted to a larger amount but not exceeding five per centum additional for supplying such city or town with water, artificial light, and sewers, when the works for supplying such water, light, and sewers shall be owned and controlled by the municipality.

SECTION 7 CREDIT NOT TO BE LOANED. No county, city, town or other municipal corporation shall hereafter give any money, or property, or loan its money, or credit to or in aid of any individual, association, company or corporation, except for the necessary support of the poor and infirm, or become directly or indirectly the owner of any stock in or bonds of any association, company or corporation.

SECTION 8 PORT EXPENDITURES — INDUSTRIAL DEVELOPMENT — PROMOTION. The use of public funds by port districts in such manner as may be prescribed by the legislature for industrial development or trade promotion and promotional hosting shall be deemed a public use for a public purpose, and shall not be deemed a gift within the provisions of section 7 of this Article. [**AMENDMENT 45,** 1965 ex.s. Senate Joint Resolution No. 25, p 2819. Approved November 8, 1966.]

SECTION 9 STATE BUILDING AUTHORITY. The legislature is empowered notwithstanding any other provision in this Constitution, to provide for a state building authority in corporate and politic form which may contract with agencies or departments of the state government to construct upon land owned by the state or its agencies, or to be acquired by the state building authority, buildings and appurtenant improvements which such state agencies or departments are hereby empowered to lease at reasonable rental rates from the Washington state building authority for terms up to seventy-five years with provisions for eventual vesting of title in the state or its agencies. This section shall not be construed as authority to provide buildings through lease or otherwise to nongovernmental entities. The legislature may authorize the state building authority to borrow funds solely upon its own credit and to issue bonds or other evidences of indebtedness therefor to be repaid from its revenues and to secure the same by pledging its income or mortgaging its leaseholds. The provisions of sections 1 and 3 of this article shall not apply to indebtedness incurred pursuant to this section. [**AMENDMENT 51,** 1967 Senate Joint Resolution No. 17; see 1969 p 2976. Approved November 5, 1968.]

Reviser's note: This section which was adopted as Sec. 8, is herein renumbered Sec. 9, to avoid confusion with Sec. 8, supra.

SECTION 10 ENERGY, WATER, OR STORMWATER OR SEWER SERVICES CONSERVATION ASSISTANCE. Notwithstanding the provisions of section 7 of this Article, any county, city, town, quasi municipal corporation, municipal corporation, or political subdivision of the state which is engaged in the sale or distribution of water, energy, or stormwater or sewer services may, as authorized by the legislature, use public moneys or credit derived from operating revenues from the sale of water, energy, or stormwater or sewer services to assist the owners of structures or equipment in financing the acquisition and installation of materials and equipment for the conservation or more efficient use of water, energy, or stormwater or sewer services in such structures or equipment. Except as provided in section 7 of this Article, an appropriate charge back shall be made for such extension of public moneys or credit and the same shall be a lien against the structure benefited or a security interest in the equipment benefited. Any financing for energy conservation authorized by this article shall only be used for conservation purposes in existing structures and shall not be used for any purpose which results in a conversion from one energy source to another. [**AMENDMENT 91,** 1997 House Joint Resolution No. 4209, p 3065. Approved November 4, 1997.]

Amendment 86 (1989) — Art. 8 Section 10 ENERGY AND WATER CONSERVATION ASSISTANCE — Notwithstanding the provisions of section 7 of this Article, any county, city, town, quasi municipal corporation, municipal corporation, or political subdivision of the state which is engaged in the sale or distribution of water or energy may, as authorized by the legislature, use public moneys or credit derived from operating revenues from the sale of water or energy to assist the owners of structures or equipment in financing the acquisition and installation of materials and equipment for the conservation or more efficient use of water or energy in such structures or equipment. Except as provided in section 7 of this Article, an appropriate charge back shall be made for such extension of public moneys or credit and the same shall be a lien against the structure benefited or a security interest in the equipment benefited. Any financing for energy conservation authorized by this article shall only be used for conservation purposes in existing structures and shall not be used for any purpose which results in a conversion from one energy source to another. [AMENDMENT 86, 1989 Senate Joint Resolution No. 8210, p 3003. Approved November 7, 1989.]

Amendment 82 (1988) — Art. 8 Section 10 RESIDENTIAL ENERGY CONSERVATION — Notwithstanding the provisions of section 7 of this Article, any county, city, town, quasi municipal corporation, municipal corporation, or political subdivision of the state which is engaged in the sale or distribution of energy may, as authorized by the legislature, use public moneys or credit derived from operating revenues from the sale of energy to assist the owners of structures or equipment in financing the acquisition and installation of materials and equipment for the conservation or more efficient use of energy in such structures or equipment.

Except as provided in section 7 of this Article, an appropriate charge back shall be made for such extension of public moneys or credit and the same shall be a lien against the structure benefited or a security interest in the equipment benefited. Any financing authorized by this article shall only be used for conservation purposes in existing structures and shall not be used for any purpose which results in a conversion from one energy source to another. [AMENDMENT 82, 1988 House Joint Resolution No. 4223, p 1552. Approved November 8, 1988.]

Amendment 70 (1979) — Art. 8 Section 10 RESIDENTIAL ENERGY CONSERVATION — Notwithstanding the provisions of section 7 of this Article, until January 1, 1990 any county, city, town, quasi municipal corporation, municipal corporation, or political subdivision of the state which is engaged in the sale or distribution of energy may, as authorized by the legislature, use public moneys or credit derived from operating revenues from the sale of energy to assist the owners of residential structures in financing the acquisition and installation of materials and equipment for the conservation or more efficient use of energy in such structures. Except as provided in section 7 of this Article, an appropriate charge back shall be made for such extension of public moneys or credit and the same shall be a lien against the residential structure benefited. Except as to contracts entered into prior thereto, this amendment to the state Constitution shall be null and void as of January 1, 1990 and shall have no further force or effect after that date. [AMENDMENT 70, Substitute Senate Joint Resolution No. 120, p 2288. Approved November 6, 1979.]

SECTION 11 AGRICULTURAL COMMODITY ASSESSMENTS — DEVELOPMENT, PROMOTION, AND HOSTING. The use of agricultural commodity assessments by agricultural commodity commissions in such manner as may be prescribed by the legislature for agricultural development or trade promotion and promotional hosting shall be deemed a public use for a public purpose, and shall not be deemed a gift within the provisions of section 5 of this article. [**AMENDMENT 76,** 1985 House Joint Resolution No. 42, p 2402. Approved November 5, 1985.]

ARTICLE IX EDUCATION

SECTION 1 PREAMBLE. It is the paramount duty of the state to make ample provision for the education of all children residing within its borders, without distinction or preference on account of race, color, caste, or sex.

SECTION 2 PUBLIC SCHOOL SYSTEM. The legislature shall provide for a general and uniform system of public schools. The public school system shall include common schools, and such high schools, normal schools, and technical schools as may hereafter be established. But the entire revenue derived from the common school fund and the state tax for common schools shall be exclusively applied to the support of the common schools.

SECTION 3 FUNDS FOR SUPPORT. The principal of the common school fund as the same existed on June 30, 1965, shall remain permanent and irreducible. The said fund shall consist of the principal amount thereof existing on June 30, 1965, and such additions thereto as may be derived after June 30, 1965, from the following named sources, to wit: Appropriations and donations by the state to this fund; donations and bequests by individuals to the state or public for common schools; the proceeds of lands and other property which revert to the state by escheat and forfeiture; the proceeds of all property granted to the state when the purpose of the grant is not specified, or is uncertain; funds accumulated in the treasury of the state for the disbursement of which provision has not been made by law; the proceeds of the sale of stone, minerals, or property other than timber and other crops from school and state lands, other than those granted for specific purposes; all moneys received from persons appropriating stone, minerals or property other than timber and other crops from school and state lands other than those granted for specific purposes, and all moneys other than rental recovered from persons trespassing on said lands; five per centum of the proceeds of the sale of public lands lying within the state, which shall be sold by the United States subsequent to the admission of the state into the Union as approved by section 13 of the act of congress enabling the admission of the state into the Union; the principal of all funds arising from the sale of lands and other property which have been, and hereafter may be granted to the state for the support of common schools. The legislature may make further provisions for enlarging said fund.

There is hereby established the common school construction fund to be used exclusively for the purpose of financing the construction of facilities for the common schools. The sources of said fund shall be: (1) Those proceeds derived from the sale or appropriation of timber and other crops from school and state lands subsequent to June 30, 1965, other than those granted for specific purposes; (2) the interest accruing on said permanent common school fund from and after July 1, 1967, together with all rentals and other revenues derived therefrom and from lands and other property devoted to the permanent common school fund from and after July 1, 1967; and (3) such other sources as the legislature may direct. That portion of the common school construction fund derived from interest on the permanent common school fund may be used to retire such bonds as may be authorized by law for the purpose of financing the construction of facilities for the common schools.

The interest accruing on the permanent common school fund together with all rentals and other revenues accruing thereto pursuant to subsection (2) of this section during the period after the effective date of this amendment and prior to July 1, 1967, shall be exclusively applied to the current use of the common schools.

To the extent that the moneys in the common school construction fund are in excess of the amount necessary to allow fulfillment of the purpose of said fund, the excess shall be available for deposit to the credit of the permanent common school fund or available for the current use of the common schools, as the legislature may direct. [**AMENDMENT 43,** 1965 ex.s. Senate Joint Resolution No. 22, part 1, p 2817. Approved November 8, 1966.]

Original text — Art. 9 Section 3 FUNDS FOR SUPPORT — The principal of the common school fund shall remain permanent and irreducible. The said fund shall be derived from the following named sources, to wit: Appropriations and donations by the state to this fund; donations and bequests by individuals to the state or public for common schools; the proceeds of lands and other property which revert to the state by escheat and forfeiture; the proceeds of all property granted to the state when the purpose of the grant is not specified, or is uncertain; funds accumulated in the treasury of the state for the disbursement of which provision has not been made by law; the proceeds of the sale of timber, stone, minerals, or other property from school and state lands, other than those granted for specific purposes; all moneys received from persons appropriating timber, stone, minerals or other property from school and state lands other than those granted for specific purposes, and all moneys other than rental recovered from persons trespassing on said lands; five per centum of the proceeds of the sale of public lands lying within the state, which shall be sold by the United States subsequent to the admission of the state into the Union as approved by section 13 of the act of congress enabling the admission of the state into the Union; the principal of all funds arising from the sale of lands and other property which have been, and hereafter may be granted to the state for the support of common schools. The legislature may make further provisions for enlarging said fund. The interest accruing on said fund together with all rentals and other revenues derived therefrom and from lands and other property devoted to the common school fund shall be exclusively applied to the current use of the common schools.

SECTION 4 SECTARIAN CONTROL OR INFLUENCE PROHIBITED. All schools maintained or supported wholly or in part by the public funds shall be forever free from sectarian control or influence.

SECTION 5 LOSS OF PERMANENT FUND TO BECOME STATE DEBT. All losses to the permanent common school or any other state educational fund, which shall be occasioned by defalcation, mismanagement or fraud of the agents or officers controlling or managing the same, shall be audited by the proper authorities of the state. The amount so audited shall be a permanent funded debt against the state in favor of the particular fund sustaining such loss, upon which not less than six per cent annual interest shall be paid. The amount of liability so created shall not be counted as a part of the indebtedness authorized and limited elsewhere in this Constitution.

Investment of permanent school fund: Art. 16 Section 5.

ARTICLE X MILITIA

SECTION 1 WHO LIABLE TO MILITARY DUTY. All able-bodied male citizens of this state between the ages of eighteen (18) and forty-five (45) years except such as are exempt by laws of the United States or by the laws of this state, shall be liable to military duty.

SECTION 2 ORGANIZATION — DISCIPLINE — OFFICERS — POWER TO CALL OUT. The legislature shall provide by law for organizing and disciplining the militia in such manner as it may deem expedient, not incompatible with the Constitution and laws of the United States. Officers of the militia shall be elected or appointed in such manner as the legislature shall from time to time direct and shall be commissioned by the governor. The governor shall have power to call forth the militia to execute the laws of the state to suppress insurrections and repel invasions.

SECTION 3 SOLDIERS' HOME. The legislature shall provide by law for the maintenance of a soldiers' home for honorably discharged Union soldiers, sailors, marines and members of the state militia disabled while in the line of duty and who are bona fidecitizens of the state.

SECTION 4 PUBLIC ARMS. The legislature shall provide by law, for the protection and safe keeping of the public arms.

SECTION 5 PRIVILEGE FROM ARREST. The militia shall, in all cases, except treason, felony and breach of the peace, be privileged from arrest during their attendance at musters and elections of officers, and in going to and returning from the same.

SECTION 6 EXEMPTION FROM MILITARY DUTY. No person or persons, having conscientious scruples against bearing arms, shall be compelled to do militia duty in time of peace: Provided, such person or persons shall pay an equivalent for such exemption.

ARTICLE XI
COUNTY, CITY, AND TOWNSHIP ORGANIZATION

SECTION 1 EXISTING COUNTIES RECOGNIZED. The several counties of the Territory of Washington existing at the time of the adoption of this Constitution are hereby recognized as legal subdivisions of this state.

SECTION 2 COUNTY SEATS — LOCATION AND REMOVAL. No county seat shall be removed unless three-fifths of the qualified electors of the county, voting on the proposition at a general election shall vote in favor of such removal, and three-fifths of all votes cast on the proposition shall be required to relocate a county seat. A proposition of removal shall not be submitted in the same county more than once in four years.

Governmental continuity during emergency periods: Art. 2 Section 42.

SECTION 3 NEW COUNTIES. No new counties shall be established which shall reduce any county to a population less than four thousand (4,000), nor shall a new county be formed containing a less population than two thousand (2,000). There shall be no territory stricken from any county unless a majority of the voters living in such territory shall petition therefor and then only under such other conditions as may be prescribed by a general law applicable to the whole state. Every county which shall be enlarged or created from territory taken from any other county or counties shall be liable for a just proportion of the existing debts and liabilities of the county or counties from which such territory shall be taken: Provided, That in such accounting neither county shall be charged with any debt or liability then existing incurred in the purchase of any county property, or in the purchase or construction of any county buildings then in use, or under construction, which shall fall within and be retained by the county: Provided further, That this shall not be construed to affect the rights of creditors.

SECTION 4 COUNTY GOVERNMENT AND TOWNSHIP ORGANIZATION. The legislature shall establish a system of county government, which shall be uniform throughout the state except as hereinafter provided, and by general laws shall provide for township organization, under which any county may organize whenever a majority of the qualified electors of such county voting at a general election shall so determine; and whenever a county shall adopt township organization, the assessment and collection of the revenue shall be made, and the business of such county and the local affairs of the several townships therein, shall be managed and transacted in the manner prescribed by such general law.

Any county may frame a "Home Rule" charter for its own government subject to the Constitution and laws of this state, and for such purpose the legislative authority of such county may cause an election to be had, at which election there shall be chosen by the qualified voters of said county not less than fifteen (15) nor more than twenty-five (25) freeholders thereof, as determined by the legislative authority, who shall have been residents of said county for a period of at least five (5) years preceding their election and who are themselves qualified electors, whose duty it shall be to convene within thirty (30) days after their election and prepare and propose a charter for such county. Such proposed charter shall be submitted to the qualified electors of said county, and if a majority of such qualified electors voting thereon ratify the same, it shall become the charter of said county and shall become the organic law thereof, and supersede any existing charter, including amendments thereto, or any existing form of county government, and all special laws inconsistent with such charter. Said proposed charter shall be published in two (2) legal newspapers published in said county, at least once a week for four (4) consecutive weeks prior to the day of submitting the same to the electors for their approval as above provided. All elections in this section authorized shall only be had upon notice, which notice shall specify the object of calling such election and shall be given for at least ten (10) days before the day of election in all election districts of said county. Said elections may be general or special elections and except as herein provided, shall be governed by the law regulating and controlling general or special elections in said county. Such charter may be amended by proposals therefor submitted by the legislative authority of said county to the electors thereof at any general election after notice of such submission published as above specified, and ratified by a majority of the qualified electors voting thereon. In submitting any such charter or amendment thereto, any alternate article or proposition may be presented for the choice of the voters and may be voted on separately without prejudice to others.

Any home rule charter proposed as herein provided, may provide for such county officers as may be deemed necessary to carry out and perform all county functions as provided by charter or by general law, and for their compensation, but shall not affect the election of the prosecuting attorney, the county superintendent of schools, the judges of the superior court, and the justices of the peace, or the jurisdiction of the courts.

Notwithstanding the foregoing provision for the calling of an election by the legislative authority of such county for the election of freeholders to frame a county charter, registered voters equal in number to ten (10) per centum of the voters of any such county voting at the last preceding general election, may at any time propose by petition the calling of an election of freeholders. The petition shall be filed with the county auditor of the county at least three (3) months before any general election and the proposal that a board of freeholders be elected for the purpose of framing a county charter shall be submitted to the vote of the people at said general election, and at the same election a board of freeholders of not less than fifteen (15) or more than twenty-five (25), as fixed in the petition calling for the election, shall be chosen to draft the new charter. The procedure for the nomination of qualified electors as candidates for said board of freeholders shall be prescribed by the legislative authority of the county, and the procedure for the framing of the charter and the submission of the charter as framed shall be the same as in the case of a board of freeholders chosen at an election initiated by the legislative authority of the county.

In calling for any election of freeholders as provided in this section, the legislative authority of the county shall apportion the number of freeholders to be elected in accordance with either the legislative districts or the county commissioner districts, if any, within said county, the number of said freeholders to be elected from each of said districts to be in proportion to the population of said districts as nearly as may be.

Should the charter proposed receive the affirmative vote of the majority of the electors voting thereon, the legislative authority of the county shall immediately call such special election as may be provided for therein, if any, and the county government shall be established in accordance with the terms of said charter not more than six (6) months after the election at which the charter was adopted.

The terms of all elective officers, except the prosecuting attorney, the county superintendent of schools, the judges of the superior court, and the justices of the peace, who are in office at the time of the adoption of a Home Rule Charter shall terminate as provided in the charter. All appointive officers in office at the time the charter goes into effect, whose positions are not abolished thereby, shall continue until their successors shall have qualified.

After the adoption of such charter, such county shall continue to have all the rights, powers, privileges and benefits then possessed or thereafter conferred by general law. All the powers, authority and duties granted to and imposed on county officers by general law, except the prosecuting attorney, the county superintendent of schools, the judges of the superior court and the justices of the peace, shall be vested in the legislative authority of the county unless expressly vested in specific officers by the charter. The legislative authority may by resolution delegate any of its executive or administrative powers, authority or duties not expressly vested in specific officers by the charter, to any county officer or officers or county employee or employees.

The provisions of sections 5, 6, 7, and the first sentence of section 8 of this Article as amended shall not apply to counties in which the government has been established by charter adopted under the provisions hereof. The authority conferred on the board of county commissioners by Section 15 of Article II as amended, shall be exercised by the legislative authority of the county. [**AMENDMENT 21,** 1947 Senate Joint Resolution No. 5, p 1372. Approved November 2, 1948.]

Original text — Art. 11 Section 4 COUNTY GOVERNMENT AND TOWNSHIP ORGANIZATION — The legislature shall establish a system of county government which shall be uniform throughout the state, and by general laws shall provide for township organization, under which any county may organize whenever a majority of the qualified electors of such county voting at a general election shall so determine, and whenever a county shall adopt township organization the assessment and collection of the revenue shall be made and the business of such county, and the local affairs of the several townships therein shall be managed and transacted in the manner prescribed by such general laws.

SECTION 5 COUNTY GOVERNMENT. The legislature, by general and uniform laws, shall provide for the election in the several counties of boards of county commissioners, sheriffs, county clerks, treasurers, prosecuting attorneys and other county, township or precinct and district officers, as public convenience may require, and shall prescribe their duties, and fix their terms of office: Provided,That the legislature may, by general laws, classify the counties by population and provide for the election in certain classes of counties certain officers who shall exercise the powers and perform the duties of two or more officers. It shall regulate the compensation of all such officers, in proportion to their duties, and for that purpose may classify the counties by population: Provided, That it may delegate to the legislative authority of the counties the right to prescribe the salaries of its own members and the salaries of other county officers. And it shall provide for the strict accountability of such officers for all fees which may be collected by them and for all public moneys which may be paid to them, or officially come into their possession. [**AMENDMENT 57,** part, 1971 Senate Joint Resolution No. 38, part, p 1829. Approved November, 1972.]

Amendment 12 (1924) — Art. 11 Section 5 COUNTY GOVERNMENT — The legislature, by general and uniform laws, shall provide for the election in the several counties of boards of county commissioners, sheriffs, county clerks, treasurers, prosecuting attorneys and other county, township or precinct and district officers, as public convenience may require, and shall prescribe their duties, and fix their terms of office: Provided, That the legislature may, by general laws, classify the counties by population and provide for the election in certain classes of counties certain officers who shall exercise the powers and perform the duties of two or more officers. It shall regulate the compensation of all such officers, in proportion to their duties, and for that purpose may classify the counties by population. And it shall provide for the strict accountability of such officers for all fees which may be collected by them and for all public moneys which may be paid to them, or officially come into their possession. [AMENDMENT 12, 1923 p 255 Section 1. Approved November, 1924.]

Original text — Art. 11 Section 5 ELECTION AND COMPENSATION OF COUNTY OFFICERS — The legislature by general and uniform laws shall provide for the election in the several counties of boards of county commissioners, sheriffs, county clerks, treasurers, prosecuting attorneys, and other county, township or precinct and district officers as public convenience may require, and shall prescribe their duties, and fix their terms of office. It shall regulate the compensation of all such officers, in proportion to their duties, and for that purpose may classify the counties by population. And it shall provide for the strict accountability of such officers for all fees which may be collected by them, and for all public moneys which may be paid to them, or officially come into their possession.

SECTION 6 VACANCIES IN TOWNSHIP, PRECINCT OR ROAD DISTRICT OFFICE. The board of county commissioners in each county shall fill all vacancies occurring in any township, precinct or road district office of such county by appointment, and officers thus appointed shall hold office till the next general election, and until their successors are elected and qualified. [**AMENDMENT 52,** part, 1967 Senate Joint Resolution No. 24, part. Approved November 5, 1968.]

Governmental continuity during emergency periods: Art. 2 Section 42.
Vacancies in legislature and in partisan county elective office: Art. 2 Section 15.

Original text — Art. 11 Section 6 VACANCIES IN COUNTY, ETC., OFFICES, HOW FILLED — The board of county commissioners in each county shall fill all vacancies occurring in any county, township, precinct or road district office of such county by appointment, and officers thus appointed shall hold office till the next general election, and until their successors are elected and qualified.

SECTION 7 TENURE OF OFFICE LIMITED TO TWO TERMS. [Repealed by AMENDMENT 22, 1947 House Joint Resolution No. 4, p 1385. Approved November 2, 1948.]

Original text — Art. 11 Section 7 TENURE OF OFFICE LIMITED TO TWO TERMS — No county officer shall be eligible to hold his office more than two terms in succession.

SECTION 8 SALARIES AND LIMITATIONS AFFECTING. The salary of any county, city, town, or municipal officers shall not be increased except as provided in section 1 of Article XXX or diminished after his election, or during his term of office; nor shall the term of any such officer be extended beyond the period for which he is elected or appointed. [**AMENDMENT 57,** part, 1971 Senate Joint Resolution No. 38, part, p 1829. Approved November, 1972.]

Original text — Art. 11 Section 8 SALARIES AND LIMITATIONS AFFECTING — The legislature shall fix the compensation by salaries of all county officers, and of constables in cities having a population of five thousand and upwards; except that public administrators, surveyors and coroners may or may not be salaried officers. The salary of any county, city, town, or municipal officers shall not be increased or diminished after his election, or during his term of office; nor shall the term of any such officer be extended beyond the period for which he is elected or appointed.

SECTION 9 STATE TAXES NOT TO BE RELEASED OR COMMUTED. No county, nor the inhabitants thereof, nor the property therein, shall be released or discharged from its or their proportionate share of taxes to be levied for state purposes, nor shall commutation for such taxes be authorized in any form whatever.

SECTION 10 INCORPORATION OF MUNICIPALITIES. Corporations for municipal purposes shall not be created by special laws; but the legislature, by general laws, shall provide for the incorporation, organization and classification in proportion to population, of cities and towns, which laws may be altered, amended or repealed. Cities and towns heretofore organized, or incorporated may become organized under such general laws whenever a majority of the electors voting at a general election, shall so determine, and shall organize in conformity therewith; and cities or towns heretofore or hereafter organized, and all charters thereof framed or adopted by authority of this Constitution shall be subject to and controlled by general laws. Any city containing a population of ten thousand inhabitants, or more, shall be permitted to frame a charter for its own government, consistent with and subject to the Constitution and laws of this state, and for such purpose the legislative authority of such city may cause an election to be had at which election there shall be chosen by the qualified electors of said city, fifteen freeholders thereof, who shall have been residents of said city for a period of at least two years preceding their election and qualified electors, whose duty it shall be to convene within ten days after their election, and prepare and propose a charter for such city. Such proposed charter shall be submitted to the qualified electors of said city, and if a majority of such qualified electors voting thereon ratify the same, it shall become the charter of said city, and shall become the organic law thereof, and supersede any existing charter including amendments thereto, and all special laws inconsistent with such charter. Said proposed charter shall be published in the daily newspaper of largest general circulation published in the area to be incorporated as a first class city under the charter or, if no daily newspaper is published therein, then in the newspaper having the largest general circulation within such area at least once each week for four weeks next preceding the day of submitting the same to the electors for their approval, as above provided. All elections in this section authorized shall only be had upon notice, which notice shall specify the object of calling such election, and shall be given as required by law. Said elections may be general or special elections, and except as herein provided shall be governed by the law regulating and controlling general or special elections in said city. Such charter may be amended by proposals therefor submitted by the legislative authority of such city to the electors thereof at any general election after notice of said submission published as above specified, and ratified by a majority of the qualified electors voting thereon. In submitting any such charter, or amendment thereto, any alternate article or proposition may be presented for the choice of the voters, and may be voted on separately without prejudice to others. [**AMENDMENT 40,** 1963 ex.s. Senate Joint Resolution No. 1, p 1526. Approved November 3, 1964.]

Original text — Art. 11 Section 10 INCORPORATION OF MUNICIPALITIES — Corporations for municipal purposes shall not be created by special laws; but the legislature, by general laws, shall provide for the incorporation, organization and classification in proportion to population, of cities and towns, which laws may be altered, amended or repealed. Cities and towns heretofore organized, or incorporated may become organized under such general laws whenever a majority of the electors voting at a general election, shall so determine, and shall organize in conformity therewith; and cities or towns heretofore or hereafter organized, and all charters thereof framed or adopted by authority of this Constitution shall be subject to, and controlled by general laws. Any city containing a population of twenty thousand inhabitants, or more, shall be permitted to frame a charter for its own government, consistent with and subject to the Constitution and laws of this state, and for such purpose the legislative authority of such city may cause an election to be had at which election there shall be chosen by the qualified electors of said city, fifteen freeholders thereof, who shall have been residents of said city for a period of at least two years preceding their election and qualified electors, whose duty it shall be to convene within ten days after their election, and prepare and propose a charter for such city. Such proposed charter shall be submitted to the qualified electors of said city, and if a majority of such qualified electors voting thereon ratify the same, it shall become the charter of said city, and shall become the organic law thereof, and supersede any existing charter including amendments thereto, and all special laws inconsistent with such charter. Said proposed charter shall be published in two daily newspapers published in said city, for at least thirty days prior to the day of submitting the same to the electors for their approval, as above provided. All elections in this section authorized shall only be had upon notice, which notice shall specify the object of calling such election, and shall be given for at least ten days before the day of election, in all election districts of said city. Said elections may be general or special elections, and except as herein provided shall be governed by the law regulating and controlling general or special elections in said city. Such charter may be amended by proposals therefore submitted by the legislative authority of such city to the electors thereof at any general election after notice of said submission published as above specified, and ratified by a majority of the qualified electors voting thereon. In submitting any such charter, or amendment thereto, any alternate article or proposition may be presented for the choice of the voters, and may be voted on separately without prejudice to others.

Authority to incur and limit of indebtedness: Art. 8 Section 6.

SECTION 11 POLICE AND SANITARY REGULATIONS. Any county, city, town or township may make and enforce within its limits all such local police, sanitary and other regulations as are not in conflict with general laws.

SECTION 12 ASSESSMENT AND COLLECTION OF TAXES IN MUNICIPALITIES. The legislature shall have no power to impose taxes upon counties, cities, towns or other municipal corporations, or upon the inhabitants or property thereof, for county, city, town, or other municipal purposes, but may, by general laws, vest in the corporate authorities thereof, the power to assess and collect taxes for such purposes.

SECTION 13 PRIVATE PROPERTY, WHEN MAY BE TAKEN FOR PUBLIC DEBT. Private property shall not be taken or sold for the payment of the corporate debt of any public or municipal corporation, except in the mode provided by law for the levy and collection of taxes.

SECTION 14 PRIVATE USE OF PUBLIC FUNDS PROHIBITED. The making of profit out of county, city, town, or other public money, or using the same for any purpose not authorized by law, by any officer having the possession or control thereof, shall be a felony, and shall be prosecuted and punished as prescribed by law.

SECTION 15 DEPOSIT OF PUBLIC FUNDS. All moneys, assessments and taxes belonging to or collected for the use of any county, city, town or other public or municipal corporation, coming into the hands of any officer thereof, shall immediately be deposited with the treasurer, or other legal depositary to the credit of such city, town, or other corporation respectively, for the benefit of the funds to which they belong.

SECTION 16 COMBINED CITY-COUNTY. Any county may frame a "Home Rule" charter subject to the Constitution and laws of this state to provide for the formation and government of combined city and county municipal corporations, each of which shall be known as "city-county". Registered voters equal in number to ten (10) percent of the voters of any such county voting at the last preceding general election may at any time propose by a petition the calling of an election of freeholders. The provisions of section 4 of this Article with respect to a petition calling for an election of freeholders to frame a county home rule charter, the election of freeholders, and the framing and adoption of a county home rule charter pursuant to such petition shall apply to a petition proposed under this section for the election of freeholders to frame a city-county charter, the election of freeholders, and to the framing and adoption of such city-county charter pursuant to such petition. Except as otherwise provided in this section, the provisions of section 4 applicable to a county home rule charter shall apply to a city-county charter. If there are not sufficient legal newspapers published in the county to meet the requirements for publication of a proposed charter under section 4 of this Article, publication in a legal newspaper circulated in the county may be substituted for publication in a legal newspaper published in the county. No such "city-county" shall be formed except by a majority vote of the qualified electors voting thereon in the county. The charter shall designate the respective officers of such city-county who shall perform the duties imposed by law upon county officers. Every such city-county shall have and enjoy all rights, powers and privileges asserted in its charter, and in addition thereto, such rights, powers and privileges as may be granted to it, or to any city or county or class or classes of cities and counties. In the event of a conflict in the constitutional provisions applying to cities and those applying to counties or of a conflict in the general laws applying to cities and those applying to counties, a city-county shall be authorized to exercise any powers that are granted to either the cities or the counties.

No legislative enactment which is a prohibition or restriction shall apply to the rights, powers and privileges of a city-county unless such prohibition or restriction shall apply equally to every other city, county, and city-county.

The provisions of sections 2, 3, 5, 6, and 8 and of the first paragraph of section 4 of this article shall not apply to any such city-county.

Municipal corporations may be retained or otherwise provided for within the city-county. The formation, powers and duties of such municipal corporations shall be prescribed by the charter.

No city-county shall for any purpose become indebted in any manner to an amount exceeding three per centum of the taxable property in such city-county without the assent of three-fifths of the voters therein voting at an election to be held for that purpose, nor in cases requiring such assent shall the total indebtedness at any time exceed ten per centum of the value of the taxable property therein, to be ascertained by the last assessment for city-county purposes previous to the incurring of such indebtedness: Provided,That no part of the indebtedness allowed in this section shall be incurred for any purpose other than strictly city-county or other municipal purposes: Provided further, That any city-county, with such assent may be allowed to become indebted to a larger amount, but not exceeding five per centum additional for supplying such city-county with water, artificial light, and sewers, when the works for supplying such water, light, and sewers shall be owned and controlled by the city-county.

No municipal corporation which is retained or otherwise provided for within the city-county shall for any purpose become indebted in any manner to an amount exceeding one and one-half per centum of the taxable property in such municipal corporation without the assent of three-fifths of the voters therein voting at an election to be held for that purpose, nor shall the total indebtedness at any time exceed five per centum of the value of the taxable property therein, to be ascertained by the last assessment for city-county purposes previous to the incurring of such indebtedness: Provided, That no part of the indebtedness allowed in this section shall be incurred for any purpose other than strictly municipal purposes: Provided further, That any such municipal corporation, with such assent, may be allowed to become indebted to a larger amount, but not exceeding five per centum additional for supplying such municipal corporation with water, artificial light, and sewers, when the works for supplying such water, light, and sewers shall be owned and controlled by the municipal corporation. All taxes which are levied and collected within a municipal corporation for a specific purpose shall be expended within that municipal corporation.

The authority conferred on the city-county government shall not be restricted by the second sentence of Article 7, section 1, or by Article 8, section 6 of this Constitution.
[**AMENDMENT 58,** 1971 House Joint Resolution No. 21, p 1831. Approved November, 1972.]

Amendment 23 (1948) — Art. 11 Section 16 COMBINED CITY AND COUNTY — The legislature shall, by general law, provide for the formation of combined city and county municipal corporations, and for the manner of determining the territorial limits thereof, each of which shall be known as a "city and county," and, when organized, shall contain a population of at least three hundred thousand (300,000) inhabitants. No such city and county shall be formed except by a majority vote of the qualified electors of the area proposed to be included therein and also by a majority vote of the qualified electors of the remainder of that county from which such area is to be taken. Any such city and county shall be permitted to frame a charter for its own government, and amend the same, in the manner provided for cities by section 10 of this article: Provided, however, That the first charter of such city and county shall be framed and adopted in a manner to be specified in the general law authorizing the formation of such corporations: Provided further, That every such charter shall designate the respective officers of such city and county who shall perform the duties imposed by law upon county officers. Every such city and county shall have and enjoy all rights, powers and privileges asserted in its charter, not inconsistent with general laws, and in addition thereto, such rights, powers and privileges as may be granted to it, or possessed and enjoyed by cities and counties of like population separately organized.

No county or county government existing outside the territorial limits of such county and city shall exercise any police, taxation or other powers within the territorial limits of such county and city, but all such powers shall be exercised by the city and county and the officers thereof, subject to such constitutional provisions and general laws as apply to either cities or counties: Provided, That the provisions of sections 2, 3, 4, 5, 6, 7, and 8 of this article shall not apply to any such city and county: Provided further, That the salary of any elective or appointive officer of a city and county shall not be changed after his election or appointment or during his term of office; nor shall the term of any such officer be extended beyond the period for which he is elected or appointed. In case an existing county is divided in the formation of a city and county, such city and county shall be liable for a just proportion of the existing debts or liabilities of the former county, and shall account for and pay the county remaining a just proportion of the value of any real estate or other property owned by the former county and taken over by the county and city, the method of determining such just proportion to be prescribed by general law, but such division shall not affect the rights of creditors. The officers of a city and county, their compensation, qualifications, term of office and manner of election or appointment shall be as provided for in its charter, subject to general laws and applicable constitutional provisions. [AMENDMENT 23, 1947 House Joint Resolution No. 13, p 1386. Approved November 2, 1948.]

ARTICLE XII CORPORATIONS OTHER THAN MUNICIPAL

SECTION 1 CORPORATIONS, HOW FORMED. Corporations may be formed under general laws, but shall not be created by special acts. All laws relating to corporations may be altered, amended or repealed by the legislature at any time, and all corporations doing business in this state may, as to such business, be regulated, limited or restrained by law.

SECTION 2 EXISTING CHARTERS. All existing charters, franchises, special or exclusive privileges, under which an actual and bona fide organization shall not have taken place, and business been commenced in good faith, at the time of the adoption of this Constitution shall thereafter have no validity.

SECTION 3 EXISTING CHARTERS NOT TO BE EXTENDED NOR FORFEITURE REMITTED. The legislature shall not extend any franchise or charter, nor remit the forfeiture of any franchise or charter of any corporation now existing, or which shall hereafter exist under the laws of this state.

SECTION 4 LIABILITY OF STOCKHOLDERS. Each stockholder in all incorporated companies, except corporations organized for banking or insurance purposes, shall be liable for the debts of the corporation to the amount of his unpaid stock and no more; and one or more stockholders may be joined as parties defendant in suits to recover upon this liability.

SECTION 5 TERM "CORPORATION," DEFINED — RIGHT TO SUE AND BE SUED. The term corporations, as used in this article, shall be construed to include all associations and joint stock companies having any powers or privileges of corporations not possessed by individuals or partnerships, and all corporations shall have the right to sue and shall be subject to be sued, in all courts, in like cases as natural persons.

SECTION 6 LIMITATIONS UPON ISSUANCE OF STOCK. Corporations shall not issue stock, except to bona fide subscribers therefor, or their assignees; nor shall any corporation issue any bond, or other obligation, for the payment of money, except for money or property received or labor done. The stock of corporations shall not be increased, except in pursuance of a general law, nor shall any law authorize the increase of stock, without the consent of the person or persons holding the larger amount in value of the stock, nor without due notice of the proposed increase having been previously given in such manner as may be prescribed by law. All fictitious increase of stock or indebtedness shall be void.

SECTION 7 FOREIGN CORPORATIONS. No corporation organized outside the limits of this state shall be allowed to transact business within the state on more favorable conditions than are prescribed by law to similar corporations organized under the laws of this state.

SECTION 8 ALIENATION OF FRANCHISE NOT TO RELEASE LIABILITIES. No corporation shall lease or alienate any franchise, so as to relieve the franchise, or property held thereunder, from the liabilities of the lessor, or grantor, lessee, or grantee, contracted or incurred in the operation, use, or enjoyment of such franchise or any of its privileges.

SECTION 9 STATE NOT TO LOAN ITS CREDIT OR SUBSCRIBE FOR STOCK. The state shall not in any manner loan its credit, nor shall it subscribe to, or be interested in the stock of any company, association or corporation.

SECTION 10 EMINENT DOMAIN AFFECTING. The exercise of the right of eminent domain shall never be so abridged or construed as to prevent the legislature from taking the property and franchises of incorporated companies, and subjecting them to public use the same as the property of individuals.

SECTION 11 STOCKHOLDER LIABILITY. No corporation, association, or individual shall issue or put in circulation as money anything but the lawful money of the United States. Each stockholder of any banking or insurance corporation or joint stock association shall be individually and personally liable equally and ratably, and not one for another, for all contracts, debts, and engagements of such corporation or association accruing while they remain such stockholders, to the extent of the amount of their stock therein at the par value thereof, in addition to the amount invested in such shares.

The legislature may provide that stockholders of banking corporations organized under the laws of this state which shall provide and furnish, either through membership in the Federal Deposit Insurance Corporation, or through membership in any other instrumentality of the government of the United States, insurance or security for the payment of the debts and obligations of such banking corporation equivalent to that required by the laws of the United States to be furnished and provided by national banking associations, shall be relieved from liability for the debts and obligations of such banking corporation to the same extent that stockholders of national banking associations are relieved from liability for the debts and obligations of such national banking associations under the laws of the United States.
[**AMENDMENT 16,** 1939 Senate Joint Resolution No. 8, p 1024. Approved November, 1940.]

Original text — Art. 12 Section 11 PROHIBITION AGAINST ISSUANCE OF MONEY AND LIABILITY OF STOCKHOLDERS IN BANKS — No corporation, association, or individual shall issue or put in circulation as money anything but the lawful money of the United States. Each stockholder of any banking or insurance corporation or joint stock association, shall be individually and personally liable equally and ratably and not one for another, for all contracts, debts and engagements of such corporation or association accruing while they remain such stockholders to the extent of the amount of their stock therein at the par value thereof, in addition to the amount invested in such shares.

SECTION 12 RECEIVING DEPOSITS BY BANK AFTER INSOLVENCY. Any president, director, manager, cashier, or other officer of any banking institution, who shall receive or assent to the reception of deposits, after he shall have knowledge of the fact that such banking institution is insolvent or in failing circumstances, shall be individually responsible for such deposits so received.

SECTION 13 COMMON CARRIERS, REGULATION OF. All railroad, canal and other transportation companies are declared to be common carriers and subject to legislative control. Any association or corporation organized for the purpose, under the laws of this state, shall have the right to connect at the state line with railroads of other states. Every railroad company shall have the right with its road, whether the same be now constructed or may hereafter be constructed, to intersect, cross or connect with any other railroad, and when such railroads are of the same or similar gauge they shall at all crossings and at all points, where a railroad shall begin or terminate at or near any other railroad, form proper connections so that the cars of any such railroad companies may be speedily transferred from one railroad to another. All railroad companies shall receive and transport each the other's passengers, tonnage and cars without delay or discrimination.

SECTION 14 PROHIBITION AGAINST COMBINATIONS BY CARRIERS. [Repealed by AMENDMENT 67, 1977 House Joint Resolution No. 57, p 1714. Approved November 8, 1977.]

Original text — Art. 12 Section 14 PROHIBITION AGAINST COMBINATIONS BY CARRIERS — No railroad company, or other common carrier, shall combine or make any contract with the owners of any vessel that leaves port or makes port in this state, or with any common carrier, by which combination or contract the earnings of one doing the carrying are to be shared by the other not doing the carrying.

SECTION 15 PROHIBITION AGAINST DISCRIMINATING CHARGES. No discrimination in charges or facilities for transportation shall be made by any railroad or other transportation company between places or persons, or in the facilities for the transportation of the same classes of freight or passengers within this state, or coming from or going to any other state. Persons and property transported over any railroad, or by any other transportation company, or individual, shall be delivered at any station, landing or port, at charges not exceeding the charges for the transportation of persons and property of the same class, in the same direction, to any more distant station, port or landing. Excursion and commutation tickets may be issued at special rates.

SECTION 16 PROHIBITION AGAINST CONSOLIDATING OF COMPETING LINES. No railroad corporation shall consolidate its stock, property or franchises with any other railroad corporation owning a competing line.

SECTION 17 ROLLING STOCK, PERSONALTY FOR PURPOSE OF TAXATION. The rolling stock and other movable property belonging to any railroad company or corporation in this state, shall be considered personal property, and shall be liable to taxation and to execution and sale in the same manner as the personal property of individuals and such property shall not be exempted from execution and sale.

SECTION 18 RATES FOR TRANSPORTATION. The legislature may pass laws establishing reasonable rates of charges for the transportation of passengers and freight, and to correct abuses and prevent discrimination and extortion in the rates of freight and passenger tariffs on the different railroads and other common carriers in the state, and shall enforce such laws by adequate penalties. A railroad and transportation commission may be established and its powers and duties fully defined by law. [**AMENDMENT 66,** 1977 House Joint Resolution No. 55, p 1713. Approved November 8, 1977.]

Original text — Art. 12 Section 18 MAXIMUM RATES FOR TRANSPORTATION — The legislature shall pass laws establishing reasonable maximum rates of charges for the transportation of passengers and freight, and to correct abuses and prevent discrimination and extortion in the rates of freight and passenger tariffs on the different railroads and other common carriers in the state, and shall enforce such laws by adequate penalties. A railroad and transportation commission may be established and its powers and duties fully defined by law.

SECTION 19 TELEGRAPH AND TELEPHONE COMPANIES. Any association or corporation, or the lessees or managers thereof, organized for the purpose, or any individual, shall have the right to construct and maintain lines of telegraph and telephone within this state, and said companies shall receive and transmit each other's messages without delay or discrimination and all of such companies are hereby declared to be common carriers and subject to legislative control. Railroad corporations organized or doing business in this state shall allow telegraph and telephone corporations and companies to construct and maintain telegraph lines on and along the rights of way of such railroads and railroad companies, and no railroad corporation organized or doing business in this state shall allow any telegraph corporation or company any facilities, privileges or rates for transportation of men or material or for repairing their lines not allowed to all telegraph companies. The right of eminent domain is hereby extended to all telegraph and telephone companies. The legislature shall, by general law of uniform operation, provide reasonable regulations to give effect to this section.

Eminent domain: Art. 1 Section 16.

SECTION 20 PROHIBITION AGAINST FREE TRANSPORTATION FOR PUBLIC OFFICERS. No railroad or other transportation company shall grant free passes, or sell tickets or passes at a discount, other than as sold to the public generally, to any member of the legislature, or to any person holding any public office within this state. The legislature shall pass laws to carry this provision into effect.

SECTION 21 EXPRESS COMPANIES. Railroad companies now or hereafter organized or doing business in this state, shall allow all express companies organized or doing business in this state, transportation over all lines of railroad owned or operated by such railroad companies upon equal terms with any other express company, and no railroad corporation organized or doing business in this state shall allow any express corporation or company any facilities, privileges or rates for transportation of men or materials or property carried by them or for doing the business of such express companies not allowed to all express companies.

SECTION 22 MONOPOLIES AND TRUSTS. Monopolies and trusts shall never be allowed in this state, and no incorporated company, copartnership, or association of persons in this state shall directly or indirectly combine or make any contract with any other incorporated company, foreign or domestic, through their stockholders, or the trustees or assignees of such stockholders, or with any copartnership or association of persons, or in any manner whatever for the purpose of fixing the price or limiting the production or regulating the transportation of any product or commodity. The legislature shall pass laws for the enforcement of this section by adequate penalties, and in case of incorporated companies, if necessary for that purpose, may declare a forfeiture of their franchises.

ARTICLE XIII STATE INSTITUTIONS

SECTION 1 EDUCATIONAL, REFORMATORY, AND PENAL INSTITUTIONS. Educational, reformatory, and penal institutions; those for the benefit of youth who are blind or deaf or otherwise disabled; for persons who are mentally ill or developmentally disabled; and such other institutions as the public good may require, shall be fostered and supported by the state, subject to such regulations as may be provided by law. The regents, trustees, or commissioners of all such institutions existing at the time of the adoption of this Constitution, and of such as shall thereafter be established by law, shall be appointed by the governor, by and with the advice and consent of the senate; and upon all nominations made by the governor, the question shall be taken by ayes and noes, and entered upon the journal. [**AMENDMENT 83,** 1988 House Joint Resolution No. 4231, p 1553. Approved November 8, 1988.]

Original text — Art. 13 Section 1 EDUCATIONAL, REFORMATORY AND PENAL INSTITUTIONS — Educational, reformatory and penal institutions; those for the benefit of blind, deaf, dumb, or otherwise defective youth; for the insane or idiotic; and such other institutions as the public good may require, shall be fostered and supported by the state, subject to such regulations as may be provided by law. The regents, trustees, or commissioners of all such institutions existing at the time of the adoption of this Constitution, and of such as shall thereafter be established by law, shall be appointed by the governor, by and with the advice and consent of the senate; and upon all nominations made by the governor, the question shall be taken by ayes and noes, and entered upon the journal.

ARTICLE XIV SEAT OF GOVERNMENT

SECTION 1 STATE CAPITAL, LOCATION OF. The legislature shall have no power to change, or to locate the seat of government of this state; but the question of the permanent location of the seat of government of the state shall be submitted to the qualified electors of the Territory, at the election to be held for the adoption of this Constitution. A majority of all the votes cast at said election, upon said question, shall be necessary to determine the permanent location of the seat of government for the state; and no place shall ever be the seat of government which shall not receive a majority of the votes cast on that matter. In case there shall be no choice of location at said first election the legislature shall, at its first regular session after the adoption of this Constitution, provide for submitting to the qualified electors of the state, at the next succeeding general election thereafter, the question of choice of location between the three places for which the highest number of votes shall have been cast at the said first election. Said legislature shall provide further that in case there shall be no choice of location at said second election, the question of choice between the two places for which the highest number of votes shall have been cast, shall be submitted in like manner to the qualified electors of the state at the next ensuing general election: Provided, That until the seat of government shall have been permanently located as herein provided, the temporary location thereof shall remain at the city of Olympia.

SECTION 2 CHANGE OF STATE CAPITAL. When the seat of government shall have been located as herein provided, the location thereof shall not thereafter be changed except by a vote of two-thirds of all the qualified electors of the state voting on that question, at a general election, at which the question of location of the seat of government shall have been submitted by the legislature.

Governmental continuity during emergency periods: Art. 2 Section 42.

SECTION 3 RESTRICTIONS ON APPROPRIATIONS FOR CAPITOL BUILDINGS. The legislature shall make no appropriations or expenditures for capitol buildings or grounds, except to keep the Territorial capitol buildings and grounds in repair, and for making all necessary additions thereto, until the seat of government shall have been permanently located, and the public buildings are erected at the permanent capital in pursuance of law.

ARTICLE XV HARBORS AND TIDE WATERS

SECTION 1 HARBOR LINE COMMISSION AND RESTRAINT ON DISPOSITION. The legislature shall provide for the appointment of a commission whose duty it shall be to locate and establish harbor lines in the navigable waters of all harbors, estuaries, bays and inlets of this state, wherever such navigable waters lie within or in front of the corporate limits of any city, or within one mile thereof on either side. Any harbor line so located or established may thereafter be changed, relocated or reestablished by the commission pursuant to such provision as may be made therefor by the legislature. The state shall never give, sell or lease to any private person, corporation, or association any rights whatever in the waters beyond such harbor lines, nor shall any of the area lying between any harbor line and the line of ordinary high water, and within not less than fifty feet nor more than two thousand feet of such harbor line (as the commission shall determine) be sold or granted by the state, nor its rights to control the same relinquished, but such area shall be forever reserved for landings, wharves, streets, and other conveniences of navigation and commerce. [**AMENDMENT 15,** 1931 p 417 Section 1. Approved November, 1932.]

Tide lands: Art. 17.

Original text — Art. 15 Section 1 HARBOR LINE COMMISSION AND RESTRAINT ON DISPOSITION OF CERTAIN TIDE LANDS — The legislature shall provide for the appointment of a commission whose duty it shall be to locate and establish harbor lines in the navigable waters of all harbors, estuaries, bays and inlets of this state, wherever such navigable waters lie within or in front of the corporate limits of any city or within one mile thereof on either side. The state shall never give, sell or lease to any private person, corporation or association any rights whatever in the waters beyond such harbor lines, nor shall any of the area lying between any harbor line and the line of ordinary high tide, and within not less than fifty feet nor more than six hundred feet of such harbor line (as the commission shall determine) be sold or granted by the state, nor its right to control the same relinquished, but such area shall be forever reserved for landings, wharves, streets and other conveniences of navigation and commerce.

SECTION 2 LEASING AND MAINTENANCE OF WHARVES, DOCKS, ETC. The legislature shall provide general laws for the leasing of the right to build and maintain wharves, docks and other structures, upon the areas mentioned in section one of this article, but no lease shall be made for any term longer than thirty years, or the legislature may provide by general laws for the building and maintaining upon such area wharves, docks, and other structures.

SECTION 3 EXTENSION OF STREETS OVER TIDE LANDS. Municipal corporations shall have the right to extend their streets over intervening tide lands to and across the area reserved as herein provided.

ARTICLE XVI SCHOOL AND GRANTED LANDS

SECTION 1 DISPOSITION OF. All the public lands granted to the state are held in trust for all the people and none of such lands, nor any estate or interest therein, shall ever be disposed of unless the full market value of the estate or interest disposed of, to be ascertained in such manner as may be provided by law, be paid or safely secured to the state; nor shall any lands which the state holds by grant from the United States (in any case in which the manner of disposal and minimum price are so prescribed) be disposed of except in the manner and for at least the price prescribed in the grant thereof, without the consent of the United States.

SECTION 2 MANNER AND TERMS OF SALE. None of the lands granted to the state for educational purposes shall be sold otherwise than at public auction to the highest bidder, the value thereof, less the improvements shall, before any sale, be appraised by a board of appraisers to be provided by law, the terms of payment also to be prescribed by law, and no sale shall be valid unless the sum bid be equal to the appraised value of said land. In estimating the value of such lands for disposal, the value of the improvements thereon shall be excluded: Provided, That the sale of all school and university land heretofore made by the commissioners of any county or the university commissioners when the purchase price has been paid in good faith, may be confirmed by the legislature.

SECTION 3 LIMITATIONS ON SALES. No more than one-fourth of the land granted to the state for educational purposes shall be sold prior to January 1, 1895, and not more than one-half prior to January 1, 1905: provided, that nothing herein shall be so construed as to prevent the state from selling the timber or stone off of any of the state lands in such manner and on such terms as may be prescribed by law: and provided, further, that no sale of timber lands shall be valid unless the full value of such lands is paid or secured to the state.

SECTION 4 HOW MUCH MAY BE OFFERED IN CERTAIN CASES — PLATTING OF. No more than one hundred and sixty (160) acres of any granted lands of the state shall be offered for sale in one parcel, and all lands within the limits of any incorporated city or within two miles of the boundary of any incorporated city where the valuation of such land shall be found by appraisement to exceed one hundred dollars ($100) per acre shall, before the same be sold, be platted into lots and blocks of not more than five acres in a block, and not more than one block shall be offered for sale in one parcel.

SECTION 5 INVESTMENT OF PERMANENT COMMON SCHOOL FUND. The permanent common school fund of this state may be invested as authorized by law. [**AMENDMENT 44,** 1965 ex.s. Senate Joint Resolution No. 22, part 2, p 2817. Approved November 8, 1966.]

Amendment 1 (1894) — Art. 16 Section 5 INVESTMENT OF SCHOOL FUND — None of the permanent school fund of this state shall ever be loaned to private persons or corporations, but it may be invested in national, state, county, municipal or school district bonds. [AMENDMENT 1, 1893 p 9 Section 1. Approved November, 1894.]

Original text — Art. 16 Section 5 INVESTMENT OF PERMANENT SCHOOL FUND — None of the permanent school fund shall ever be loaned to private persons or corporations, but it may be invested in national, state, county or municipal bonds.

Funds for support of education: Art. 9 Section 3.

SECTION 6 INVESTMENT OF HIGHER EDUCATION PERMANENT FUNDS. Notwithstanding the provisions of Article VIII, sections 5 and 7 and Article XII, section 9, or any other section or article of the Constitution of the state of Washington, the moneys of the permanent funds established for any of the institutions of higher education in this state may be invested as authorized by law. Without limitation, this shall include the authority to invest permanent funds held for the benefit of institutions of higher education in stocks or bonds issued by any association, company, or corporation if authorized by law. [**AMENDMENT 102,** 2007 Substitute House Joint Resolution No. 4215, p 3145. Approved November 6, 2007.]

ARTICLE XVII TIDE LANDS

SECTION 1 DECLARATION OF STATE OWNERSHIP. The state of Washington asserts its ownership to the beds and shores of all navigable waters in the state up to and including the line of ordinary high tide, in waters where the tide ebbs and flows, and up to and including the line of ordinary high water within the banks of all navigable rivers and lakes: Provided, that this section shall not be construed so as to debar any person from asserting his claim to vested rights in the courts of the state.

Harbors and tide waters: Art. 15.

SECTION 2 DISCLAIMER OF CERTAIN LANDS. The state of Washington disclaims all title in and claim to all tide, swamp and overflowed lands, patented by the United States: Provided, the same is not impeached for fraud.

ARTICLE XVIII STATE SEAL

SECTION 1 SEAL OF THE STATE. The seal of the State of Washington shall be, a seal encircled with the words: "The Seal of the State of Washington," with the vignette of General George Washington as the central figure, and beneath the vignette the figures "1889."

Custody of seal: Art. 3 Section 18.State seal: RCW 1.20.080.

ARTICLE XIX

EXEMPTIONS
SECTION 1 EXEMPTIONS — HOMESTEADS, ETC. The legislature shall protect by law from forced sale a certain portion of the homestead and other property of all heads of families.

ARTICLE XX
PUBLIC HEALTH AND VITAL STATISTICS
SECTION 1 BOARD OF HEALTH AND BUREAU OF VITAL STATISTICS. There shall be established by law a state board of health and a bureau of vital statistics in connection therewith, with such powers as the legislature may direct.

SECTION 2 REGULATIONS CONCERNING MEDICINE, SURGERY AND PHARMACY. The legislature shall enact laws to regulate the practice of medicine and surgery, and the sale of drugs and medicines.

ARTICLE XXI
WATER AND WATER RIGHTS
SECTION 1 PUBLIC USE OF WATER. The use of the waters of this state for irrigation, mining and manufacturing purposes shall be deemed a public use.

ARTICLE XXII
LEGISLATIVE APPORTIONMENT
SECTION 1 SENATORIAL APPORTIONMENT. Until otherwise provided by law, the state shall be divided into twenty-four (24) senatorial districts, and said districts shall be constituted and numbered as follows: The counties of Stevens and Spokane shall constitute the first district, and be entitled to one senator; the county of Spokane shall constitute the second district, and be entitled to three senators; the county of Lincoln shall constitute the third district, and be entitled to one senator; the counties of Okanogan, Lincoln, Adams and Franklin shall constitute the fourth district, and be entitled to one senator; the county of Whitman shall constitute the fifth district, and be entitled to three senators; the counties of Garfield and Asotin shall constitute the sixth district, and be entitled to one senator; the county of Columbia shall constitute the seventh district, and be entitled to one senator; the county of Walla Walla shall constitute the eighth district, and be entitled to two senators; the counties of Yakima and Douglas shall constitute the ninth district, and be entitled to one senator; the county of Kittitas shall constitute the tenth district and be entitled to one senator; the counties of Klickitat, and Skamania shall constitute the eleventh district, and be entitled to one senator; the county of Clarke shall constitute the twelfth district, and be entitled to one senator; the county of Cowlitz shall constitute the thirteenth district, and be entitled to one senator; the county of Lewis shall constitute the fourteenth district, and be entitled to one senator; the counties of Pacific and Wahkiakum shall constitute the fifteenth district, and be entitled to one senator; the county of Thurston shall constitute the sixteenth district, and be entitled to one senator; the county of Chehalis shall constitute the seventeenth district, and be entitled to one senator; the county of Pierce shall constitute the eighteenth district, and be entitled to three senators; the county of King shall constitute the nineteenth district, and be entitled to five senators; the counties of Mason and Kitsap shall constitute the twentieth district, and be entitled to one senator; the counties of Jefferson, Clallam and San Juan shall constitute the twenty-first district, and be entitled to one senator; the county of Snohomish shall constitute the twenty-second district, and shall be entitled to one senator; the counties of Skagit and Island shall constitute the twenty-third district, and be entitled to one senator; the county of Whatcom shall constitute the twenty-fourth district, and be entitled to one senator.

Districts and apportionment: Chapter 44.07D RCW.

SECTION 2 APPORTIONMENT OF REPRESENTATIVES. Until otherwise provided by law the representatives shall be divided among the several counties of the state in the following manner; the county of Adams shall have one representative; the county of Asotin shall have one representative; the county of Chehalis shall have two representatives; the county of Clarke shall have three representatives; the county of Clallam shall have one representative; the county of Columbia shall have two representatives; the county of Cowlitz shall have one representative; the county of Douglas shall have one representative; the county of Franklin shall have one representative; the county of Garfield shall have one representative; the county of Island shall have one representative; the county of Jefferson shall have two representatives; the county of King shall have eight representatives; the county of Klickitat shall have two representatives; the county of Kittitas shall have two representatives; the county of Kitsap shall have one representative; the county of Lewis shall have two representatives; the county of Lincoln shall have two representatives; the county of Mason shall have one representative; the county of Okanogan shall have one representative; the county of Pacific shall have one representative; the county of Pierce shall have six representatives; the county of San Juan shall have one representative; the county of Skamania shall have one representative; the county of Snohomish shall have two representatives; the county of Skagit shall have two representatives; the county of Spokane shall have six representatives; the county of Stevens shall have one representative; the county of Thurston shall have two representatives; the county of Walla Walla shall have three representatives; the county of Wahkiakum shall have one representative; the county of Whatcom shall have two representatives; the county of Whitman shall have five representatives; the county of Yakima shall have one representative.

Districts and apportionment: Chapter 44.07D RCW.

ARTICLE XXIII AMENDMENTS

SECTION 1 HOW MADE. Any amendment or amendments to this Constitution may be proposed in either branch of the legislature; and if the same shall be agreed to by two-thirds of the members elected to each of the two houses, such proposed amendment or amendments shall be entered on their journals, with the ayes and noes thereon, and be submitted to the qualified electors of the state for their approval, at the next general election; and if the people approve and ratify such amendment or amendments, by a majority of the electors voting thereon, the same shall become part of this Constitution, and proclamation thereof shall be made by the governor: Provided, That if more than one amendment be submitted, they shall be submitted in such a manner that the people may vote for or against such amendments separately. The legislature shall also cause notice of the amendments that are to be submitted to the people to be published at least four times during the four weeks next preceding the election in every legal newspaper in the state: Provided, That failure of any newspaper to publish this notice shall not be interpreted as affecting the outcome of the election.
[**AMENDMENT 37,** 1961 Senate Joint Resolution No. 25, p 2753. Approved November, 1962.]

Original text — Art. 23 Section 1 HOW MADE — Any amendment or amendments to this Constitution may be proposed in either branch of the legislature; and if the same shall be agreed to by two-thirds of the members elected to each of the two houses, such proposed amendment or amendments shall be entered on their journals, with the ayes and noes thereon, and be submitted to the qualified electors of the state for their approval, at the next general election; and if the people approve and ratify such amendment or amendments, by a majority of the electors voting thereon, the same shall become part of this Constitution, and proclamation thereof shall be made by the governor: Provided, that if more than one amendment be submitted, they shall be submitted in such a manner that the people may vote for or against such amendments separately. The legislature shall also cause the amendments that are to be submitted to the people to be published for at least three months next preceding the election, in some weekly newspaper, in every county where a newspaper is published throughout the state.

SECTION 2 CONSTITUTIONAL CONVENTIONS. Whenever two-thirds of the members elected to each branch of the legislature shall deem it necessary to call a convention to revise or amend this Constitution, they shall recommend to the electors to vote at the next general election, for or against a convention, and if a majority of all the electors voting at said election shall have voted for a convention, the legislature shall at the next session, provide by law for calling the same; and such convention shall consist of a number of members, not less than that of the most numerous branch of the legislature.

SECTION 3 SUBMISSION TO THE PEOPLE. Any Constitution adopted by such convention shall have no validity until it has been submitted to and adopted by the people.

ARTICLE XXIV BOUNDARIES

SECTION 1 STATE BOUNDARIES. The boundaries of the state of Washington shall be as follows: Beginning at a point in the Pacific ocean one marine league due west of and opposite the middle of the mouth of the north ship channel of the Columbia river thence running easterly to and up the middle channel of said river and where it is divided by islands up the middle of the widest channel thereof to where the forty-sixth parallel of north latitude crosses said river near the mouth of the Walla Walla river; thence east on said forty-sixth parallel of latitude to the middle of the main channel of Shoshone or Snake river, thence follow down the middle of the main channel of Snake river to a point opposite the mouth of the Kooskooskia or Clear Water river, thence due north to the forty-ninth parallel of north latitude, thence west along said forty-ninth parallel of north latitude to the middle of the channel which separates Vancouver's island from the continent, that is to say to a point in longitude 123 degrees, 19 minutes and 15 seconds west, thence following the boundary line between the United States and British possessions through the channel which separates Vancouver's island from the continent to the termination of the boundary line between the United States and British possessions at a point in the Pacific ocean equidistant between Bonnilla point on Vancouver's island and Tatoosh island light house, thence running in a southerly course and parallel with the coast line, keeping one marine league off shore to place of beginning; until such boundaries are modified by appropriate interstate compacts duly approved by the Congress of the United States. [**AMENDMENT 33,** 1957 Senate Joint Resolution No. 10, p 1292. Approved November 4, 1958.]

Original text — Art. 24 Section 1 STATE BOUNDARIES — The boundaries of the State of Washington shall be as follows: Beginning at a point in the Pacific ocean one marine league due west of and opposite the middle of the mouth of the north ship channel of the Columbia river thence running easterly to and up the middle channel of said river and where it is divided by islands up the middle of the widest channel thereof to where the forty-sixth parallel of north latitude crosses said river near the mouth of the Walla Walla river; thence east on said forty-sixth parallel of latitude to the middle of the main channel of the Shoshone or Snake river, thence follow down the middle of the main channel of Snake river to a point opposite the mouth of the Kooskooskia or Clear Water river, thence due north to the forty-ninth parallel of north latitude, thence west along said forty-ninth parallel of north latitude to the middle of the channel which separates Vancouver's island from the continent, that is to say to a point in longitude 123 degrees, 19 minutes and 15 seconds west, thence following the boundary line between the United States and British possessions through the channel which separates Vancouver's island from the continent to the termination of the boundary line between the United States and British possessions at a point in the Pacific ocean equi distant between Bonnilla point on Vancouver's island and Tatoosh island light house, thence running in a southerly course and parallel with the coast line, keeping one marine league off shore to place of beginning.

ARTICLE XXV JURISDICTION

SECTION 1 AUTHORITY OF THE UNITED STATES. The consent of the State of Washington is hereby given to the exercise, by the congress of the United States, of exclusive legislation in all cases whatsoever over such tracts or parcels of land as are now held or reserved by the government of the United States for the purpose of erecting or maintaining thereon forts, magazines, arsenals, dockyards, lighthouses and other needful buildings, in accordance with the provisions of the seventeenth paragraph of the eighth section of the first article of the Constitution of the United States, so long as the same shall be so held and reserved by the United States. Provided: That a sufficient description by metes and bounds, and an accurate plat or map of each such tract or parcel of land be filed in the proper office of record in the county in which the same is situated, together with copies of the orders, deeds, patents or other evidences in writing of the title of the United States: and provided, That all civil process issued from the courts of this state and such criminal process as may issue under the authority of this state against any person charged with crime in cases arising outside of such reservations, may be served and executed thereon in the same mode and manner, and by the same officers, as if the consent herein given had not been made.

ARTICLE XXVI COMPACT WITH THE UNITED STATES

The following ordinance shall be irrevocable without the consent of the United States and the people of this state:

First. That perfect toleration of religious sentiment shall be secured and that no inhabitant of this state shall ever be molested in person or property on account of his or her mode of religious worship.

Second. That the people inhabiting this state do agree and declare that they forever disclaim all right and title to the unappropriated public lands lying with the boundaries of this state, and to all lands lying within said limits owned or held by any Indian or Indian tribes; and that until the title thereto shall have been extinguished by the United States, the same shall be and remain subject to the disposition of the United States, and said Indian lands shall remain under the absolute jurisdiction and control of the congress of the United States and that the lands belonging to citizens of the United States residing without the limits of this state shall never be taxed at a higher rate than the lands belonging to residents thereof; and that no taxes shall be imposed by the state on lands or property therein, belonging to or which may be hereafter purchased by the United States or reserved for use: Provided, That nothing in this ordinance shall preclude the state from taxing as other lands are taxed any lands owned or held by any Indian who has severed his tribal relations, and has obtained from the United States or from any person a title thereto by patent or other grant, save and except such lands as have been or may be granted to any Indian or Indians under any act of congress containing a provision exempting the lands thus granted from taxation, which exemption shall continue so long and to such an extent as such act of congress may prescribe.

Third. The debts and liabilities of the Territory of Washington and payment of the same are hereby assumed by this state.

Fourth. Provision shall be made for the establishment and maintenance of systems of public schools free from sectarian control which shall be open to all the children of said state.

ARTICLE XXVII SCHEDULE

In order that no inconvenience may arise by reason of a change from a Territorial to a State government, it is hereby declared and ordained as follows:

SECTION 1 EXISTING RIGHTS, ACTIONS, AND CONTRACTS SAVED. No existing rights, actions, suits, proceedings, contracts or claims shall be affected by a change in the form of government, but all shall continue as if no such change had taken place; and all process which may have been issued under the authority of the Territory of Washington previous to its admission into the Union shall be as valid as if issued in the name of the state.

SECTION 2 LAWS IN FORCE CONTINUED. All laws now in force in the Territory of Washington, which are not repugnant to this Constitution, shall remain in force until they expire by their own limitation, or are altered or repealed by the legislature: Provided, That this section shall not be so construed as to validate any act of the legislature of Washington Territory granting shore or tide lands to any person, company or any municipal or private corporation.

SECTION 3 DEBTS, FINES, ETC., TO INURE TO THE STATE. All debts, fines, penalties and forfeitures, which have accrued, or may hereafter accrue, to the Territory of Washington, shall inure to the State of Washington.

SECTION 4 RECOGNIZANCES. All recognizances heretofore taken, or which may be taken before the change from a territorial to a state government shall remain valid, and shall pass to, and may be prosecuted in the name of the state; and all bonds executed to the Territory of Washington or to any county or municipal corporation, or to any officer or court in his or its official capacity, shall pass to the state authorities and their successors in office, for the uses therein expressed, and may be sued for and recovered accordingly, and all the estate, real, personal and mixed, and all judgments decrees, bonds, specialties, choses in action, and claims or debts, of whatever description, belonging to the Territory of Washington, shall inure to and vest in the State of Washington, and may be sued for and recovered in the same manner, and to the same extent, by the State of Washington, as the same could have been by the Territory of Washington.

SECTION 5 CRIMINAL PROSECUTIONS AND PENAL ACTIONS. All criminal prosecutions and penal actions which may have arisen, or which may arise, before the change from a territorial to a state government, and which shall then be pending, shall be prosecuted to judgment, and execution in the name of the state. All offenses committed against the laws of the Territory of Washington, before the change from a territorial to a state government, and which shall not be prosecuted before such change, may be prosecuted in the name and by the authority of the State of Washington, with like effect as though such change had not taken place; and all penalties incurred shall remain the same as if this Constitution had not been adopted. All actions at law and suits in equity which may be pending in any of the courts of the Territory of Washington, at the time of the change from a territorial to a state government, shall be continued, and transferred to the court of the state having jurisdiction of the subject matter thereof.

SECTION 6 RETENTION OF TERRITORIAL OFFICERS. All officers now holding their office under the authority of the United States, or of the Territory of Washington, shall continue to hold and exercise their respective offices until they shall be superseded by the authority of the state.

SECTION 7 CONSTITUTIONAL OFFICERS, WHEN ELECTED. All officers provided for in this Constitution including a county clerk for each county when no other time is fixed for their election, shall be elected at the election to be held for the adoption of this Constitution on the first Tuesday of October, 1889.

SECTION 8 CHANGE OF COURTS - TRANSFER OF CAUSES. Whenever the judge of the superior court of any county, elected or appointed under the provisions of this Constitution shall have qualified the several causes then pending in the district court of the territory except such causes as would have been within the exclusive jurisdiction of the United States district court had such court existed at the time of the commencement of such causes, within such county, and the records, papers and proceedings of said district court, and the seal and other property pertaining thereto, shall pass into the jurisdiction and possession of the superior court for such county. And where the same judge is elected for two or more counties, it shall be the duty of the clerk of the district court having custody of such papers and records to transmit to the clerk of such county, or counties, other than that in which such records are kept the original papers in all cases pending in such district court and belonging to the jurisdiction of such county or counties together with transcript of so much of the records of said district court as relate to the same; and until the district courts of the Territory shall be superseded in manner aforesaid, the said district courts and the judges thereof, shall continue with the same jurisdiction and powers, to be exercised in the same judicial districts respectively, as heretofore constituted under the laws of the Territory. Whenever a quorum of the judges of the supreme court of the state shall have been elected and qualified, the causes then pending in the supreme court of the Territory, except such causes as would have been within the exclusive jurisdiction of the United States, circuit court had such court existed at the time of the commencement of such causes, and the papers, records and proceedings of said court and the seal and other property pertaining thereto, shall pass into the jurisdiction and possession of the supreme court of the state, and until so superseded, the supreme court of the Territory and the judges thereof, shall continue with like powers and jurisdiction as if this Constitution had not been adopted.

SECTION 9 SEALS OF COURTS AND MUNICIPALITIES. Until otherwise provided by law, the seal now in use in the supreme court of the Territory shall be the seal of the supreme court of the state. The seals of the superior courts of the several counties of the state shall be, until otherwise provided by law, the vignette of General George Washington with the words: "Seal of the Superior Court of ———— county" surrounding the vignette. The seal of municipalities, and of all county officers of the Territory, shall be the seals of such municipalities, and county officers respectively under the state, until otherwise provided by law.

SECTION 10 PROBATE COURT, TRANSFER OF. When the state is admitted into the Union, and the superior courts in the respective counties organized, the books, records, papers and proceedings of the probate court in each county, and all causes and matters of administration pending therein, shall, upon the expiration of the term of office of the probate judges, on the second Monday in January, 1891, pass into the jurisdiction and possession of the superior court of the same county created by this Constitution, and the said court shall proceed to final judgment or decree, order or other determination in the several matters and causes, as the territorial probate court might have done, if this Constitution had not been adopted. And until the expiration of the term of office of the probate judges, such probate judges shall perform the duties now imposed upon them by the laws of the Territory. The superior courts shall have appellate and revisory jurisdiction over the decisions of the probate courts, as now provided by law, until such latter courts expire by limitation.

SECTION 11 DUTIES OF FIRST LEGISLATURE. The legislature, at its first session, shall provide for the election of all officers whose election is not provided for elsewhere in this Constitution, and fix the time for the commencement and duration of their term.

SECTION 12 ELECTION CONTESTS FOR SUPERIOR JUDGES, HOW DECIDED. In case of a contest of election between candidates, at the first general election under this Constitution, for judges of the superior courts, the evidence shall be taken in the manner prescribed by the Territorial laws, and the testimony so taken shall be certified to the secretary of state; and said officer, together with the governor and treasurer of state, shall review the evidence and determine who is entitled to the certificate of election.

SECTION 13 REPRESENTATION IN CONGRESS. [Repealed by AMENDMENT 74, 1983 Substitute Senate Joint Resolution No. 103. Approved November 8, 1983.]

Original text — Art. 27 Section 13 REPRESENTATION IN CONGRESS — One representative in the congress of the United States shall be elected from the state at large, at the first election provided for in this Constitution; and, thereafter, at such times and places, and in such manner, as may be prescribed by law. When a new apportionment shall be made by congress, the legislature shall divide the state into congressional districts, in accordance with such apportionment. The vote cast for representative in congress, at the first election, shall be canvassed, and the result determined in the manner provided for by the laws of the Territory for the canvass of the vote for delegate in congress.

SECTION 14 DURATION OF TERM OF CERTAIN OFFICERS. All district, county and precinct officers, who may be in office at the time of the adoption of this Constitution, and the county clerk of each county elected at the first election, shall hold their respective offices until the second Monday of January, A. D., 1891, and until such time as their successors may be elected and qualified, in accordance with the provisions of this Constitution; and the official bonds of all such officers shall continue in full force and effect as though this Constitution had not been adopted. And such officers shall continue to receive the compensation now provided, until the same be changed by law.

SECTION 15 ELECTION ON ADOPTION OF CONSTITUTION, HOW TO BE CONDUCTED. The election held at the time of the adoption of this Constitution shall be held and conducted in all respects according to the laws of the Territory, and the votes cast at said election for all officers (where no other provisions are made in this Constitution), and for the adoption of this Constitution and the several separate articles and the location of the state capital, shall be canvassed and returned in the several counties in the manner provided by Territorial law, and shall be returned to the secretary of the Territory in the manner provided by the Enabling Act.

SECTION 16 WHEN CONSTITUTION TO TAKE EFFECT. The provisions of this Constitution shall be in force from the day on which the president of the United States shall issue his proclamation declaring the State of Washington admitted into the Union, and the terms of all officers elected at the first election under the provisions of this Constitution shall commence on the Monday next succeeding the issue of said proclamation, unless otherwise provided herein.

SECTION 17 SEPARATE ARTICLES. The following separate articles shall be submitted to the people for adoption or rejection at the election for the adoption of this Constitution:

SEPARATE ARTICLE, NO. 1

"All persons male and female of the age of twenty-one years or over, possessing the other qualifications, provided by this Constitution, shall be entitled to vote at all elections."

SEPARATE ARTICLE, NO. 2

"It shall not be lawful for any individual, company or corporation, within the limits of this state, to manufacture, or cause to be manufactured, or to sell, or offer for sale, or in any manner dispose of any alcoholic, malt or spirituous liquors, except for medicinal, sacramental or scientific purposes."

If a majority of the ballots cast at said election on said separate articles be in favor of the adoption of either of said separate articles, then such separate article so receiving a majority shall become a part of this Constitution and shall govern and control any provision of the Constitution in conflict therewith.

SECTION 18 BALLOT. The form of ballot to be used in voting for or against this Constitution, or for or against the separate articles, or for the permanent location of the seat of government, shall be:

1. For the Constitution- - - -
   Against the Constitution- - - -
2. For Woman Suffrage Article- - - -
   Against Woman Suffrage Article- - - -
3. For Prohibition Article- - - -
   Against Prohibition Article- - - -
4. For the Permanent Location of the Seat of Government (Name of place voted for)- - - -

The result of the election was against both woman suffrage and prohibition.

SECTION 19 APPROPRIATION. The legislature is hereby authorized to appropriate from the state treasury sufficient money to pay any of the expenses of this convention not provided for by the Enabling Act of Congress.

ARTICLE XXVIII COMPENSATION OF STATE OFFICERS

SECTION 1 SALARIES FOR LEGISLATURE, ELECTED STATE OFFICIALS, AND JUDGES — INDEPENDENT COMMISSION — REFERENDUM. Salaries for members of the legislature, elected officials of the executive branch of state government, and judges of the state's supreme court, court of appeals, superior courts, and district courts shall be fixed by an independent commission created and directed by law to that purpose. No state official, public employee, or person required by law to register with a state agency as a lobbyist, or immediate family member of the official, employee, or lobbyist, may be a member of that commission.

As used in this section the phrase "immediate family" has the meaning that is defined by law.

Any change of salary shall be filed with the secretary of state and shall become law ninety days thereafter without action of the legislature or governor, but shall be subject to referendum petition by the people, filed within the ninety-day period. Referendum measures under this section shall be submitted to the people at the next following general election, and shall be otherwise governed by the provisions of this Constitution generally applicable to referendum measures. The salaries fixed pursuant to this section shall supersede any other provision for the salaries of members of the legislature, elected officials of the executive branch of state government, and judges of the state's supreme court, court of appeals, superior courts, and district courts. The salaries for such officials in effect on January 12, 1987, shall remain in effect until changed pursuant to this section.

After the initial adoption of a law by the legislature creating the independent commission, no amendment to such act which alters the composition of the commission shall be valid unless the amendment is enacted by a favorable vote of two-thirds of the members elected to each house of the legislature and is subject to referendum petition.

The provisions of section 14 of Article IV, sections 14, 16, 17, 19, 20, 21, and 22 of Article III, and section 23 of Article II, insofar as they are inconsistent herewith, are hereby superseded. The provisions of section 1 of Article II relating to referendum procedures, insofar as they are inconsistent herewith, are hereby superseded with regard to the salaries governed by this section. [**AMENDMENT 78,** 1986 Substitute House Joint Resolution No. 49, p 1529. Approved November 4, 1986.]

Authorizing compensation increase during term: Art. 30 Section 1.

Amendment 20 (1948) — Art. 28 Section 1 COMPENSATION OF STATE OFFICERS — All elected state officials shall each severally receive such compensation as the legislature may direct. The compensation of any state officer shall not be increased or diminished during his term of office, except that the legislature, at its thirty-first regular session, may increase or diminish the compensation of all state officers whose terms exist on the Thursday after the second Monday in January, 1949.

The provisions of sections 14, 16, 17, 19, 20, 21, and 22 of Article III and section 23 of Article II in so far as they are inconsistent herewith, are hereby repealed. [AMENDMENT 20, 1947 Senate Joint Resolution No. 4, p 1371. Approved November 2, 1948.]

ARTICLE XXIX INVESTMENTS OF PUBLIC PENSION AND RETIREMENT FUNDS

SECTION 1 MAY BE INVESTED AS AUTHORIZED BY LAW. Notwithstanding the provisions of sections 5, and 7 of Article VIII and section 9 of Article XII or any other section or article of the Constitution of the state of Washington, the moneys of any public pension or retirement fund, industrial insurance trust fund, or fund held in trust for the benefit of persons with developmental disabilities may be invested as authorized by law. [**AMENDMENT 93,** 2000 Senate Joint Resolution No. 8214, p 1919. Approved November 7, 2000.]

Amendment 75 (1985) — Art. 29 Section 1 MAY BE INVESTED AS AUTHORIZED BY LAW — Notwithstanding the provisions of sections 5, and 7 of Article VIII and section 9 of Article XII or any other section or article of the Constitution of the state of Washington, the moneys of any public pension or retirement fund or industrial insurance trust fund may be invested as authorized by law.[AMENDMENT 75, 1985 House Joint Resolution No. 12, p 2398. Approved November 5, 1985.]

Amendment 49 (1968) — Art. 29 Section 1 MAY BE INVESTED AS AUTHORIZED BY LAW — Notwithstanding the provisions of sections 5, and 7 of Article VIII and section 9 of Article XII or any other section or article of the Constitution of the state of Washington, the moneys of any public pension or retirement fund may be invested as authorized by law. [AMENDMENT 49, 1967 Senate Joint Resolution No. 5; see 1969 p 2975. Approved November 5, 1968.]

ARTICLE XXX COMPENSATION OF PUBLIC OFFICERS

SECTION 1 AUTHORIZING COMPENSATION INCREASE DURING TERM. The compensation of all elective and appointive state, county, and municipal officers who do not fix their own compensation, including judges of courts of record and the justice courts may be increased during their terms of office to the end that such officers and judges shall each severally receive compensation for their services in accordance with the law in effect at the time the services are being rendered.

The provisions of section 25 of Article II (Amendment 35), section 25 of Article III (Amendment 31), section 13 of Article IV, section 8 of Article XI, and section 1 of Article XXVIII (Amendment 20) insofar as they are inconsistent herewith are hereby repealed. [**AMENDMENT 54,** 1967 House Joint Resolution No. 13; see 1969 p 2976. Approved November 5, 1968.]

Reviser's note: (1) Amendment 49 (1967 SJR No. 5) and Amendment 54 (1967 HJR No. 13) each added a new Article XXIX to the Constitution. Amendment 49 is carried herein as Article XXIX while Amendment 54 has been herein redesignated as Article XXX.

(2) The name of this Article has been supplied by the reviser.

ARTICLE XXXI SEX EQUALITY - RIGHTS AND RESPONSIBILITIES

SECTION 1 EQUALITY NOT DENIED BECAUSE OF SEX. Equality of rights and responsibility under the law shall not be denied or abridged on account of sex.

SECTION 2 ENFORCEMENT POWER OF LEGISLATURE. The legislature shall have the power to enforce, by appropriate legislation, the provisions of this article. [**AMENDMENT 61,** 1972 House Joint Resolution No. 61, p 526. Approved November, 1972.]

The name of this Article and the captions have been supplied by the reviser.

ARTICLE XXXII SPECIAL REVENUE FINANCING

SECTION 1 SPECIAL REVENUE FINANCING. The legislature may enact laws authorizing the state, counties, cities, towns, port districts, or public corporations established thereby to issue nonrecourse revenue bonds or other nonrecourse revenue obligations and to apply the proceeds thereof in the manner and for the purposes heretofore or hereafter authorized by law, subject to the following limitations:

(a) Nonrecourse revenue bonds and other nonrecourse revenue obligations issued pursuant to this section shall be payable only from money or other property received as a result of projects financed by the nonrecourse revenue bonds or other nonrecourse revenue obligations and from money and other property received from private sources.

(b) Nonrecourse revenue bonds and other nonrecourse revenue obligations issued pursuant to this section shall not be payable from or secured by any tax funds or governmental revenue or by all or part of the faith and credit of the state or any unit of local government.

(c) Nonrecourse revenue bonds or other nonrecourse revenue obligations issued pursuant to this section may be issued only if the issuer certifies that it reasonably believes that the interest paid on the bonds or obligations will be exempt from income taxation by the federal government.

(d) Nonrecourse revenue bonds or other nonrecourse revenue obligations may only be used to finance industrial development projects as defined in legislation.

(e) The state, counties, cities, towns, port districts, or public corporations established thereby, shall never exercise their respective attributes of sovereignty, including but not limited to, the power to tax, the power of eminent domain, and the police power on behalf of any industrial development project authorized pursuant to this section.

After the initial adoption of a law by the legislature authorizing the issuance of nonrecourse revenue bonds or other nonrecourse revenue obligations, no amendment to such act which expands the definition of industrial development project shall be valid unless the amendment is enacted by a favorable vote of three-fifths of the members elected to each house of the legislature and is subject to referendum petition.

Sections 5 and 7 of Article VIII and section 9 of Article XII shall not be construed as a limitation upon the authority granted by this section. The proceeds of revenue bonds and other revenue obligations issued pursuant to this section for the purpose of financing privately owned property or loans to private persons or corporations shall be subject to audit by the state but shall not otherwise be deemed to be public money or public property for purposes of this Constitution. This section is supplemental to and shall not be construed as a repeal of or limitation on any other authority lawfully exercisable under the Constitution and laws of this state, including, among others, any existing authority to issue revenue bonds. [**AMENDMENT 73,** 1981 Substitute House Joint Resolution No. 7, p 1794. Approved November 3, 1981.]

The name of this Article has been supplied by the reviser.

CERTIFICATE

We, the undersigned, members of the convention to form a Constitution for the State of Washington; which is to be submitted to the people for their adoption or rejection, do hereby declare this to be the Constitution formed by us, and in testimony thereof, do hereunto set our hands, this twenty-second day of August Anno Domini, one thousand eight hundred and eighty-nine.

John P. Hoyt,	Edward Eldridge
President	George H. Stevenson
J. J. Browne	Louis Sohns
N. G. Blalock	A. A. Lindsley

John F. Gowey

Frank M. Dallam

James Z. Moore

E. H. Sullivan

George Turner

Austin Mires

M. M. Godman

Gwin Hicks

Wm. F. Prosser

C. H. Warner

J. P. T. McCroskey

S. G. Cosgrove

Thos. Hayton

Charles P. Coey

Robert F. Sturdevant

John A. Shoudy

Allen Weir

W. B. Gray

Trusten P. Dyer

Geo. H. Jones

B. L. Sharpstein

H. M. Lillis

James A. Burk

John McReavy

R. O. Dunbar

Morgan Morgans

Jas. Power

B. B. Glascock

O. A. Bowen

Sam'l H. Berry

D. J. Crowley

J. T. McDonald

John M. Reed

J. J. Weisenburger

P. C. Sullivan

R. S. More

Thomas T. Minor

J. J. Travis

Arnold J. West

Charles T. Fay

George W. Tibbetts

H. W. Fairweather

Thomas C. Griffitts

J. F. Van Name

Albert Schooley

H. C. Willison

T. M. Reed

S. H. Manly

Richard Jeffs

Francis Henry

George Comegys

Oliver H. Joy

David E. Durie

D. Buchanan

John R. Kinnear

Sylvious A. Dickey

Henry Winsor

Theodore L. Stiles

Harrison Clothier

Matt. J. McElroy

J. T. Eshelman

Robert Jamieson

Hiram E. Allen

H. F. Suksdorf

J. C. Kellogg

J. A. Hungate

Attest: JNO. I. BOOGE, Chief Clerk

The above names are not in the order in which subscribed to the Constitution.

(B) Constitutional Amendments
(In Order of Adoption)

1	Art. 16	§ 5	Investment of school fund.
2	Art. 6	§ 1	Qualifications of voters. (original) Taxation—
3	Art. 7	§ 2	Uniformity and equality— Exemption.
4	Art. 1	§ 11	Religious freedom.
5	Art. 6	§ 1	Qualifications of electors.
6	Art. 3	§ 10	Vacancy in office of governor.

AMENDMENT 1

Art. 16 Section 5 INVESTMENT OF SCHOOL FUND. None of the permanent school fund of this state shall ever be loaned to private persons or corporations, but it may be invested in national, state, county, municipal or school district bonds. [1893 p 9 Section 1. Adopted November, 1894.]

Art. 16 Section 5 was later amended by Amendment 44.

AMENDMENT 2

Art. 6 Section 1 QUALIFICATIONS OF VOTERS. All male persons of the age of twenty-one years or over, possessing the following qualifications, shall be entitled to vote at all elections: They shall be citizens of the United States; they shall have lived in the state one year, and in the county ninety days, and in the city, town, ward or precinct thirty days immediately preceding the election at which they offer to vote; they shall be able to read and speak the English language: Provided, That Indians not taxed shall never be allowed the elective franchise: And further provided, That this amendment shall not effect [affect] the right of franchise of any person who is now a qualified elector of this state. The legislature shall enact laws defining the manner of ascertaining the qualifications of voters as to their ability to read and speak the English language, and providing for punishment of persons voting or registering in violation of the provisions of this section. [1895 p 60 Section 1. Approved November, 1896.]

Art. 6 Section 1 was later amended by Amendment 5.

AMENDMENT 3

Art. 7 Section 2 was amended by adding the following proviso: "And provided further, That the legislature shall have power, by appropriate legislation, to exempt personal property to the amount of three hundred dollars ($300) for each head of a family liable to assessment and taxation under the provisions of the laws of this state of which the individual is the actual and bona fide owner." [1899 p 121 Section 1. Approved November, 1900.]

Original Art. 7 Section 2 and Amendment 3 were stricken by Amendment 14.

AMENDMENT 4

Art. 1 Section 11 RELIGIOUS FREEDOM. Absolute freedom of conscience in all matters of religious sentiment, belief and worship, shall be guaranteed to every individual, and no one shall be molested or disturbed in person or property on account of religion; but the liberty of conscience hereby secured shall not be so construed as to excuse acts of licentiousness or justify practices inconsistent with the peace and safety of the state. No public money or property shall be appropriated for or applied to any religious worship, exercise or instruction, or the support of any religious establishment. Provided, however, That this article shall not be so construed as to forbid the employment by the state of a chaplain for the state penitentiary, and for such of the state reformatories as in the discretion of the legislature may seem justified. No religious qualification shall be required for any public office or employment, nor shall any person be incompetent as a witness or juror, in consequence of his opinion on matters of religion, nor be questioned in any court of justice touching his religious belief to affect the weight of his testimony. [1903 p 283 Section 1. Approved November, 1904.]

Art. 1 Section 11 was later amended by Amendments 34 and 88.

AMENDMENT 5

Article 6 was amended by striking from said article all of sections one (1) and two (2) and inserting in lieu thereof the following, to be known as section one (1):

Art. 6 Section 1 QUALIFICATIONS OF ELECTORS. All person of the age of twenty-one years or over, possessing the following qualifications, shall be entitled to vote at all elections: They shall be citizens of the United States; they shall have lived in the state one year, and in the county ninety days, and in the city, town, ward or precinct thirty days immediately preceding the election at which they offer to vote; they shall be able to read and speak the English language: Provided, That Indians not taxed shall never be allowed the elective franchise: And further provided, That this amendment shall not affect the rights of franchise of any person who is now a qualified elector of this state. The legislative authority shall enact laws defining the manner of ascertaining the qualifications of voters as to their ability to read and speak the English language, and providing for punishment of persons voting or registering in violation of the provision of this section. There shall be no denial of the elective franchise at any election on account of sex. [1909 p 26 Section 1. Approved November, 1910.]

Prior amendment of Art. 6, see Amendment 2.

Art. 6. Section 1 was later amended by Amendment 63.

AMENDMENT 6

Art. 3 Section 10 VACANCY IN OFFICE OF GOVERNOR. In case of the removal, resignation, death or disability of the governor, the duties of the office shall devolve upon the lieutenant governor; and in case of a vacancy in both the offices of governor and lieutenant governor, the duties of the governor shall devolve upon the secretary of state. In addition to the line of succession to the office and duties of governor as hereinabove indicated, if the necessity shall arise, in order to fill the vacancy in the office of governor, the following state officers shall succeed to the duties of governor and in the order named, viz.: Treasurer, auditor, attorney general, superintendent of public instruction and commissioner of public lands. In case of the death, disability, failure or refusal of the person regularly elected to the office of governor to qualify at the time provided by law, the duties of the office shall devolve upon the person regularly elected to and qualified for the office of lieutenant governor, who shall act as governor until the disability be removed, or a governor be elected; and in case of the death, disability, failure or refusal of both the governor and the lieutenant governor elect to qualify, the duties of the governor shall devolve upon the secretary of state; and in addition to the line of succession to the office and duties of governor as hereinabove indicated, if there shall be the failure or refusal of any officer named above to qualify, and if the necessity shall arise by reason thereof, then in that event in order to fill the vacancy in the office of governor, the following state officers shall succeed to the duties of governor in the order named, viz.: Treasurer, auditor, attorney general, superintendent of public instruction and commissioner of public lands. Any person succeeding to the office of governor as in this section provided, shall perform the duties of such office only until the disability be removed, or a governor be elected and qualified; and if a vacancy occur more than thirty days before the next general election occurring within two years after the commencement of the term, a person shall be elected at such election to fill the office of governor for the remainder of the unexpired term. [1909 p 642 Section 1. Approved November, 1910.]

AMENDMENT 7

Article 2 was amended by striking all of sections 1 and 31, and inserting in lieu thereof as section 1 the following, so that the same shall read as follows:

Art. 2 Section 1 LEGISLATIVE POWERS, WHERE VESTED. The legislative authority of the state of Washington shall be vested in the legislature, consisting of a senate and house of representatives, which shall be called the legislature of the state of Washington, but the people reserve to themselves the power to propose bills, laws, and to enact or reject the same at the polls, independent of the legislature, and also reserve power, at their own option, to approve or reject at the polls any act, item, section or part of any bill, act or law passed by the legislature.

(a) Initiative: The first power reserved by the people is the initiative. Ten per centum, but in no case more than fifty thousand, of the legal voters shall be required to propose any measure by such petition, and every such petition shall include the full text of the measure so proposed. Initiative petitions shall be filed with the secretary of state not less than four months before the election at which they are to be voted upon, or not less than ten days before any regular session of the legislature. If filed at least four months before the election at which they are to be voted upon, he shall submit the same to the vote of the people at the said election. If such petitions are filed not less than ten days before any regular session of the legislature, he shall transmit the same to the legislature as soon as it convenes and organizes. Such initiative measure shall take precedence over all other measures in the legislature except appropriation bills and shall be either enacted or rejected without change or amendment by the legislature before the end of such regular session. If any such initiative measure shall be enacted by the legislature it shall be subject to the referendum petition, or it may be enacted and referred by the legislature to the people for approval or rejection at the next regular election. If it is rejected or if no action is taken upon it by the legislature before the end of such regular session, the secretary of state shall submit it to the people for approval or rejection at the next ensuing regular general election. The legislature may reject any measure so proposed by initiative petition and propose a different one dealing with the same subject, and in such event both measures shall be submitted by the secretary of state to the people for approval or rejection at the next ensuing regular general election. When conflicting measures are submitted to the people the ballots shall be so printed that a voter can express separately by making one cross (X) for each, two preferences, first, as between either measure and neither, and secondly, as between one and the other. If the majority of those voting on the first issue is for neither, both fail, but in that case the votes on the second issue shall nevertheless be carefully counted and made public. If a majority voting on the first issue is for either, then the measure receiving a majority of the votes on the second issue shall be law.

Portion of subdivision (a) is superseded by Amendment 30.

(b) Referendum. The second power reserved by the people is the referendum, and it may be ordered on any act, bill, law, or any part thereof passed by the legislature, except such laws as may be necessary for the immediate preservation of the public peace, health or safety, support of the state government and its existing public institutions, either by petition signed by the required percentage of the legal voters, or by the legislature as other bills are enacted. Six per centum, but in no case more than thirty thousand, of the legal voters shall be required to sign and make a valid referendum petition.

Portion of subdivision (b) is superseded by Amendment 30.

(c) No act, law, or bill subject to referendum shall take effect until ninety days after the adjournment of the session at which it was enacted. No act, law, or bill approved by a majority of the electors voting thereon shall be amended or repealed by the legislature within a period of two years following such enactment. But such enactment may be amended or repealed at any general regular or special election by direct vote of the people thereon.

Subdivision (c) is superseded by Amendment 26.

(d) The filing of a referendum petition against one or more items, sections or parts of any act, law or bill shall not delay the remainder of the measure from becoming operative. Referendum petitions against measures passed by the legislature shall be filed with the secretary of state not later than ninety days after the final adjournment of the session of the legislature which passed the measure on which the referendum is demanded. The veto power of the governor shall not extend to measures initiated by or referred to the people. All elections on measures referred to the people of the state shall be had at the biennial regular elections, except when the legislature shall order a special election. Any measure initiated by the people or referred to the people as herein provided shall take effect and become the law if it is approved by a majority of the votes cast thereon: Provided, That the vote cast upon such question or measure shall equal one-third of the total votes cast at such election and not otherwise. Such measure shall be in operation on and after the thirtieth day after the election at which it is approved. The style of all bills proposed by initiative petition shall be: "Be it enacted by the people of the State of Washington." This section shall not be construed to deprive any member of the legislature of the right to introduce any measure. The whole number of electors who voted for governor at the regular gubernatorial election last preceding the filing of any petition for the initiative or for the referendum shall be the basis on which the number of legal voters necessary to sign such petition shall be counted. All such petitions shall be filed with the secretary of state, who shall be guided by the general laws in submitting the same to the people until additional legislation shall especially provide therefor. This section is self-executing, but legislation may be enacted especially to facilitate its operation.

The legislature shall provide methods of publicity of all laws or parts of laws, and amendments to the constitution referred to the people with arguments for and against the laws and amendments so referred, so that each voter of the state shall receive the publication at least fifty days before the election at which they are to be voted upon. [1911 p 136 Section 1. Approved November, 1912.]

Last paragraph is superseded by Amendment 36.

Art. 2 Section 1 was later amended by Amendment 72.

AMENDMENT 8

Article 1 was amended by adding the two following sections:

Art. 1 Section 33 RECALL OF ELECTIVE OFFICERS. Every elective public officer in the state of Washington expect [except] judges of courts of record is subject to recall and discharge by the legal voters of the state, or of the political subdivision of the state, from which he was elected whenever a petition demanding his recall, reciting that such officer has committed some act or acts of malfeasance or misfeasance while in office, or who has violated his oath of office, stating the matters complained of, signed by the percentages of the qualified electors thereof, hereinafter provided, the percentage required to be computed from the total number of votes cast for all candidates for his said office to which he was elected at the preceding election, is filed with the officer with whom a petition for nomination, or certificate for nomination, to such office must be filed under the laws of this state, and the same officer shall call a special election as provided by the general election laws of this state, and the result determined as therein provided.

Art. 1 Section 34 SAME. The legislature shall pass the necessary laws to carry out the provisions of section thirty-three (33) of this article, and to facilitate its operation and effect without delay: Provided, That the authority hereby conferred upon the legislature shall not be construed to grant to the legislature any exclusive power of law-making nor in any way limit the initiative and referendum powers reserved by the people. The percentages required shall be, state officers, other than judges, senators and representatives, city officers of cities of the first class, school district boards in cities of the first class; county officers of counties of the first, second and third classes, twenty-five per cent. Officers of all other political subdivisions, cities, towns, townships, precincts and school districts not herein mentioned, and state senators and representatives, thirty-five per cent. [1911 p 504 Section 1. Approved November, 1912.]

AMENDMENT 9

Art. 1 Section 16 EMINENT DOMAIN. Private property shall not be taken for private use, except for private ways of necessity, and for drains, flumes, or ditches on or across the lands of others for agricultural, domestic, or sanitary purposes. No private property shall be taken or damaged for public or private use without just compensation having been first made, or paid into court for the owner, and no right-of-way shall be appropriated to the use of any corporation other than municipal until full compensation therefor be first made in money, or ascertained and paid into court for the owner, irrespective of any benefit from any improvement proposed by such corporation, which compensation shall be ascertained by a jury, unless a jury be waived, as in other civil cases in courts of record, in the manner prescribed by law. Whenever an attempt is made to take private property for a use alleged to be public, the question whether the contemplated use be really public shall be a judicial question, and determined as such, without regard to any legislative assertion that the use is public: Provided, that the taking of private property by the state for land reclamation and settlement purposes is hereby declared to be for public use. [1919 p 385 Section 1. Approved November, 1920.]

AMENDMENT 10

Art. 1 Section 22 RIGHTS OF THE ACCUSED. In criminal prosecutions the accused shall have the right to appear and defend in person, or by counsel, to demand the nature and cause of the accusation against him, to have a copy thereof, to testify in his own behalf, to meet the witnesses against him face to face, to have compulsory process to compel the attendance of witnesses in his own behalf, to have a speedy public trial by an impartial jury of the county in which the offense is charged to have been committed and the right to appeal in all cases: Provided, The route traversed by any railway coach, train or public conveyance, and the water traversed by any boat shall be criminal districts; and the jurisdiction of all public offenses committed on any such railway car, coach, train, boat or other public conveyance, or at any station or depot upon such route, shall be in any county through which the said car, coach, train, boat or other public conveyance may pass during the trip or voyage, or in which the trip or voyage may begin or terminate. In no instance shall any accused person before final judgment be compelled to advance money or fees to secure the rights herein guaranteed. [1921 p 79 Section 1. Approved November, 1922.]

AMENDMENT 11

Art. 8 Section 4 MONEYS DISBURSED ONLY BY APPROPRIATIONS. No moneys shall ever be paid out of the treasury of this state, or any of its funds, or any of the funds under its management, except in pursuance of an appropriation by law; nor unless such payment be made within one calendar month after the end of the next ensuing fiscal biennium, and every such law making a new appropriation, or continuing or reviving an appropriation, shall distinctly specify the sum appropriated, and the object to which it is to be applied, and it shall not be sufficient for such law to refer to any other law to fix such sum. [1921 p 80 Section 1. Approved November, 1922.]

AMENDMENT 12

Art. 11 Section 5 COUNTY GOVERNMENT. The legislature, by general and uniform laws, shall provide for the election in the several counties of boards of county commissioners, sheriffs, county clerks, treasurers, prosecuting attorneys and other county, township or precinct and district officers, as public convenience may require, and shall prescribe their duties, and fix their terms of office: Provided, That the legislature may, by general laws, classify the counties by population and provide for the election in certain classes of counties certain officers who shall exercise the powers and perform the duties of two or more officers. It shall regulate the compensation of all such officers, in proportion to their duties, and for that purpose may classify the counties by population. And it shall provide for the strict accountability of such officers for all fees which may be collected by them and for all public moneys which may be paid to them, or officially come into their possession. [1923 p 255 Section 1. Approved November, 1924.]
Art. 11 Section 5 was later amended by Amendment 57.

AMENDMENT 13

Art. 2 Section 15 VACANCIES IN LEGISLATURE. Such vacancies as may occur in either house of the legislature shall be filled by appointment by the board of county commissioners of the county in which the vacancy occurs, and the person so appointed shall hold office until his successor is elected at the next general election, and shall have qualified: Provided, That in case of a vacancy occurring in the office of joint senator, the vacancy shall be filled by appointment by the joint action of the boards of county commissioners of the counties composing the joint senatorial district. [1929 p 690. Approved November, 1930.]
Art. 2 Section 15 was later amended by Amendments 32, 52, and 96.

AMENDMENT 14

Article 7 is amended by striking out all of sections 1, 2, 3 and 4, and inserting in lieu thereof the following, to be known as section 1:
Art. 7 Section 1 TAXATION. The power of taxation shall never be suspended, surrendered or contracted away. All taxes shall be uniform upon the same class of property within the territorial limits of the authority levying the tax and shall be levied and collected for public purposes only. The word "property" as used herein shall mean and include everything, whether tangible or intangible, subject to ownership. All real estate shall constitute one class: Provided, That the legislature may tax mines and mineral resources and lands devoted to reforestation by either a yield tax or an ad valorem tax at such rate as it may fix, or by both. Such property as the legislature may by general laws provide shall be exempt from taxation. Property of the United States and of the state, counties, school districts and other municipal corporations, and credits secured by property actually taxed in this state, not exceeding in value the value of such property, shall be exempt from taxation. The legislature shall have power, by appropriate legislation, to exempt personal property to the amount of three hundred ($300.00) dollars for each head of a family liable to assessment and taxation under the provisions of the laws of this state of which the individual is the actual bona fide owner. [1929 p 499 Section 1. Approved November, 1930.]

Amendment 17 added a new Section 2.

Amendment 19 added a new Section 3.

Art. 7 Section 1 was later amended by Amendments 81 and 98.

AMENDMENT 15

Art. 15 Section 1 HARBOR LINE COMMISSION AND RESTRAINT ON DISPOSITION. The legislature shall provide for the appointment of a commission whose duty it shall be to locate and establish harbor lines in the navigable waters of all harbors, estuaries, bays and inlets of this state, wherever such navigable waters lie within or in front of the corporate limits of any city, or within one mile thereof on either side. Any harbor line so located or established may thereafter be changed, relocated or reestablished by the commission pursuant to such provision as may be made therefor by the legislature. The state shall never give, sell or lease to any private person, corporation, or association any rights whatever in the waters beyond such harbor lines, nor shall any of the area lying between any harbor line and the line of ordinary high water, and within not less than fifty feet nor more than two thousand feet of such harbor line (as the commission shall determine) be sold or granted by the state, nor its rights to control the same relinquished, but such area shall be forever reserved for landings, wharves, streets, and other conveniences of navigation and commerce. [1931 p 417 Section 1. Approved November, 1932.]

AMENDMENT 16

Art. 12 Section 11 STOCKHOLDER LIABILITY. No corporation, association, or individual shall issue or put in circulation as money anything but the lawful money of the United States. Each stockholder of any banking or insurance corporation or joint stock association shall be individually and personally liable equally and ratably, and not one for another, for all contracts, debts, and engagements of such corporation or association accruing while they remain such stockholders, to the extent of the amount of their stock therein at the par value thereof, in addition to the amount invested in such shares.

The legislature may provide that stockholders of banking corporations organized under the laws of this state which shall provide and furnish, either through membership in the Federal Deposit Insurance Corporation, or through membership in any other instrumentality of the government of the United States, insurance or security for the payment of the debts and obligations of such banking corporation equivalent to that required by the laws of the United States to be furnished and provided by national banking associations, shall be relieved from liability for the debts and obligations of such banking corporation to the same extent that stockholders of national banking associations are relieved from liability for the debts and obligations of such national banking associations under the laws of the United States. [1939 Senate Joint Resolution No. 8, p 1024. Approved November, 1940.]

AMENDMENT 17

Art. 7 Section 2 FORTY MILL LIMIT. Except as hereinafter provided and notwithstanding any other provision of this Constitution, the aggregate of all tax levies upon real and personal property by the state and all taxing districts now existing or hereafter created, shall not in any year exceed forty mills on the dollar of assessed valuation, which assessed valuation shall be fifty per centum of the true and fair value of such property in money: Provided, however, That nothing herein shall prevent levies at the rates now provided by law by or for any port or public utility district. The term "taxing district" for the purposes of this section shall mean any political subdivision, municipal corporation, district, or other governmental agency authorized by law to levy, or have levied for it, ad valorem taxes on property, other than a port or public utility district. Such aggregate limitation or any specific limitation imposed by law in conformity therewith may be exceeded only

(a) By any taxing district when specifically authorized so to do by a majority of at least three-fifths of the electors thereof voting on the proposition to levy such additional tax submitted not more than twelve months prior to the date on which the proposed levy is to be made and not oftener than twice in such twelve month period, either at a special election or at the regular election of such taxing district, at which election the number of persons voting on the proposition shall constitute not less than forty per centum of the total number of votes cast in such taxing district at the last preceding general election;

(b) By any taxing district otherwise authorized by law to issue general obligation bonds for capital purposes, for the sole purpose of making the required payments of principal and interest on general obligation bonds issued solely for capital purposes, other than the replacement of equipment, when authorized so to do by majority of at least three-fifths of the electors thereof voting on the proposition to issue such bonds and to pay the principal and interest thereon by an annual tax levy in excess of the limitation herein provided during the term of such bonds, submitted not oftener than twice in any calendar year, at an election held in the manner provided by law for bond elections in such taxing district, at which election the total number of persons voting on the proposition shall constitute not less than forty per centum of the total number of votes cast in such taxing district at the last preceding general election: Provided, That any such taxing district shall have the right by vote of its governing body to refund any general obligation bonds of said district issued for capital purposes only, and to provide for the interest thereon and amortization thereof by annual levies in excess of the tax limitation provided for herein, and Provided further, That the provisions of this section shall also be subject to the limitations contained in Article VIII, Section 6, of this Constitution;

(c) By the state or any taxing district for the purpose of paying the principal or interest on general obligation bonds outstanding on December 6, 1934; or for the purpose of preventing the impairment of the obligation of a contract when ordered so to do by a court of last resort. [1943 House Joint Resolution No. 1, p 936. Approved November, 1944.]

Art. 7 Section 2 was later amended by Amendments 55, 59, 64, 79, 90, 95, and 101.

AMENDMENT 18

Art. 2 Section 40 HIGHWAY FUNDS. All fees collected by the State of Washington as license fees for motor vehicles and all excise taxes collected by the State of Washington on the sale, distribution or use of motor vehicle fuel and all other state revenue intended to be used for highway purposes, shall be paid into the state treasury and placed in a special fund to be used exclusively for highway purposes. Such highway purposes shall be construed to include the following:

(a) The necessary operating, engineering and legal expenses connected with the administration of public highways, county roads and city streets;

(b) The construction, reconstruction, maintenance, repair, and betterment of public highways, county roads, bridges and city streets; including the cost and expense of (1) acquisition of rights-of-way, (2) installing, maintaining and operating traffic signs and signal lights, (3) policing by the state of public highways, (4) operation of movable span bridges, (5) operation of ferries which are a part of any public highway, county road, or city street;

(c) The payment or refunding of any obligation of the State of Washington, or any political subdivision thereof, for which any of the revenues described in section 1 may have been legally pledged prior to the effective date of this act;

(d) Refunds authorized by law for taxes paid on motor vehicle fuels;

(e) The cost of collection of any revenues described in this section:

Provided, That this section shall not be construed to include revenue from general or special taxes or excises not levied primarily for highway purposes, or apply to vehicle operator's license fees or any excise tax imposed on motor vehicles or the use thereof in lieu of a property tax thereon, or fees for certificates of ownership of motor vehicles. [1943 House Joint Resolution No. 4, p 938. Approved November, 1944.]

AMENDMENT 19

Art. 7 Section 3 TAXATION OF FEDERAL AGENCIES AND PROPERTY. The United States and its agencies and instrumentalities, and their property, may be taxed under any of the tax laws of this state, whenever and in such manner as such taxation may be authorized or permitted under the laws of the United States, notwithstanding anything to the contrary in the Constitution of this state. [1945 House Joint Resolution No. 9, p 932. Approved November, 1946.]

AMENDMENT 20

Art. 28 Section 1 COMPENSATION OF STATE OFFICERS. All elected state officials shall each severally receive such compensation as the legislature may direct. The compensation of any state officer shall not be increased or diminished during his term of office, except that the legislature, at its thirty-first regular session, may increase or diminish the compensation of all state officers whose terms exist on the Thursday after the second Monday in January, 1949.

The provisions of sections 14, 16, 17, 19, 20, 21, and 22 of Article III and section 23 of Article II in so far as they are inconsistent herewith, are hereby repealed. [1947 Senate Joint Resolution No. 4, p 1371. Approved November 2, 1948.]

Art. 28 Section 1 was later amended by Amendment 78.

Authorizing compensation increase during term: See Amendment 54.

AMENDMENT 21

Art. 11 Section 4 COUNTY GOVERNMENT AND TOWNSHIP ORGANIZATION. The legislature shall establish a system of county government, which shall be uniform throughout the state except as hereinafter provided, and by general laws shall provide for township organization, under which any county may organize whenever a majority of the qualified electors of such county voting at a general election shall so determine; and whenever a county shall adopt township organization, the assessment and collection of the revenue shall be made, and the business of such county and the local affairs of the several townships therein, shall be managed and transacted in the manner prescribed by such general law.

Any county may frame a "Home Rule" charter for its own government subject to the Constitution and laws of this state, and for such purpose the legislative authority of such county may cause an election to be had, at which election there shall be chosen by the qualified voters of said county not less than fifteen (15) nor more than twenty-five (25) freeholders thereof, as determined by the legislative authority, who shall have been residents of said county for a period of at least five (5) years preceding their election and who are themselves qualified electors, whose duty it shall be to convene within thirty (30) days after their election and prepare and propose a charter for such county. Such proposed charter shall be submitted to the qualified electors of said county, and if a majority of such qualified electors voting thereon ratify the same, it shall become the charter of said county and shall become the organic law thereof, and supersede any existing charter, including amendments thereto, or any existing form of county government, and all special laws inconsistent with such charter. Said proposed charter shall be published in two (2) legal newspapers published in said county, at least once a week for four (4) consecutive weeks prior to the day of submitting the same to the electors for their approval as above provided. All elections in this section authorized shall only be had upon notice, which notice shall specify the object of calling such election and shall be given for at least ten (10) days before the day of election in all election districts of said county. Said elections may be general or special elections and except as herein provided, shall be governed by the law regulating and controlling general or special elections in said county. Such charter may be amended by proposals therefor submitted by the legislative authority of said county to the electors thereof at any general election after notice of such submission published as above specified, and ratified by a majority of the qualified electors voting thereon. In submitting any such charter or amendment thereto, any alternate article or proposition may be presented for the choice of the voters and may be voted on separately without prejudice to others.

Any home rule charter proposed as herein provided, may provide for such county officers as may be deemed necessary to carry out and perform all county functions as provided by charter or by general law, and for their compensation, but shall not affect the election of the prosecuting attorney, the county superintendent of schools, the judges of the superior court, and the justices of the peace, or the jurisdiction of the courts.

Notwithstanding the foregoing provision for the calling of an election by the legislative authority of such county for the election of freeholders to frame a county charter, registered voters equal in number to ten (10) per centum of the voters of any such county voting at the last preceding general election, may at any time propose by petition the calling of an election of freeholders. The petition shall be filed with the county auditor of the county at least three (3) months before any general election and the proposal that a board of freeholders be elected for the purpose of framing a county charter shall be submitted to the vote of the people at said general election, and at the same election a board of freeholders of not less than fifteen (15) or more than twenty-five (25), as fixed in the petition calling for the election, shall be chosen to draft the new charter. The procedure for the nomination of qualified electors as candidates for said board of freeholders shall be prescribed by the legislative authority of the county, and the procedure for the framing of the charter and the submission of the charter as framed shall be the same as in the case of a board of freeholders chosen at an election initiated by the legislative authority of the county.

In calling for any election of freeholders as provided in this section, the legislative authority of the county shall apportion the number of freeholders to be elected in accordance with either the legislative districts or the county commissioner districts, if any, within said county, the number of said freeholders to be elected from each of said districts to be in proportion to the population of said districts as nearly as may be.

Should the charter proposed receive the affirmative vote of the majority of the electors voting thereon, the legislative authority of the county shall immediately call such special election as may be provided for therein, if any, and the county government shall be established in accordance with the terms of said charter not more than six (6) months after the election at which the charter was adopted.

The terms of all elective officers, except the prosecuting attorney, the county superintendent of schools, the judges of the superior court, and the justices of the peace, who are in office at the time of the adoption of a Home Rule Charter shall terminate as provided in the charter. All appointive officers in office at the time the charter goes into effect, whose positions are not abolished thereby, shall continue until their successors shall have qualified.

108

After the adoption of such charter, such county shall continue to have all the rights, powers, privileges and benefits then possessed or thereafter conferred by general law. All the powers, authority and duties granted to and imposed on county officers by general law, except the prosecuting attorney, the county superintendent of schools, the judges of the superior court and the justices of the peace, shall be vested in the legislative authority of the county unless expressly vested in specific officers by the charter. The legislative authority may by resolution delegate any of its executive or administrative powers, authority or duties not expressly vested in specific officers by the charter, to any county officer or officers or county employee or employees.

The provisions of sections 5, 6, 7, and the first sentence of section 8 of this Article as amended shall not apply to counties in which the government has been established by charter adopted under the provisions hereof. The authority conferred on the board of county commissioners by Section 15 of Article II as amended, shall be exercised by the legislative authority of the county. [1947 Senate Joint Resolution No. 5, p 1372. Approved November 2, 1948.]

AMENDMENT 22

Section 7, Article XI, Constitution of the State of Washington is hereby repealed. [1947 House Joint Resolution No. 4, p 1385. Approved November 2, 1948.]

AMENDMENT 23

Art. 11 Section 16 COMBINED CITY AND COUNTY. The legislature shall, by general law, provide for the formation of combined city and county municipal corporations, and for the manner of determining the territorial limits thereof, each of which shall be known as a "city and county," and, when organized, shall contain a population of at least three hundred thousand (300,000) inhabitants. No such city and county shall be formed except by a majority vote of the qualified electors of the area proposed to be included therein and also by a majority vote of the qualified electors of the remainder of that county from which such area is to be taken. Any such city and county shall be permitted to frame a charter for its own government, and amend the same, in the manner provided for cities by section 10 of this article: Provided, however, That the first charter of such city and county shall be framed and adopted in a manner to be specified in the general law authorizing the formation of such corporations: Provided further, That every such charter shall designate the respective officers of such city and county who shall perform the duties imposed by law upon county officers. Every such city and county shall have and enjoy all rights, powers and privileges asserted in its charter, not inconsistent with general laws, and in addition thereto, such rights, powers and privileges as may be granted to it, or possessed and enjoyed by cities and counties of like population separately organized.

No county or county government existing outside the territorial limits of such county and city shall exercise any police, taxation or other powers within the territorial limits of such county and city, but all such powers shall be exercised by the city and county and the officers thereof, subject to such constitutional provisions and general laws as apply to either cities or counties: Provided, That the provisions of sections 2, 3, 4, 5, 6, 7, and 8 of this article shall not apply to any such city and county: Provided further, That the salary of any elective or appointive officer of a city and county shall not be changed after his election or appointment or during his term of office; nor shall the term of any such officer be extended beyond the period for which he is elected or appointed. In case an existing county is divided in the formation of a city and county, such city and county shall be liable for a just proportion of the existing debts or liabilities of the former county, and shall account for and pay the county remaining a just proportion of the value of any real estate or other property owned by the former county and taken over by the county and city, the method of determining such just proportion to be prescribed by general law, but such division shall not affect the rights of creditors. The officers of a city and county, their compensation, qualifications, term of office and manner of election or appointment shall be as provided for in its charter, subject to general laws and applicable constitutional provisions. [1947 House Joint Resolution No. 13, p 1386. Approved November 2, 1948.]

Art. 11 Section 16 was later amended by Amendment 58.

AMENDMENT 24

[Repealed by AMENDMENT 42, 1965 ex.s. Senate Joint Resolution No. 20, p 2816. Approved November 8, 1966.]

Text of Amendment 24 - Art. 2 Section 33 ALIEN OWNERSHIP - The ownership of lands by aliens, other than those who in good faith have declared their intention to become citizens of the United States, is prohibited in this state, except where acquired by inheritance, under mortgage or in good faith in the ordinary course of justice in the collection of debts; and all conveyances of lands hereafter made to any alien directly, or in trust for such alien, shall be void: Provided, That the provisions of this section shall not apply to lands containing valuable deposits of minerals, metals, iron, coal, or fire clay, and the necessary land for mills and machinery to be used in the development thereof and the manufacture of the products therefrom: And provided further, That the provisions of this section shall not apply to the citizens of such of the Provinces of the Dominion of Canada as do not expressly or by implication prohibit ownership of provincial lands by citizens of this state. Every corporation, the majority of the capital stock of which is owned by aliens, shall be considered an alien for the purposes of this prohibition. [1949 Senate Joint Resolution No. 9, p 999. Approved November 7, 1950.]

Art. 2 Section 33 was also amended by Amendment 29.

AMENDMENT 25

Article 4 was amended by adding the following section:

Art. 4 Section 3(a) RETIREMENT OF SUPREME COURT AND SUPERIOR COURT JUDGES. A judge of the supreme court or the superior court shall retire from judicial office at the end of the calendar year in which he attains the age of seventy-five years. The legislature may, from time to time, fix a lesser age for mandatory retirement, not earlier than the end of the calendar year in which any such judge attains the age of seventy years, as the legislature deems proper. This provision shall not affect the term to which any such judge shall have been elected or appointed prior to, or at the time of, approval and ratification of this provision. Notwithstanding the limitations of this section, the legislature may by general law authorize or require the retirement of judges for physical or mental disability, or any cause rendering judges incapable of performing their judicial duties. [1951 House Joint Resolution No. 6, p 960. Approved November 4, 1952.]

AMENDMENT 26

Article 2 was amended by adding the following section:

Art. 2 Section 41 LAWS, EFFECTIVE DATE. INITIATIVE, REFERENDUM - AMENDMENT OR REPEAL. No act, law, or bill subject to referendum shall take effect until ninety days after the adjournment of the session at which it was enacted. No act, law or bill approved by a majority of the electors voting thereon shall be amended or repealed by the legislature within a period of two years following such enactment: Provided, That any such act, law or bill may be amended within two years after such enactment at any regular or special session of the legislature by a vote of two-thirds of all the members elected to each house with full compliance with section 12, Article III, of the Washington Constitution, and no amendatory law adopted in accordance with this provision shall be subject to referendum. But such enactment may be amended or repealed at any general regular or special election by direct vote of the people thereon. These provisions supersede the provisions of subsection (c) of section 1 of this article as amended by the seventh amendment to the Constitution of this state. [1951 Substitute Senate Joint Resolution No. 7, p 959. Approved November 4, 1952.]

Reviser's note: In third sentence, comma between "general" and "regular" omitted in conformity with enrolled resolution.

AMENDMENT 27

Art. 8 Section 6 LIMITATIONS UPON MUNICIPAL INDEBTEDNESS. No county, city, town, school district, or other municipal corporation shall for any purpose become indebted in any manner to an amount exceeding one and one-half per centum of the taxable property in such county, city, town, school district, or other municipal corporation, without the assent of three-fifths of the voters therein voting at an election to be held for that purpose, nor in cases requiring such assent shall the total indebtedness at any time exceed five per centum on the value of the taxable property therein, to be ascertained by the last assessment for state and county purposes previous to the incurring of such indebtedness, except that in incorporated cities the assessment shall be taken from the last assessment for city purposes: Provided, That no part of the indebtedness allowed in this section shall be incurred for any purpose other than strictly county, city, town, school district, or other municipal purposes: Provided further, That (a) any city or town, with such assent, may be allowed to become indebted to a larger amount, but not exceeding five per centum additional for supplying such city or town with water, artificial light, and sewers, when the works for supplying such water, light, and sewers shall be owned and controlled by the municipality and (b) any school district with such assent, may be allowed to become indebted to a larger amount but not exceeding five per centum additional for capital outlays. [1951 House Joint Resolution No. 8, p 961. Approved November 4, 1952.]

AMENDMENT 28

Art. 4 Section 6 JURISDICTION OF SUPERIOR COURTS. The superior court shall have original jurisdiction in all cases in equity and in all cases at law which involve the title or possession of real property, or the legality of any tax, impost, assessment, toll, or municipal fine, and in all other cases in which the demand or the value of the property in controversy amounts to one thousand dollars, or a lesser sum in excess of the jurisdiction granted to justices of the peace and other inferior courts, and in all criminal cases amounting to felony, and in all cases of misdemeanor not otherwise provided for by law; of actions of forcible entry and detainer; of proceedings in insolvency; of actions to prevent or abate a nuisance; of all matters of probate, of divorce, and for annulment of marriage; and for such special cases and proceedings as are not otherwise provided for. The superior court shall also have original jurisdiction in all cases and of all proceedings in which jurisdiction shall not have been by law vested exclusively in some other court; and said court shall have the power of naturalization and to issue papers therefor. They shall have such appellate jurisdiction in cases arising in justices' and other inferior courts in their respective counties as may be prescribed by law. They shall always be open, except on nonjudicial days, and their process shall extend to all parts of the state. Said courts and their judges shall have power to issue writs of mandamus, quo warranto, review, certiorari, prohibition, and writs of habeas corpus, on petition by or on behalf of any person in actual custody in their respective counties. Injunctions and writs of prohibition and of habeas corpus may be issued and served on legal holidays and nonjudicial days.

Later amendment to Art. 4 Section 6, see Amendment 87.

Art. 4 Section 10 JUSTICES OF THE PEACE. The legislature shall determine the number of justices of the peace to be elected and shall prescribe by law the powers, duties and jurisdiction of justices of the peace: Provided, That such jurisdiction granted by the legislature shall not trench upon the jurisdiction of superior or other courts of record, except that justices of the peace may be made police justices of incorporated cities and towns. Justices of the peace shall have original jurisdiction in cases where the demand or value of the property in controversy is less than three hundred dollars or such greater sum, not to exceed one thousand dollars, as shall be prescribed by the legislature. In incorporated cities or towns having more than five thousand inhabitants, the justices of the peace shall receive such salary as may be provided by law, and shall receive no fees for their own use. [1951 Substitute House Joint Resolution No. 13, p 962. Approved November 4, 1952.]

Later amendment to Art. 4 Section 6 and Section 10, see Amendment 65.

AMENDMENT 29

[Repealed by AMENDMENT 42, 1965 ex.s. Senate Joint Resolution No. 20, p 2816. Approved November 8, 1966.]

Text of Amendment 29 - Art. 2 Section 33 Alien Ownership - The ownership of lands by aliens, other than those who in good faith have declared their intention to become citizens of the United States, is prohibited in this state, except where acquired by inheritance, under mortgage or in good faith in the ordinary course of justice in the collection of debts; and all conveyances of lands hereafter made to any alien directly, or in trust for such alien, shall be void: Provided, That the provisions of this section shall not apply to lands containing valuable deposits of minerals, metals, iron, coal, or fire clay, and the necessary land for mills and machinery to be used in the development thereof and the manufacture of the products therefrom: And provided further, That the provisions of this section shall not apply to the citizens of such of the Provinces of the Dominion of Canada as do not expressly or by implication prohibit ownership of provincial lands by citizens of this state. [1953 House Joint Resolution No. 16, p 853. Approved November 2, 1954.]

Prior amendment of Art. 2 Section 33, see Amendment 24.

AMENDMENT 30

[Stricken by AMENDMENT 72, 1981 Substitute Senate Joint Resolution No. 133, p 1796. Approved November 3, 1981.]

Text of Amendment 30 - Art. 2 Section 1(a) INITIATIVE AND REFERENDUM, SIGNATURES REQUIRED - Hereafter, the number of valid signatures of legal voters required upon a petition for an initiative measure shall be equal to eight per centum of the number of voters registered and voting for the office of governor at the last preceding regular gubernatorial election. Hereafter, the number of valid signatures of legal voters required upon a petition for a referendum of an act of the legislature or any part thereof, shall be equal to four per centum of the number of voters registered and voting for the office of governor at the last preceding regular gubernatorial election. These provisions supersede the requirements specified in section 1 of this article as amended by the seventh amendment to the Constitution of this state. [1955 Senate Joint Resolution No. 4, p 1860. Approved November 6, 1956.]

AMENDMENT 31

Art. 3 Section 25 QUALIFICATIONS, COMPENSATION, OFFICES WHICH MAY BE ABOLISHED. No person, except a citizen of the United States and a qualified elector of this state, shall be eligible to hold any state office. The compensation for state officers shall not be increased or diminished during the term for which they shall have been elected. The legislature may in its discretion abolish the offices of the lieutenant governor, auditor and commissioner of public lands. [1955 Senate Joint Resolution No. 6, p 1861. Approved November 6, 1956.] Authorizing compensation increase during term: See Amendment 54.

AMENDMENT 32

Art. 2 Section 15 VACANCIES IN LEGISLATURE AND IN PARTISAN COUNTY ELECTIVE OFFICE. Such vacancies as may occur in either house of the legislature or in any partisan county elective office shall be filled by appointment by the board of county commissioners of the county in which the vacancy occurs: Provided, That the person appointed to fill the vacancy must be from the same legislative district and the same political party as the legislator whose office has been vacated, and shall be one of three persons who shall be nominated by the county central committee of that party, and the person so appointed shall hold office until his successor is elected at the next general election, and shall have qualified: Provided, That in case of a vacancy occurring in the office of joint senator, or joint representative, the vacancy shall be filled from a list of three nominees selected by the state central committee, by appointment by the joint action of the boards of county commissioners of the counties composing the joint senatorial or joint representative district, the person appointed to fill the vacancy must be from the same legislative district and of the same political party as the legislator whose office has been vacated, and in case a majority of said county commissioners do not agree upon the appointment within sixty days after the vacancy occurs, the governor shall within thirty days thereafter, and from the list of nominees provided for herein, appoint a person who shall be from the same legislative district and of the same political party as the legislator whose office has been vacated. [1955 Senate Joint Resolution No. 14, p 1862. Approved November 6, 1956.]

Prior amendment of Art. 2 Section 15, see Amendment 13.

Later amendment of Art. 2 Section 15, see Amendments 52 and 96.

AMENDMENT 33

Art. 24 Section 1 STATE BOUNDARIES. The boundaries of the state of Washington shall be as follows: Beginning at a point in the Pacific ocean one marine league due west of and opposite the middle of the mouth of the north ship channel of the Columbia river thence running easterly to and up the middle channel of said river and where it is divided by islands up the middle of the widest channel thereof to where the forty-sixth parallel of north latitude crosses said river near the mouth of the Walla Walla river; thence east on said forty-sixth parallel of latitude to the middle of the main channel of the Shoshone or Snake river, thence follow down the middle of the main channel of Snake river to a point opposite the mouth of the Kooskooskia or Clear Water river, thence due north to the forty-ninth parallel of north latitude, thence west along said forty-ninth parallel of north latitude to the middle of the channel which separates Vancouver's island from the continent, that is to say to a point in longitude 123 degrees, 19 minutes and 15 seconds west, thence following the boundary line between the United States and British possessions through the channel which separates Vancouver's island from the continent to the termination of the boundary line between the United States and British possessions at a point in the Pacific ocean equidistant between Bonnilla point on Vancouver's island and Tatoosh island light house, thence running in a southerly course and parallel with the coast line, keeping one marine league off shore to place of beginning; until such boundaries are modified by appropriate interstate compacts duly approved by the Congress of the United States. [1957 Senate Joint Resolution No. 10, p 1292. Approved November 4, 1958.]

AMENDMENT 34

Art. 1 Section 11 RELIGIOUS FREEDOM. Absolute freedom of conscience in all matters of religious sentiment, belief and worship, shall be guaranteed to every individual, and no one shall be molested or disturbed in person or property on account of religion; but the liberty of conscience hereby secured shall not be so construed as to excuse acts of licentiousness or justify practices inconsistent with the peace and safety of the state. No public money or property shall be appropriated for or applied to any religious worship, exercise or instruction, or the support of any religious establishment: Provided, however, That this article shall not be so construed as to forbid the employment by the state of a chaplain for such of the state custodial, correctional and mental institutions as in the discretion of the legislature may seem justified. No religious qualification shall be required for any public office or employment, nor shall any person be incompetent as a witness or juror, in consequence of his opinion on matters of religion, nor be questioned in any court of justice touching his religious belief to affect the weight of his testimony. [1957 Senate Joint Resolution No. 14, p 1299. Approved November 4, 1958.]

Prior amendment of Art. 1 Section 11, see Amendment 4.

Art. 1 Section 11 was later amended by Amendment 88.

AMENDMENT 35

Art. 2 Section 25 EXTRA COMPENSATION PROHIBITED. The legislature shall never grant any extra compensation to any public officer, agent, employee, servant, or contractor, after the services shall have been rendered, or the contract entered into, nor shall the compensation of any public officer be increased or diminished during his term of office. Nothing in this section shall be deemed to prevent increases in pensions after such pensions shall have been granted. [1957 Senate Joint Resolution No. 18, p 1301. Approved November 4, 1958.] Increase during term in compensation of certain officers authorized: See Amendment 54.

AMENDMENT 36

Article 2, section 1 (LEGISLATIVE POWERS, WHERE VESTED) as amended by AMENDMENT 7 was amended by adding the following subsection:

Article 2, section 1, subsection (e). The legislature shall provide methods of publicity of all laws or parts of laws, and amendments to the Constitution referred to the people with arguments for and against the laws and amendments so referred. The secretary of state shall send one copy of the publication to each individual place of residence in the state and shall make such additional distribution as he shall determine necessary to reasonably assure that each voter will have an opportunity to study the measures prior to election. These provisions supersede the provisions set forth in the last paragraph of section 1 of this article as amended by the seventh amendment to the Constitution of this state. [1961 Senate Joint Resolution No. 9, p 2751. Approved November, 1962.]

AMENDMENT 37

Art. 23 Section 1 HOW MADE. Any amendment or amendments to this Constitution may be proposed in either branch of the legislature; and if the same shall be agreed to by two-thirds of the members elected to each of the two houses, such proposed amendment or amendments shall be entered on their journals, with the ayes and noes thereon, and be submitted to the qualified electors of the state for their approval, at the next general election; and if the people approve and ratify such amendment or amendments, by a majority of the electors voting thereon, the same shall become part of this Constitution, and proclamation thereof shall be made by the governor: Provided, That if more than one amendment be submitted, they shall be submitted in such a manner that the people may vote for or against such amendments separately. The legislature shall also cause notice of the amendments that are to be submitted to the people to be published at least four times during the four weeks next preceding the election in every legal newspaper in the state: Provided, That failure of any newspaper to publish this notice shall not be interpreted as affecting the outcome of the election. [1961 Senate Joint Resolution No. 25, p 2753. Approved November, 1962.]

AMENDMENT 38

Article 4 was amended by adding the following section:
Art. 4 Section 2(a) TEMPORARY PERFORMANCE OF JUDICIAL DUTIES. When necessary for the prompt and orderly administration of justice a majority of the Supreme Court is empowered to authorize judges or retired judges of courts of record of this state, to perform, temporarily, judicial duties in the Supreme Court, and to authorize any superior court judge to perform judicial duties in any superior court of this state. [1961 House Joint Resolution No. 6, p 2757. Approved November, 1962.]

AMENDMENT 39

Art. 2 Section 42 GOVERNMENTAL CONTINUITY DURING EMERGENCY PERIODS. The legislature, in order to insure continuity of state and local governmental operations in periods of emergency resulting from enemy attack, shall have the power and the duty, immediately upon and after adoption of this amendment, to enact legislation providing for prompt and temporary succession to the powers and duties of public offices of whatever nature and whether filled by election or appointment, the incumbents and legal successors of which may become unavailable for carrying on the powers and duties of such offices; the legislature shall likewise enact such other measures as may be necessary and proper for insuring the continuity of governmental operations during such emergencies. Legislation enacted under the powers conferred by this amendment shall in all respects conform to the remainder of the Constitution: Provided, That if, in the judgment of the legislature at the time of disaster, conformance to the provisions of the Constitution would be impracticable or would admit of undue delay, such legislation may depart during the period of emergency caused by enemy attack only, from the following sections of the Constitution:
Article 14, Sections 1 and 2, Seat of Government;
Article 2, Sections 8, 15 (Amendments 13 and 32), and 22, Membership, Quorum of Legislature and Passage of Bills;
Article 3, Section 10 (Amendment 6), Succession to Governorship: Provided, That the legislature shall not depart from Section 10, Article III, as amended by Amendment 6, of the state Constitution relating to the Governor's office so long as any successor therein named is available and capable of assuming the powers and duties of such office as therein prescribed;
Article 3, Section 13, Vacancies in State Offices;
Article 11, Section 6, Vacancies in County Offices;
Article 11, Section 2, Seat of County Government;
Article 3, Section 24, State Records. [1961 House Joint Resolution No. 9, p 2758. Approved November, 1962.]

AMENDMENT 40

Art. 11 Section 10 INCORPORATION OF MUNICIPALITIES. Corporations for municipal purposes shall not be created by special laws; but the legislature, by general laws, shall provide for the incorporation, organization and classification in proportion to population, of cities and towns, which laws may be altered, amended or repealed. Cities and towns heretofore organized, or incorporated may become organized under such general laws whenever a majority of the electors voting at a general election, shall so determine, and shall organize in conformity therewith; and cities or towns heretofore or hereafter organized, and all charters thereof framed or adopted by authority of this Constitution shall be subject to, and controlled by general laws. Any city containing a population of ten thousand inhabitants, or more, shall be permitted to frame a charter for its own government, consistent with and subject to the Constitution and laws of this state, and for such purpose the legislative authority of such city may cause an election to be had at which election there shall be chosen by the qualified electors of said city, fifteen freeholders thereof, who shall have been residents of said city for a period of at least two years preceding their election and qualified electors, whose duty it shall be to convene within ten days after their election, and prepare and propose a charter for such city. Such proposed charter shall be submitted to the qualified electors of said city, and if a majority of such qualified electors voting thereon ratify the same, it shall become the charter of said city, and shall become the organic law thereof, and supersede any existing charter including amendments thereto, and all special laws inconsistent with such charter. Said proposed charter shall be published in the daily newspaper of largest general circulation published in the area to be incorporated as a first class city under the charter or, if no daily newspaper is published therein, then in the newspaper having the largest general circulation within such area at least once each week for four weeks next preceding the day of submitting the same to the electors for their approval, as above provided. All elections in this section authorized shall only be had upon notice, which notice shall specify the object of calling such election, and shall be given as required by law. Said elections may be general or special elections, and except as herein provided shall be governed by the law regulating and controlling general or special elections in said city. Such charter may be amended by proposals therefor submitted by the legislative authority of such city to the electors thereof at any general election after notice of said submission published as above specified, and ratified by a majority of the qualified electors voting thereon. In submitting any such charter, or amendment thereto, any alternate article or proposition may be presented for the choice of the voters, and may be voted on separately without prejudice to others. [1963 ex.s. Senate Joint Resolution No. 1, p 1526. Approved November 3, 1964.]

AMENDMENT 41

Art. 4 Section 29 ELECTION OF SUPERIOR COURT JUDGES. Notwithstanding any provision of this Constitution to the contrary, if, after the last day as provided by law for the withdrawal of declarations of candidacy has expired, only one candidate has filed for any single position of superior court judge in any county containing a population of one hundred thousand or more, no primary or election shall be held as to such position, and a certificate of election shall be issued to such candidate. If, after any contested primary for superior court judge in any county, only one candidate is entitled to have his name printed on the general election ballot for any single position, no election shall be held as to such position, and a certificate of election shall be issued to such candidate: Provided, That in the event that there is filed with the county auditor within ten days after the date of the primary, a petition indicating that a write in campaign will be conducted for such single position and signed by one hundred registered voters qualified to vote with respect of the office, then such single position shall be subject to the general election. Provisions for the contingency of the death or disqualification of a sole candidate between the last date for withdrawal and the time when the election would be held but for the provisions of this section, and such other provisions as may be deemed necessary to implement the provisions of this section, may be enacted by the legislature. [1965 ex.s. Substitute Senate Joint Resolution No. 6, p 2815. Approved November 8, 1966.]

AMENDMENT 42

Section 33, Article II and Amendments 24 and 29 amendatory thereof, of the Constitution of the State of Washington are each hereby repealed. [1965 ex.s. Senate Joint Resolution No. 20, p 2816. Approved November 8, 1966.]

AMENDMENT 43

Art. 9 Section 3 FUNDS FOR SUPPORT. The principal of the common school fund as the same existed on June 30, 1965, shall remain permanent and irreducible. The said fund shall consist of the principal amount thereof existing on June 30, 1965, and such additions thereto as may be derived after June 30, 1965, from the following named sources, to wit: Appropriations and donations by the state to this fund; donations and bequests by individuals to the state or public for common schools; the proceeds of lands and other property which revert to the state by escheat and forfeiture; the proceeds of all property granted to the state when the purpose of the grant is not specified, or is uncertain; funds accumulated in the treasury of the state for the disbursement of which provision has not been made by law; the proceeds of the sale of stone, minerals, or property other than timber and other crops from school and state lands, other than those granted for specific purposes; all moneys received from persons appropriating stone, minerals or property other than timber and other crops from school and state lands other than those granted for specific purposes, and all moneys other than rental recovered from persons trespassing on said lands; five per centum of the proceeds of the sale of public lands lying within the state, which shall be sold by the United States subsequent to the admission of the state into the Union as approved by section 13 of the act of congress enabling the admission of the state into the Union; the principal of all funds arising from the sale of lands and other property which have been, and hereafter may be granted to the state for the support of common schools. The legislature may make further provisions for enlarging said fund.

There is hereby established the common school construction fund to be used exclusively for the purpose of financing the construction of facilities for the common schools. The sources of said fund shall be: (1) Those proceeds derived from the sale or appropriation of timber and other crops from school and state lands subsequent to June 30, 1965, other than those granted for specific purposes; (2) the interest accruing on said permanent common school fund from and after July 1, 1967, together with all rentals and other revenues derived therefrom and from lands and other property devoted to the permanent common school fund from and after July 1, 1967; and (3) such other sources as the legislature may direct. That portion of the common school construction fund derived from interest on the permanent common school fund may be used to retire such bonds as may be authorized by law for the purpose of financing the construction of facilities for the common schools.

The interest accruing on the permanent common school fund together with all rentals and other revenues accruing thereto pursuant to subsection (2) of this section during the period after the effective date of this amendment and prior to July 1, 1967, shall be exclusively applied to the current use of the common schools.

To the extent that the moneys in the common school construction fund are in excess of the amount necessary to allow fulfillment of the purpose of said fund, the excess shall be available for deposit to the credit of the permanent common school fund or available for the current use of the common schools, as the legislature may direct. [1965 ex.s. Senate Joint Resolution No. 22, part 1, p 2817. Approved November 8, 1966.]

AMENDMENT 44

Art. 16 Section 5 INVESTMENT OF PERMANENT COMMON SCHOOL FUND. The permanent common school fund of this state may be invested as authorized by law. [1965 ex.s. Senate Joint Resolution No. 22, part 2, p 2817. Approved November 8, 1966.]
Prior amendment of Art. 16 Section 5, see Amendment 1.

AMENDMENT 45

Art. 8 Section 8 PORT EXPENDITURES - INDUSTRIAL DEVELOPMENT - PROMOTION. The use of public funds by port districts in such manner as may be prescribed by the legislature for industrial development or trade promotion and promotional hosting shall be deemed a public use for a public purpose, and shall not be deemed a gift within the provisions of section 7 of this Article. [1965 ex.s. Senate Joint Resolution No. 25, p 2819. Approved November 8, 1966.]

AMENDMENT 46

Art. 6 Section 1A VOTER QUALIFICATIONS FOR PRESIDENTIAL ELECTIONS. In consideration of those citizens of the United States who become residents of the state of Washington during the year of a presidential election with the intention of making this state their permanent residence, this section is for the purpose of authorizing such persons who can meet all qualifications for voting as set forth in section 1 of this article, except for residence, to vote for presidential electors or for the office of President and Vice-President of the United States, as the case may be, but no other: Provided, That such persons have resided in the state at least sixty days immediately preceding the presidential election concerned.
The legislature shall establish the time, manner and place for such persons to cast such presidential ballots. [1965 ex.s. Substitute Joint House Resolution No. 4, p 2820. Approved November 8, 1966.]

Art. 6 Section 1A was later amended by Amendment 105.

AMENDMENT 47

Art. 7 Section 10 RETIRED PERSONS PROPERTY TAX EXEMPTION. Notwithstanding the provisions of Article 7, section 1 (Amendment 14) and Article 7, section 2 (Amendment 17), the following tax exemption shall be allowed as to real property:
The legislature shall have the power, by appropriate legislation, to grant to retired property owners relief from the property tax on the real property occupied as a residence by those owners. The legislature may place such restrictions and conditions upon the granting of such relief as it shall deem proper. Such restrictions and conditions may include, but are not limited to, the limiting of the relief to those property owners below a specific level of income and

those fulfilling certain minimum residential requirements. [1965 ex.s. House Joint Resolution No. 7, p 2821. Approved November 8, 1966.]

AMENDMENT 48

Art. 8 Section 3 SPECIAL INDEBTEDNESS, HOW AUTHORIZED. Except the debt specified in sections one and two of this article, no debts shall hereafter be contracted by, or on behalf of this state, unless such debt shall be authorized by law for some single work or object to be distinctly specified therein, which law shall provide ways and means, exclusive of loans, for the payment of the interest on such debt as it falls due, and also to pay and discharge the principal of such debt within twenty years from the time of the contracting thereof. No such law shall take effect until it shall, at a general election, have been submitted to the people and have received a majority of all the votes cast for and against it at such election, and all moneys raised by authority of such law shall be applied only to the specific object therein stated, or to the payment of the debt thereby created, and notice that such law will be submitted to the people shall be published at least four times during the four weeks next preceding the election in every legal newspaper in the state: Provided, That failure of any newspaper to publish this notice shall not be interpreted as affecting the outcome of the election. [1965 ex.s. House Joint Resolution No. 39, p 2822. Approved November 8, 1966.]

Art. 8 Section 3 was later amended by Amendment 60.

AMENDMENT 49

The Constitution was amended by adding the following new article and section 1 thereof:

ARTICLE XXIX INVESTMENTS OF PUBLIC PENSION AND
RETIREMENT FUNDS

Art. 29 Section 1 MAY BE INVESTED AS AUTHORIZED BY LAW. Notwithstanding the provisions of sections 5, and 7 of Article VIII and section 9 of Article XII or any other section or article of the Constitution of the state of Washington, the moneys of any public pension or retirement fund may be invested as authorized by law. [1967 Senate Joint Resolution No. 5; see 1969 p 2975. Approved November 5, 1968.]

Art. 29 Section 1 was later amended by Amendments 75 and 93.

AMENDMENT 50

Article 4 was amended by adding the following section:

Art. 4 Section 30 COURT OF APPEALS. (1) Authorization. In addition to the courts authorized in section 1 of this article, judicial power is vested in a court of appeals, which shall be established by statute.

(2) Jurisdiction. The jurisdiction of the court of appeals shall be as provided by statute or by rules authorized by statute.

(3) Review of Superior Court. Superior court actions may be reviewed by the court of appeals or by the supreme court as provided by statute or by rule authorized by statute.

(4) Judges. The number, manner of election, compensation, terms of office, removal and retirement of judges of the court of appeals shall be as provided by statute.

(5) Administration and Procedure. The administration and procedures of the court of appeals shall be as provided by rules issued by the supreme court.

(6) Conflicts. The provisions of this section shall supersede any conflicting provisions in prior sections of this article. [1967 Senate Joint Resolution No. 6; see 1969 p 2975. Approved November 5, 1968.]

Reviser's note: This section which was adopted as Art. 4 Section 29 is herein renumbered Art. 4 Section 30 to avoid confusion with Amendment 41.

AMENDMENT 51

Article 8 was amended by adding the following section:

Art. 8 Section 9 STATE BUILDING AUTHORITY. The legislature is empowered notwithstanding any other provision in this Constitution, to provide for a state building authority in corporate and politic form which may contract with agencies or departments of the state government to construct upon land owned by the state or its agencies, or to be acquired by the state building authority, buildings and appurtenant improvements which such state agencies or departments are hereby empowered to lease at reasonable rental rates from the Washington state building authority for terms up to seventy-five years with provisions for eventual vesting of title in the state or its agencies. This section shall not be construed as authority to provide buildings through lease or otherwise to nongovernmental entities. The legislature may authorize the state building authority to borrow funds solely upon its own credit and to issue bonds or other evidences of indebtedness therefor to be repaid from its revenues and to secure the same by pledging its income or mortgaging its leaseholds. The provisions of sections 1 and 3 of this article shall not apply to indebtedness incurred pursuant to this section. [1967 Senate Joint Resolution No. 17; see 1969 p 2976. Approved November 5, 1968.]

Reviser's note: This section which was adopted as Art. 8 Section 8 is herein renumbered as Art. 8 Section 9 to avoid confusion with Amendment 45.

AMENDMENT 52

Art. 2 Section 15 VACANCIES IN LEGISLATURE AND IN PARTISAN COUNTY ELECTIVE OFFICE. Such vacancies as may occur in either house of the legislature or in any partisan county elective office shall be filled by appointment by the board of county commissioners of the county in which the vacancy occurs: Provided, That the person appointed to fill the vacancy must be from the same legislative district, county or county commissioner district and the same political party as the legislator or partisan county elective officer whose office has been vacated, and shall be one of three persons who shall be nominated by the county central committee of that party, and in case a majority of said county commissioners do not agree upon the appointment within sixty days after the vacancy occurs, the governor shall within thirty days thereafter, and from the list of nominees provided for herein, appoint a person who shall be from the same legislative district, county or county commissioner district and of the same political party as the legislator or partisan county elective officer whose office has been vacated, and the person so appointed shall hold office until his successor is elected at the next general election, and shall have qualified: Provided, That in case of a vacancy occurring in the office of joint senator, or joint representative, the vacancy shall be filled from a list of three nominees selected by the state central committee, by appointment by the joint action of the boards of county commissioners of the counties composing the joint senatorial or joint representative district, the person appointed to fill the vacancy must be from the same legislative district and of the same political party as the legislator whose office has been vacated, and in case a majority of said county commissioners do not agree upon the appointment within sixty days after the vacancy occurs, the governor shall within thirty days thereafter, and from the list of nominees provided for herein, appoint a person who shall be from the same legislative district and of the same political party as the legislator whose office has been vacated.

Art. 11 Section 6 VACANCIES IN TOWNSHIP, PRECINCT OR ROAD DISTRICT OFFICE. The board of county commissioners in each county shall fill all vacancies occurring in any township, precinct or road district office of such county by appointment, and officers thus appointed shall hold office till the next general election, and until their successors are elected and qualified. [1967 Senate Joint Resolution No. 24; see 1969 p 2976. Approved November 5, 1968.]

Prior amendment of Art. 2 Section 15, see Amendments 13 and 32.

Later amendment of Art. 2 Section 15, see Amendment 96.

AMENDMENT 53

Article 7 was amended by adding the following section:
Art. 7 Section 11 TAXATION BASED ON ACTUAL USE. Nothing in this Article VII as amended shall prevent the legislature from providing, subject to such conditions as it may enact, that the true and fair value in money (a) of farms, agricultural lands, standing timber and timberlands, and (b) of other open space lands which are used for recreation or for enjoyment of their scenic or natural beauty shall be based on the use to which such property is currently applied, and such values shall be used in computing the assessed valuation of such property in the same manner as the assessed valuation is computed for all property. [1967 House Joint Resolution No. 1; see 1969 p 2976. Approved November 5, 1968.]

AMENDMENT 54

The Constitution was amended by adding the following new article and section 1 thereof:

ARTICLE XXX*
COMPENSATION OF PUBLIC OFFICERS**

Art. 30 Section 1 AUTHORIZING COMPENSATION INCREASE DURING TERM. The compensation of all elective and appointive state, county, and municipal officers who do not fix their own compensation, including judges of courts of record and the justice courts may be increased during their terms of office to the end that such officers and judges shall each severally receive compensation for their services in accordance with the law in effect at the time the services are being rendered.

The provisions of section 25 of Article II (Amendment 35), section 25 of Article III (Amendment 31), section 13 of Article IV, section 8 of Article XI, and section 1 of Article XXVIII (Amendment 20) insofar as they are inconsistent herewith are hereby repealed. [1967 House Joint Resolution No. 13; see 1969 p 2976. Approved November 5, 1968.]

Reviser's note: *(1) Amendment 49 (1967 SJR No. 5) and Amendment 54 (1967 HJR No. 13) each added a new Article XXIX to the Constitution. Amendment 49 is carried herein as Article XXIX while Amendment 54 has been herein redesignated as Article XXX.

**(2) The name of this Article has been supplied by the reviser.

AMENDMENT 55

Art. 7 Section 2 LIMITATION ON LEVIES. Except as hereinafter provided and notwithstanding any other provision of this Constitution, the aggregate of all tax levies upon real and personal property by the state and all taxing districts now existing or hereafter created, shall not in any year exceed one percentum of the true and fair value of such property in money: Provided, however, That nothing herein shall prevent levies at the rates now provided by law by or for any port or public utility district. The term "taxing district" for the purposes of this section shall mean any political subdivision, municipal corporation, district, or other governmental agency authorized by law to levy, or have levied for it, ad valorem taxes on property, other than a port or public utility district. Such aggregate limitation or any specific limitation imposed by law in conformity therewith may be exceeded only

(a) By any taxing district when specifically authorized so to do by a majority of at least three-fifths of the electors thereof voting on the proposition to levy such additional tax submitted not more than twelve months prior to the date on which the proposed levy is to be made and not oftener than twice in such twelve month period, either at a special election or at the regular election of such taxing district, at which election the number of persons voting on the proposition shall constitute not less than forty per centum of the total number of votes cast in such taxing district at the last preceding general election;

(b) By any taxing district otherwise authorized by law to issue general obligation bonds for capital purposes, for the sole purpose of making the required payments of principal and interest on general obligation bonds issued solely for capital purposes, other than the replacement of equipment, when authorized so to do by majority of at least three-fifths of the electors thereof voting on the proposition to issue such bonds and to pay the principal and interest thereon by an annual tax levy in excess of the limitation herein provided during the term of such bonds, submitted not oftener than twice in any calendar year, at an election held in the manner provided by law for bond elections in such taxing district, at which election the total number of persons voting on the proposition shall constitute not less than forty per centum of the total number of votes cast in such taxing district at the last preceding general election: Provided, That any such taxing district shall have the right by vote of its governing body to refund any general obligation bonds of said district issued for capital purposes only, and to provide for the interest thereon and amortization thereof by annual levies in excess of the tax limitation provided for herein, And Provided Further, That the provisions of this section shall also be subject to the limitations contained in Article VIII, section 6, of this Constitution;

(c) By the state or any taxing district for the purpose of paying the principal or interest on general obligation bonds outstanding on December 6, 1934; or for the purpose of preventing the impairment of the obligation of a contract when ordered so to do by a court of last resort. [1971 Senate Joint Resolution No. 1, p 1827. Approved November 7, 1972.]

Reviser's note: Art. 7 Section 2 was also amended at the November 7, 1972 general election by Amendment 59. (HJR 47.)

Prior amendment of Art. 7 Section 2, see Amendment 17.

Art. 7 Section 2 was later amended by Amendments 59, 64, 79, 90, 95, and 101.

AMENDMENT 56

Art. 2 Section 24 LOTTERIES AND DIVORCE. The legislature shall never grant any divorce. Lotteries shall be prohibited except as specifically authorized upon the affirmative vote of sixty percent of the members of each house of the legislature or, notwithstanding any other provision of this Constitution, by referendum or initiative approved by a sixty percent affirmative vote of the electors voting thereon. [1971 Senate Joint Resolution No. 5, p 1828. Approved November 7, 1972.]

AMENDMENT 57

Art. 11 Section 5 COUNTY GOVERNMENT. The legislature, by general and uniform laws, shall provide for the election in the several counties of boards of county commissioners, sheriffs, county clerks, treasurers, prosecuting attorneys and other county, township or precinct and district officers, as public convenience may require, and shall prescribe their duties, and fix their terms of office: Provided, That the legislature may, by general laws, classify the counties by population and provide for the election in certain classes of counties certain officers who shall exercise the powers and perform the duties of two or more officers. It shall regulate the compensation of all such officers, in proportion to their duties, and for that purpose may classify the counties by population: Provided,That it may delegate to the legislative authority of the counties the right to prescribe the salaries of its own members and the salaries of other county officers. And it shall provide for the strict accountability of such officers for all fees which may be collected by them and for all public moneys which may be paid to them, or officially come into their possession.

Art. 11 Section 8 SALARIES AND LIMITATIONS AFFECTING. The salary of any county, city, town, or municipal officers shall not be increased except as provided in section 1 of Article XXX or diminished after his election, or during his term of office; nor shall the term of any such officer be extended beyond the period for which he is elected or appointed. [1971 Senate Joint Resolution No. 38, p 1829. Approved November 7, 1972.]

Prior amendment of Art. 11 Section 5, see Amendment 12.

AMENDMENT 58

Art. 11 Section 16 COMBINED CITY-COUNTY. Any county may frame a "Home Rule" charter subject to the Constitution and laws of this state to provide for the formation and government of combined city and county municipal corporations, each of which shall be known as "city-county". Registered voters equal in number to ten (10) percent of the voters of any such county voting at the last preceding general election may at any time propose by a petition the calling of an election of freeholders. The provisions of section 4 of this Article with respect to a petition calling for an election of freeholders to frame a county home rule charter, the election of freeholders, and the framing and adoption of a county home rule charter pursuant to such petition shall apply to a petition proposed under this section for the election of freeholders to frame a city-county charter, the election of freeholders, and to the framing and adoption of such city-county charter pursuant to such petition. Except as otherwise provided in this section, the provisions of section 4 applicable to a county home rule charter shall apply to a city-county charter. If there are not sufficient legal newspapers published in the county to meet the requirements for publication of a proposed charter under section 4 of this Article, publication in a legal newspaper circulated in the county may be substituted for publication in a legal newspaper published in the county. No such "city-county" shall be formed except by a majority vote of the qualified electors voting thereon in the county. The charter shall designate the respective officers of such city-county who shall perform the duties imposed by law upon county officers. Every such city-county shall have and enjoy all rights, powers and privileges asserted in its charter, and in addition thereto, such rights, powers and privileges as may be granted to it, or to any city or county or class or classes of cities and counties. In the event of a conflict in the constitutional provisions applying to cities and those applying to counties or of a conflict in the general laws applying to cities and those applying to counties, a city-county shall be authorized to exercise any powers that are granted to either the cities or the counties.

No legislative enactment which is a prohibition or restriction shall apply to the rights, powers and privileges of a city-county unless such prohibition or restriction shall apply equally to every other city, county, and city-county.

The provisions of sections 2, 3, 5, 6, and 8 and of the first paragraph of section 4 of this Article shall not apply to any such city-county.

Municipal corporations may be retained or otherwise provided for within the city-county. The formation, powers and duties of such municipal corporations shall be prescribed by the charter.

No city-county shall for any purpose become indebted in any manner to an amount exceeding three per centum of the taxable property in such city-county without the assent of three-fifths of the voters therein voting at an election to be held for that purpose, nor in cases requiring such assent shall the total indebtedness at any time exceed ten per centum of the value of the taxable property therein, to be ascertained by the last assessment for city-county purposes previous to the incurring of such indebtedness: Provided,That no part of the indebtedness allowed in this section shall be incurred for any purpose other than strictly city-county or other municipal purposes: Provided further, That any city-county, with such assent may be allowed to become indebted to a larger amount, but not exceeding five per centum additional for supplying such city-county with water, artificial light, and sewers, when the works for supplying such water, light, and sewers shall be owned and controlled by the city-county.

No municipal corporation which is retained or otherwise provided for within the city-county shall for any purpose become indebted in any manner to an amount exceeding one and one-half per centum of the taxable property in such municipal corporation without the assent of three-fifths of the voters therein voting at an election to be held for that purpose, nor shall the total indebtedness at any time exceed five per centum of the value of the taxable property therein, to be ascertained by the last assessment for city-county purposes previous to the incurring of such indebtedness: Provided, That no part of the indebtedness allowed in this section shall be incurred for any purpose other than strictly municipal purposes: Provided further, That any such municipal corporation, with such assent, may be allowed to become indebted to a larger amount, but not exceeding five per centum additional for supplying such municipal corporation with water, artificial light, and sewers, when the works for supplying such water, light, and sewers shall be owned and controlled by the municipal corporation. All taxes which are levied and collected within a municipal corporation for a specific purpose shall be expended within that municipal corporation.

The authority conferred on the city-county government shall not be restricted by the second sentence of Article 7, section 1, or by Article 8, section 6 of this Constitution. [1971 House Joint Resolution No. 21, p 1831. Approved November 7, 1972.]

Prior amendment of Art. 11 Section 16, see Amendment 23.

AMENDMENT 59

Art. 7 Section 2 LIMITATION ON LEVIES. Except as hereinafter provided and notwithstanding any other provision of this Constitution, the aggregate of all tax levies upon real and personal property by the state and all taxing districts now existing or hereafter created, shall not in any year exceed forty mills on the dollar of assessed valuation, which assessed valuation shall be fifty per centum of the true and fair value of such property in money: Provided, however, That nothing herein shall prevent levies at the rates now provided by law by or for any port or public utility district. The term "taxing district" for the purposes of this section shall mean any political subdivision, municipal corporation, district, or other governmental agency authorized by law to levy, or have levied for it, ad valorem taxes on property, other than a port or public utility district. Such aggregate limitation or any specific limitation imposed by law in conformity therewith may be exceeded only:

(a) By any taxing district when specifically authorized so to do by a majority of at least three-fifths of the electors thereof voting on the proposition to levy such additional tax submitted not more than twelve months prior to the date on which the proposed levy is to be made and not oftener than twice in such twelve month period, either at a special election or at the regular election of such taxing district, at which election the number of persons voting "yes" on the proposition shall constitute three-fifths of a number equal to forty per centum of the total votes cast in such taxing district at the last preceding general election when the number of electors voting on the proposition does not exceed forty per centum of the total votes cast in such taxing district in the last preceding general election; or by a majority of at least three-fifths of the electors thereof voting on the proposition to levy when the number of electors voting on the proposition exceeds forty per centum of the total votes cast in such taxing district in the last preceding general election;

(b) By any taxing district otherwise authorized by law to issue general obligation bonds for capital purposes, for the sole purpose of making the required payments of principal and interest on general obligation bonds issued solely for capital purposes, other than the replacement of equipment, when authorized so to do by majority of at least three-fifths of the electors thereof voting on the proposition to issue such bonds and to pay the principal and interest thereon by an annual tax levy in excess of the limitation herein provided during the term of such bonds, submitted not oftener than twice in any calendar year, at an election held in the manner provided by law for bond elections in such taxing district, at which election the total number of persons voting on the proposition shall constitute not less than forty per centum of the total number of votes cast in such taxing district at the last preceding general election: Provided, That any such taxing district shall have the right by vote of its governing body to refund any general obligation bonds of said district issued for capital purposes only, and to provide for the interest thereon and amortization thereof by annual levies in excess of the tax limitation provided for herein, And provided further, That the provisions of this section shall also be subject to the limitations contained in Article VIII, section 6, of this Constitution;

(c) By the state or any taxing district for the purpose of paying the principal or interest on general obligation bonds outstanding on December 6, 1934; or for the purpose of preventing the impairment of the obligation of a contract when ordered so to do by a court of last resort. [1971 House Joint Resolution No. 47, p 1834. Approved November 7, 1972.]

Reviser's note: Art. 7 Section 2 was also amended at the November 7, 1972, general election by Amendment 55 (SJR 1). 1971 HJR No. 47 contained the following paragraph:

"Be It Further Resolved, That the foregoing amendment shall be submitted to the qualified electors of the state in such a manner that they may vote for or against it separately from the proposed amendment to Article VII, section 2, (Amendment 17) of the Constitution of the State of Washington contained in Senate Joint Resolution No. 1: Provided, That if both proposed amendments are approved and ratified, both shall become part of the Constitution."

Prior amendment of Art. 7 Section 2, see Amendments 17 and 55.

Art. 7 Section 2 was later amended by Amendments 64, 79, 90, 95, and 101.

AMENDMENT 60

Art. 8 Section 1 STATE DEBT. (a) The state may contract debt, the principal of which shall be paid and discharged within thirty years from the time of contracting thereof, in the manner set forth herein.

(b) The aggregate debt contracted by the state shall not exceed that amount for which payments of principal and interest in any fiscal year would require the state to expend more than nine percent of the arithmetic mean of its general state revenues for the three immediately preceding fiscal years as certified by the treasurer. The term "fiscal year" means that period of time commencing July 1 of any year and ending on June 30 of the following year.

(c) The term "general state revenues" when used in this section, shall include all state money received in the treasury from each and every source whatsoever except: (1) Fees and revenues derived from the ownership or operation of any undertaking, facility, or project; (2) Moneys received as gifts, grants, donations, aid, or assistance or otherwise from the United States or any department, bureau, or corporation thereof, or any person, firm, or corporation, public or private, when the terms and conditions of such gift, grant, donation, aid, or assistance require the application and disbursement of such moneys otherwise than for the general purposes of the state of Washington; (3) Moneys to be paid into and received from retirement system funds, and performance bonds and deposits; (4) Moneys to be paid into and received from trust funds including but not limited to moneys received from taxes levied for specific purposes and the several permanent and irreducible funds of the state and the moneys derived therefrom but excluding bond redemption funds; (5) Proceeds received from the sale of bonds or other evidences of indebtedness.

(d) In computing the amount required for payment of principal and interest on outstanding debt under this section, debt shall be construed to mean borrowed money represented by bonds, notes, or other evidences of indebtedness which are secured by the full faith and credit of the state or are required to be repaid, directly or indirectly, from general state revenues and which are incurred by the state, any department, authority, public corporation, or quasi public corporation of the state, any state university or college, or any other public agency created by the state but not by counties, cities, towns, school districts, or other municipal corporations, but shall not include obligations for the payment of current expenses of state government, nor shall it include debt hereafter incurred pursuant to section 3 of this Article, obligations guaranteed as provided for in subsection (f) of this section, principal of bond anticipation notes or obligations issued to fund or refund the indebtedness of the Washington state building authority.

(e) The state may, without limitation, fund or refund, at or prior to maturity, the whole or any part of any existing debt or of any debt hereafter contracted pursuant to section 1, section 2, or section 3 of this Article, including any premium payable with respect thereto and interest thereon, or fund or refund, at or prior to maturity, the whole or any part of any indebtedness incurred or authorized prior to the effective date of this amendment by any entity of the type described in subsection (g) of this section, including any premium payable with respect thereto and any interest thereon. Such funding or refunding shall not be deemed to be contracting debt by the state.

(f) Notwithstanding the limitation contained in subsection (b) of this section, the state may pledge its full faith, credit, and taxing power to guarantee the payment of any obligation payable from revenues received from any of the following sources: (1) Fees collected by the state as license fees for motor vehicles; (2) Excise taxes collected by the state on the sale, distribution or use of motor vehicle fuel; and (3) Interest on the permanent common school fund: Provided, That the legislature shall, at all times, provide sufficient revenues from such sources to pay the principal and interest due on all obligations for which said source of revenue is pledged.

(g) No money shall be paid from funds in custody of the treasurer with respect to any debt contracted after the effective date of this amendment by the Washington state building authority, the capitol committee, or any similar entity existing or operating for similar purposes pursuant to which such entity undertakes to finance or provide a facility for use or occupancy by the state or any agency, department, or instrumentality thereof.

(h) The legislature shall prescribe all matters relating to the contracting, funding or refunding of debt pursuant to this section, including: The purposes for which debt may be contracted; by a favorable vote of three-fifths of the members elected to each house, the amount of debt which may be contracted for any class of such purposes; the kinds of notes, bonds, or other evidences of debt which may be issued by the state; and the manner by which the treasurer shall determine and advise the legislature, any appropriate agency, officer, or instrumentality of the state as to the available debt capacity within the limitation set forth in this section. The legislature may delegate to any state officer, agency, or instrumentality any of its powers relating to the contracting, funding or refunding of debt pursuant to this section except its power to determine the amount and purposes for which debt may be contracted.

(i) The full faith, credit, and taxing power of the state of Washington are pledged to the payment of the debt created on behalf of the state pursuant to this section and the legislature shall provide by appropriation for the payment of the interest upon and installments of principal of all such debt as the same falls due, but in any event, any court of record may compel such payment.

(j) Notwithstanding the limitations contained in subsection (b) of this section, the state may issue certificates of indebtedness in such sum or sums as may be necessary to meet temporary deficiencies of the treasury, to preserve the best interests of the state in the conduct of the various state institutions, departments, bureaus, and agencies during each fiscal year; such certificates may be issued only to provide for appropriations already made by the legislature and such certificates must be retired and the debt discharged other than by refunding within twelve months after the date of incurrence.

(k) Bonds, notes, or other obligations issued and sold by the state of Washington pursuant to and in conformity with this Article shall not be invalid for any irregularity or defect in the proceedings of the issuance or sale thereof and shall be incontestable in the hands of a bona fide purchaser or holder thereof.

Art. 8 Section 3 SPECIAL INDEBTEDNESS, HOW AUTHORIZED. Except the debt specified in sections one and two of this Article, no debts shall hereafter be contracted by, or on behalf of this state, unless such debt shall be authorized by law for some single work or object to be distinctly specified therein. No such law shall take effect until it shall, at a general election, or a special election called for that purpose, have been submitted to the people and have received a majority of all the votes cast for and against it at such election. [1971 House Joint Resolution No. 52, p 1836. Approved November 7, 1972.]

Art 8. Section 1 was later amended by Amendments 92, 103, and 107.

Prior amendment of Art. 8 Section 3, see Amendment 48.

Art. 8 Section 3 was later amended by Amendment 92.

AMENDMENT 61

The Constitution was amended by adding the following new article and sections 1 and 2 thereof:

ARTICLE XXXI
SEX EQUALITY - RIGHTS AND RESPONSIBILITIES

Art. 31 Section 1 EQUALITY NOT DENIED BECAUSE OF SEX. Equality of rights and responsibility under the law shall not be denied or abridged on account of sex.

Art. 31 Section 2 ENFORCEMENT POWER OF LEGISLATURE. The legislature shall have the power to enforce, by appropriate legislation, the provisions of this article. [1972 House Joint Resolution No. 61, p 526. Approved November 7, 1972.]

The name of this article has been supplied by the reviser.

AMENDMENT 62

Art. 3 Section 12 VETO POWER. Every act which shall have passed the legislature shall be, before it becomes a law, presented to the governor. If he approves, he shall sign it; but if not, he shall return it, with his objections, to that house in which it shall have originated, which house shall enter the objections at large upon the journal and proceed to reconsider. If, after such reconsideration, two-thirds of the members present shall agree to pass the bill it shall be sent, together with the objections, to the other house, by which it shall likewise be reconsidered, and if approved by two-thirds of the members present, it shall become a law; but in all such cases the vote of both houses shall be determined by the yeas and nays, and the names of the members voting for or against the bill shall be entered upon the journal of each house respectively. If any bill shall not be returned by the governor within five days, Sundays excepted, after it shall be presented to him, it shall become a law without his signature, unless the general adjournment shall prevent its return, in which case it shall become a law unless the governor, within twenty days next after the adjournment, Sundays excepted, shall file such bill with his objections thereto, in the office of secretary of state, who shall lay the same before the legislature at its next session in like manner as if it had been returned by the governor: Provided, That within forty-five days next after the adjournment, Sundays excepted, the legislature may, upon petition by a two-thirds majority or more of the membership of each house, reconvene in extraordinary session, not to exceed five days duration, solely to reconsider any bills vetoed. If any bill presented to the governor contain several sections or appropriation items, he may object to one or more sections or appropriation items while approving other portions of the bill: Provided, That he may not object to less than an entire section, except that if the section contain one or more appropriation items he may object to any such appropriation item or items. In case of objection he shall append to the bill, at the time of signing it, a statement of the section or sections, appropriation item or items to which he objects and the reasons therefor; and the section or sections, appropriation item or items so objected to shall not take effect unless passed over the governor's objection, as hereinbefore provided. The provisions of Article II, section 12 insofar as they are inconsistent herewith are hereby repealed. [1974 Senate Joint Resolution No. 140, p 806. Approved November 5, 1974.]

AMENDMENT 63

Art. 6 Section 1 QUALIFICATIONS OF ELECTORS. All persons of the age of eighteen years or over who are citizens of the United States and who have lived in the state, county, and precinct thirty days immediately preceding the election at which they offer to vote, except those disqualified by Article VI, section 3 of this Constitution, shall be entitled to vote at all elections. [1974 Senate Joint Resolution No. 143, p 807. Approved November 5, 1974.]

Prior amendment of Art. 6 Section 1, see Amendments 2 and 5.

AMENDMENT 64

Art. 7 Section 2 LIMITATION ON LEVIES. Except as hereinafter provided and notwithstanding any other provision of this Constitution, the aggregate of all tax levies upon real and personal property by the state and all taxing districts now existing or hereafter created, shall not in any year exceed one per centum of the true and fair value of such property in money: Provided, however, That nothing herein shall prevent levies at the rates now provided by law by or for any port or public utility district. The term "taxing district" for the purposes of this section shall mean any political subdivision, municipal corporation, district, or other governmental agency authorized by law to levy, or have levied for it, ad valorem taxes on property, other than a port or public utility district. Such aggregate limitation or any specific limitation imposed by law in conformity therewith may be exceeded only:

(a) By any taxing district when specifically authorized so to do by a majority of at least three-fifths of the electors thereof voting on the proposition to levy such additional tax submitted not more than twelve months prior to the date on which the proposed levy is to be made and not oftener than twice in such twelve month period, either at a special election or at the regular election of such taxing district, at which election the number of persons voting "yes" on the proposition shall constitute three-fifths of a number equal to forty per centum of the total votes cast in such taxing district at the last preceding general election when the number of electors voting on the proposition does not exceed forty per centum of the total votes cast in such taxing district in the last preceding general election; or by a majority of at least three-fifths of the electors thereof voting on the proposition to levy when the number of electors voting on the proposition exceeds forty percentum of the total votes cast in such taxing district in the last preceding general election: Provided, That notwithstanding any other provision of this Constitution, any proposition pursuant to this subsection to levy additional tax for the support of the common schools may provide such support for a two year period;

(b) By any taxing district otherwise authorized by law to issue general obligation bonds for capital purposes, for the sole purpose of making the required payments of principal and interest on general obligation bonds issued solely for capital purposes, other than the replacement of equipment, when authorized so to do by majority of at least three-fifths of the electors thereof voting on the proposition to issue such bonds and to pay the principal and interest thereon by an annual tax levy in excess of the limitation herein provided during the term of such bonds, submitted not oftener than twice in any calendar year, at an election held in the manner provided by law for bond elections in such taxing district, at which election the total number of persons voting on the proposition shall constitute not less than forty per centum of the total number of votes cast in such taxing district at the last preceding general election: Provided, That any such taxing district shall have the right by vote of its governing body to refund any general obligation bonds of said district issued for capital purposes only, and to provide for the interest thereon and amortization thereof by annual levies in excess of the tax limitation provided for herein, And provided further, That the provisions of this section shall also be subject to the limitations contained in Article VIII, Section 6, of this Constitution;

(c) By the state or any taxing district for the purpose of paying the principal or interest on general obligation bonds outstanding on December 6, 1934; or for the purpose of preventing the impairment of the obligation of a contract when ordered so to do by a court of last resort. [1975-'76 2nd ex.s. Senate Joint Resolution No. 137, p 518. Approved November 2, 1976.]

Prior amendment of Art. 7 Section 2, see Amendments 17, 55, and 59.

Art. 7 Section 2 was later amended by Amendments 79, 90, 95, and 101.

AMENDMENT 65

Art. 4 Section 6 JURISDICTION OF SUPERIOR COURTS. The superior court shall have original jurisdiction in all cases in equity and in all cases at law which involve the title or possession of real property, or the legality of any tax, impost, assessment, toll, or municipal fine, and in all other cases in which the demand or the value of the property in controversy amounts to three thousand dollars or as otherwise determined by law, or a lesser sum in excess of the jurisdiction granted to justices of the peace and other inferior courts, and in all criminal cases amounting to felony, and in all cases of misdemeanor not otherwise provided for by law; of actions of forcible entry and detainer; of proceedings in insolvency; of actions to prevent or abate a nuisance; of all matters of probate, of divorce, and for annulment of marriage; and for such special cases and proceedings as are not otherwise provided for. The superior court shall also have original jurisdiction in all cases and of all proceedings in which jurisdiction shall not have been by law vested exclusively in some other court; and said court shall have the power of naturalization and to issue papers therefor. They shall have such appellate jurisdiction in cases arising in justices' and other inferior courts in their respective counties as may be prescribed by law. They shall always be open, except on nonjudicial days, and their process shall extend to all parts of the state. Said courts and their judges shall have power to issue writs of mandamus, quo warranto, review, certiorari, prohibition, and writs of habeas corpus, on petition by or on behalf of any person in actual custody in their respective counties. Injunctions and writs of prohibition and of habeas corpus may be issued and served on legal holidays and nonjudicial days. [1977 Senate Joint Resolution No. 113, p 1714. Approved November 8, 1977.]

Art. 4 Section 10 JUSTICES OF THE PEACE. The legislature shall determine the number of justices of the peace to be elected and shall prescribe by law the powers, duties and jurisdiction of justices of the peace: Provided, That such jurisdiction granted by the legislature shall not trench upon the jurisdiction of superior or other courts of record, except that justices of the peace may be made police justices of incorporated cities and towns. Justices of the peace shall have original jurisdiction in cases where the demand or value of the property in controversy is less than three hundred dollars or such greater sum, not to exceed three thousand dollars or as otherwise determined by law, as shall be prescribed by the legislature. In incorporated cities or towns having more than five thousand inhabitants, the justices of the peace shall receive such salary as may be provided by law, and shall receive no fees for their own use. [1977 Senate Joint Resolution No. 113, p 1714. Approved November 8, 1977.]

Prior amendment of Art. 4 Section 6 and Section 10, see Amendment 28.

AMENDMENT 66

Art. 12 Section 18 RATES FOR TRANSPORTATION. The legislature may pass laws establishing reasonable rates of charges for the transportation of passengers and freight, and to correct abuses and prevent discrimination and extortion in the rates of freight and passenger tariffs on the different railroads and other common carriers in the state, and shall enforce such laws by adequate penalties. A railroad and transportation commission may be established and its powers and duties fully defined by law. [1977 House Joint Resolution No. 55, p 1713. Approved November 8, 1977.]

AMENDMENT 67

Art. 12 Section 14 PROHIBITION AGAINST COMBINATIONS BY CARRIERS. [Repealed by 1977 House Joint Resolution No. 57, p 1714. Approved November 8, 1977.]

AMENDMENT 68

Art. 2 Section 12 SESSIONS, WHEN - DURATION. (1) Regular Sessions. A regular session of the legislature shall be convened each year. Regular sessions shall convene on such day and at such time as the legislature shall determine by statute. During each odd-numbered year, the regular session shall not be more than one hundred five consecutive days. During each even-numbered year, the regular session shall not be more than sixty consecutive days.

(2) Special Legislative Sessions. Special legislative sessions may be convened for a period of not more than thirty consecutive days by proclamation of the governor pursuant to Article III, section 7 of this Constitution. Special legislative sessions may also be convened for a period of not more than thirty consecutive days by resolution of the legislature upon the affirmative vote in each house of two-thirds of the members elected or appointed thereto, which vote may be taken and resolution executed either while the legislature is in session or during any interim between sessions in accordance with such procedures as the legislature may provide by law or resolution. The resolution convening the legislature shall specify a purpose or purposes for the convening of a special session, and any special session convened by the resolution shall consider only measures germane to the purpose or purposes expressed in the resolution, unless by resolution adopted during the session upon the affirmative vote in each house of two-thirds of the members elected or appointed thereto, an additional purpose or purposes are expressed. The specification of purpose by the governor pursuant to Article III, section 7 of this Constitution shall be considered by the legislature but shall not be mandatory.

(3) Committees of the Legislature. Standing and special committees of the legislature shall meet and conduct official business pursuant to such rules as the legislature may adopt. [1979 Substitute Senate Joint Resolution No. 110, p 2286. Approved November 6, 1979.]

AMENDMENT 69

Art. 2 Section 13 LIMITATION ON MEMBERS HOLDING OFFICE IN THE STATE. No member of the legislature, during the term for which he is elected, shall be appointed or elected to any civil office in the state, which shall have been created during the term for which he was elected. Any member of the legislature who is appointed or elected to any civil office in the state, the emoluments of which have been increased during his legislative term of office, shall be compensated for the initial term of the civil office at the level designated prior to the increase in emoluments. [1979 Senate Joint Resolution No. 112, p 2287. Approved November 6, 1979.]

AMENDMENT 70

Article 8 was amended by adding the following section:

Art. 8 Section 10 RESIDENTIAL ENERGY CONSERVATION. Notwithstanding the provisions of section 7 of this Article, until January 1, 1990 any county, city, town, quasi municipal corporation, municipal corporation, or political subdivision of the state which is engaged in the sale or distribution of energy may, as authorized by the legislature, use public moneys or credit derived from operating revenues from the sale of energy to assist the owners of residential structures in financing the acquisition and installation of materials and equipment for the conservation or more efficient use of energy in such structures. Except as provided in section 7 of this Article, an appropriate charge back shall be made for such extension of public moneys or credit and the same shall be a lien against the residential structure benefited. Except as to contracts entered into prior thereto, this amendment to the state Constitution shall be null and void as of January 1, 1990 and shall have no further force or effect after that date. [1979 Substitute Senate Joint Resolution No. 120, p 2288. Approved November 6, 1979.]

Art. 8 Section 10 was later amended by Amendments 82, 86, and 91.

AMENDMENT 71

Article 4 was amended by adding the following section:

Art. 4 Section 31 JUDICIAL QUALIFICATIONS COMMISSION - REMOVAL, CENSURE, SUSPENSION, OR RETIREMENT OF JUDGES OR JUSTICES. There shall be a judicial qualifications commission consisting of a judge selected by and from the court of appeals judges, a judge selected by and from the superior court judges, a judge selected by and from the district court judges, two persons admitted to the practice of law in this state selected by the state bar association, and two persons who are not attorneys appointed by the governor and confirmed by the senate.

The supreme court may censure, suspend, or remove a judge or justice for violating a rule of judicial conduct and may retire a judge or justice for disability which is permanent or is likely to become permanent and which seriously interferes with the performance of judicial duties. The office of a judge or justice retired or removed by the supreme court becomes vacant, and that person is ineligible for judicial office until eligibility is reinstated by the supreme court. The salary of a removed judge or justice shall cease.

The supreme court shall specify the effect upon salary when disciplinary action other than removal is taken. The supreme court may not discipline or retire a judge or justice until the judicial qualifications commission recommends after notice and hearing that action be taken and the supreme court conducts a hearing, after notice, to review commission proceedings and findings against a judge or justice.

The legislature shall provide for commissioners' terms of office and compensation. The commission shall establish rules of procedure for commission proceedings including due process and confidentiality of proceedings. [1980 Substitute House Joint Resolution No. 37, p 652. Approved November 4, 1980.]

Art. 4 Section 31 was later amended by Amendments 77, 85, and 97.

AMENDMENT 72

Art. 2 Section 1 LEGISLATIVE POWERS, WHERE VESTED. The legislative authority of the state of Washington shall be vested in the legislature, consisting of a senate and house of representatives, which shall be called the legislature of the state of Washington, but the people reserve to themselves the power to propose bills, laws, and to enact or reject the same at the polls, independent of the legislature, and also reserve power, at their own option, to approve or reject at the polls any act, item, section, or part of any bill, act, or law passed by the legislature.

(a) Initiative: The first power reserved by the people is the initiative. Every such petition shall include the full text of the measure so proposed. In the case of initiatives to the legislature and initiatives to the people, the number of valid signatures of legal voters required shall be equal to eight percent of the votes cast for the office of governor at the last gubernatorial election preceding the initial filing of the text of the initiative measure with the secretary of state.

Initiative petitions shall be filed with the secretary of state not less than four months before the election at which they are to be voted upon, or not less than ten days before any regular session of the legislature. If filed at least four months before the election at which they are to be voted upon, he shall submit the same to the vote of the people at the said election. If such petitions are filed not less than ten days before any regular session of the legislature, he shall certify the results within forty days of the filing. If certification is not complete by the date that the legislature convenes, he shall provisionally certify the measure pending final certification of the measure. Such initiative measures, whether certified or provisionally certified, shall take precedence over all other measures in the legislature except appropriation bills and shall be either enacted or rejected without change or amendment by the legislature before the end of such regular session. If any such initiative measures shall be enacted by the legislature it shall be subject to the referendum petition, or it may be enacted and referred by the legislature to the people for approval or rejection at the next regular election. If it is rejected or if no action is taken upon it by the legislature before the end of such regular session, the secretary of state shall submit it to the people for approval or rejection at the next ensuing regular general election. The legislature may reject any measure so proposed by initiative petition and propose a different one dealing with the same subject, and in such event both measures shall be submitted by the secretary of state to the people for approval or rejection at the next ensuing regular general election. When conflicting measures are submitted to the people the ballots shall be so printed that a voter can express separately by making one cross (X) for each, two preferences, first, as between either measure and neither, and secondly, as between one and the other. If the majority of those voting on the first issue is for neither, both fail, but in that case the votes on the second issue shall nevertheless be carefully counted and made public. If a majority voting on the first issue is for either, then the measure receiving a majority of the votes on the second issue shall be law.

(b) Referendum. The second power reserved by the people is the referendum, and it may be ordered on any act, bill, law, or any part thereof passed by the legislature, except such laws as may be necessary for the immediate preservation of the public peace, health or safety, support of the state government and its existing public institutions, either by petition signed by the required percentage of the legal voters, or by the legislature as other bills are enacted: Provided, That the legislature may not order a referendum on any initiative measure enacted by the legislature under the foregoing subsection (a). The number of valid signatures of registered voters required on a petition for referendum of an act of the legislature or any part thereof, shall be equal to or exceeding four percent of the votes cast for the office of governor at the last gubernatorial election preceding the filing of the text of the referendum measure with the secretary of state.

(c) No act, law, or bill subject to referendum shall take effect until ninety days after the adjournment of the session at which it was enacted. No act, law, or bill approved by a majority of the electors voting thereon shall be amended or repealed by the legislature within a period of two years following such enactment: Provided, That any such act, law, or bill may be amended within two years after such enactment at any regular or special session of the legislature by a vote of two-thirds of all the members elected to each house with full compliance with section 12, Article III, of the Washington Constitution, and no amendatory law adopted in accordance with this provision shall be subject to referendum. But such enactment may be amended or repealed at any general regular or special election by direct vote of the people thereon.

(d) The filing of a referendum petition against one or more items, sections, or parts of any act, law, or bill shall not delay the remainder of the measure from becoming operative. Referendum petitions against measures passed by the legislature shall be filed with the secretary of state not later than ninety days after the final adjournment of the session of the legislature which passed the measure on which the referendum is demanded. The veto power of the governor shall not extend to measures initiated by or referred to the people. All elections on measures referred to the people of the state shall be had at the next succeeding regular general election following the filing of the measure with the secretary of state, except when the legislature shall order a special election. Any measure initiated by the people or referred to the people as herein provided shall take effect and become the law if it is approved by a majority of the votes cast thereon: Provided, That the vote cast upon such question or measure shall equal one-third of the total votes cast at such election and not otherwise. Such measure shall be in operation on and after the thirtieth day after the election at which it is approved. The style of all bills proposed by initiative petition shall be: "Be it enacted by the people of the State of Washington." This section shall not be construed to deprive any member of the legislature of the right to introduce any measure. All such petitions shall be filed with the secretary of state, who shall be guided by the general laws in submitting the same to the people until additional legislation shall especially provide therefor. This section is self-executing, but legislation may be enacted especially to facilitate its operation.

(e) The legislature shall provide methods of publicity of all laws or parts of laws, and amendments to the Constitution referred to the people with arguments for and against the laws and amendments so referred. The secretary of state shall send one copy of the publication to each individual place of residence in the state and shall make such additional distribution as he shall determine necessary to reasonably assure that each voter will have an opportunity to study the measures prior to election. [1981 Substitute Senate Joint Resolution No. 133, p 1796. Approved November 3, 1981.]

Prior amendment of Art. 2 Section 1, see Amendment 7.

Addition of subsection (e) to Art. 2 Section 1, see Amendment 36.
Art. 2 Section 1(a). INITIATIVE AND REFERENDUM, SIGNATURES REQUIRED. [Stricken by 1981 Substitute Senate Joint Resolution No. 133, p 1796. Approved November 3, 1981.]

Adoption of Art. 2 Section 1(a), see Amendment 30.

AMENDMENT 73

The Constitution was amended by adding the following new article and section 1 thereof:

ARTICLE XXXII

SPECIAL REVENUE FINANCING
Art. 32 Section 1 SPECIAL REVENUE FINANCING. The legislature may enact laws authorizing the state, counties, cities, towns, port districts, or public corporations established thereby to issue nonrecourse revenue bonds or other nonrecourse revenue obligations and to

apply the proceeds thereof in the manner and for the purposes heretofore or hereafter authorized by law, subject to the following limitations:

(a) Nonrecourse revenue bonds and other nonrecourse revenue obligations issued pursuant to this section shall be payable only from money or other property received as a result of projects financed by the nonrecourse revenue bonds or other nonrecourse revenue obligations and from money and other property received from private sources.

(b) Nonrecourse revenue bonds and other nonrecourse revenue obligations issued pursuant to this section shall not be payable from or secured by any tax funds or governmental revenue or by all or part of the faith and credit of the state or any unit of local government.

(c) Nonrecourse revenue bonds or other nonrecourse revenue obligations issued pursuant to this section may be issued only if the issuer certifies that it reasonably believes that the interest paid on the bonds or obligations will be exempt from income taxation by the federal government.

(d) Nonrecourse revenue bonds or other nonrecourse revenue obligations may only be used to finance industrial development projects as defined in legislation.

(e) The state, counties, cities, towns, port districts, or public corporations established thereby, shall never exercise their respective attributes of sovereignty, including but not limited to, the power to tax, the power of eminent domain, and the police power on behalf of any industrial development project authorized pursuant to this section.

After the initial adoption of a law by the legislature authorizing the issuance of nonrecourse revenue bonds or other nonrecourse revenue obligations, no amendment to such act which expands the definition of industrial development project shall be valid unless the amendment is enacted by a favorable vote of three-fifths of the members elected to each house of the legislature and is subject to referendum petition.

Sections 5 and 7 of Article VIII and section 9 of Article XII shall not be construed as a limitation upon the authority granted by this section. The proceeds of revenue bonds and other revenue obligations issued pursuant to this section for the purpose of financing privately owned property or loans to private persons or corporations shall be subject to audit by the state but shall not otherwise be deemed to be public money or public property for purposes of this Constitution. This section is supplemental to and shall not be construed as a repeal of or limitation on any other authority lawfully exercisable under the Constitution and laws of this state, including, among others, any existing authority to issue revenue bonds. [1981 Substitute House Joint Resolution No. 7, p 1794. Approved November 3, 1981.]

The name of this Article has been supplied by the reviser.

AMENDMENT 74

Article 2 was amended by adding the following section:

Art. 2 Section 43 REDISTRICTING. (1) In January of each year ending in one, a commission shall be established to provide for the redistricting of state legislative and congressional districts.

(2) The commission shall be composed of five members to be selected as follows: The legislative leader of the two largest political parties in each house of the legislature shall appoint one voting member to the commission by January 15th of each year ending in one. By January 31st of each year ending in one, the four appointed members, by an affirmative vote of at least three, shall appoint the remaining member. The fifth member of the commission, who shall be nonvoting, shall act as its chairperson. If any appointing authority fails to make the required appointment by the date established by this subsection, within five days after that date the supreme court shall make the required appointment.

(3) No elected official and no person elected to legislative district, county, or state political party office may serve on the commission. A commission member shall not have been an elected official and shall not have been an elected legislative district, county, or state political party officer within two years of his or her appointment to the commission. The provisions of this subsection do not apply to the office of precinct committee person.

(4) The legislature shall enact laws providing for the implementation of this section, to include additional qualifications for commissioners and additional standards to govern the commission. The legislature shall appropriate funds to enable the commission to carry out its duties.

(5) Each district shall contain a population, excluding nonresident military personnel, as nearly equal as practicable to the population of any other district. To the extent reasonable, each district shall contain contiguous territory, shall be compact and convenient, and shall be separated from adjoining districts by natural geographic barriers, artificial barriers, or political subdivision boundaries. The commission's plan shall not provide for a number of legislative districts different than that established by the legislature. The commission's plan shall not be drawn purposely to favor or discriminate against any political party or group.

(6) The commission shall complete redistricting as soon as possible following the federal decennial census, but no later than January 1st of each year ending in two. At least three of the voting members shall approve such a redistricting plan. If three of the voting members of the commission fail to approve a plan within the time limitations provided in this subsection, the supreme court shall adopt a plan by April 30th of the year ending in two in conformance with the standards set forth in subsection (5) of this section.

(7) The legislature may amend the redistricting plan but must do so by a two-thirds vote of the legislators elected or appointed to each house of the legislature. Any amendment must have passed both houses by the end of the thirtieth day of the first session convened after the commission has submitted its plan to the legislature. After that day, the plan, with any legislative amendments, constitutes the state districting law.

(8) The legislature shall enact laws providing for the reconvening of a commission for the purpose of modifying a districting law adopted under this section. Such reconvening requires a two-thirds vote of the legislators elected or appointed to each house of the legislature. The commission shall conform to the standards prescribed under subsection (5) of this section and any other standards or procedures that the legislature may provide by law. At least three of the voting members shall approve such a modification. Any modification adopted by the commission may be amended by a two-thirds vote of the legislators elected and appointed to each house of the legislature. The state districting law shall include the modifications with amendments, if any.

(9) The legislature shall prescribe by law the terms of commission members and the method of filling vacancies on the commission.

(10) The supreme court has original jurisdiction to hear and decide all cases involving congressional and legislative redistricting.

(11) Legislative and congressional districts may not be changed or established except pursuant to this section. A districting plan and any legislative amendments to the plan are not subject to Article III, section 12 of this Constitution. [1983 Substitute Senate Joint Resolution No. 103, p 2202. Approved November 8, 1983.]

Art. 2 Section 43 was later amended by Amendment 108.

Art. 2 Section 3 THE CENSUS. [Repealed by 1983 Substitute Senate Joint Resolution No. 103, p 2202. Approved November 8, 1983.]

Art. 27 Section 13 REPRESENTATION IN CONGRESS. [Repealed by 1983 Substitute Senate Joint Resolution No. 103, p 2202. Approved November 8, 1983.]

AMENDMENT 75

Art. 29 Section 1 MAY BE INVESTED AS AUTHORIZED BY LAW. Notwithstanding the provisions of sections 5, and 7 of Article VIII and section 9 of Article XII or any other section or article of the Constitution of the state of Washington, the moneys of any public pension or retirement fund or industrial insurance trust fund may be invested as authorized by law. [1985 House Joint Resolution No. 12, p 2398. Approved November 5, 1985.]

Prior amendment of Art. 29 Section 1, see Amendment 49.

Art. 29 Section 1 was later amended by Amendment 93.

AMENDMENT 76

Article 8 was amended by adding the following section:

Art. 8 Section 11 AGRICULTURAL COMMODITY ASSESSMENTS - DEVELOPMENT, PROMOTION, AND HOSTING. The use of agricultural commodity assessments by agricultural commodity commissions in such manner as may be prescribed by the legislature for agricultural development or trade promotion and promotional hosting shall be deemed a public use for a public purpose, and shall not be deemed a gift within the provisions of section 5 of this article. [1985 House Joint Resolution No. 42, p 2402. Approved November 5, 1985.]

AMENDMENT 77

Art. 4 Section 31 COMMISSION ON JUDICIAL CONDUCT - REMOVAL, CENSURE, SUSPENSION, OR RETIREMENT OF JUDGES OR JUSTICES - PROCEEDINGS. There shall be a commission on judicial conduct consisting of a judge selected by and from the court of appeals judges, a judge selected by and from the superior court judges, a judge selected by and from the district court judges, two persons admitted to the practice of law in this state selected by the state bar association, and four persons who are not attorneys appointed by the governor and confirmed by the senate.

The supreme court may censure, suspend, or remove a judge or justice for violating a rule of judicial conduct and may retire a judge or justice for disability which is permanent or is likely to become permanent and which seriously interferes with the performance of judicial duties. The office of a judge or justice retired or removed by the supreme court becomes vacant, and that person is ineligible for judicial office until eligibility is reinstated by the supreme court. The salary of a removed judge or justice shall cease.

The supreme court shall specify the effect upon salary when disciplinary action other than removal is taken. The supreme court may not discipline or retire a judge or justice until the commission on judicial conduct recommends after notice and hearing that action be taken and the supreme court conducts a hearing, after notice, to review commission proceedings and findings against a judge or justice.

Whenever the commission receives a complaint against a judge or justice, it shall first conduct proceedings for the purpose of determining whether sufficient reason exists for conducting a hearing or hearings to deal with the accusations. These initial proceedings shall be confidential, unless confidentiality is waived by the judge or justice, but all subsequent hearings conducted by the commission shall be open to members of the public.

Whenever the commission adopts a recommendation that a judge or justice be removed, the judge or justice shall be suspended immediately, with salary, from his or her judicial position until a final determination is made by the supreme court.

The legislature shall provide for commissioners' terms of office and compensation. The commission shall establish rules of procedure for commission proceedings including due process and confidentiality of proceedings. [1986 Senate Joint Resolution No. 136, p 1532. Approved November 4, 1986.]

Prior amendment of Art. 4 Section 31, see Amendment 71.

Art. 4 Section 31 was later amended by Amendments 85 and 97.

AMENDMENT 78

Art. 28 Section 1 SALARIES FOR LEGISLATORS, ELECTED STATE OFFICIALS, AND JUDGES - INDEPENDENT COMMISSION - REFERENDUM. Salaries for members of the legislature, elected officials of the executive branch of state government, and judges of the state's supreme court, court of appeals, superior courts, and district courts shall be fixed by an independent commission created and directed by law to that purpose. No state official, public employee, or person required by law to register with a state agency as a lobbyist, or immediate family member of the official, employee, or lobbyist, may be a member of that commission.

As used in this section the phrase "immediate family" has the meaning that is defined by law.

Any change of salary shall be filed with the secretary of state and shall become law ninety days thereafter without action of the legislature or governor, but shall be subject to referendum petition by the people, filed within the ninety-day period. Referendum measures under this section shall be submitted to the people at the next following general election, and shall be otherwise governed by the provisions of this Constitution generally applicable to referendum measures. The salaries fixed pursuant to this section shall supersede any other provision for the salaries of members of the legislature, elected officials of the executive branch of state government, and judges of the state's supreme court, court of appeals, superior courts, and district courts. The salaries for such officials in effect on January 12, 1987, shall remain in effect until changed pursuant to this section.

After the initial adoption of a law by the legislature creating the independent commission, no amendment to such act which alters the composition of the commission shall be valid unless the amendment is enacted by a favorable vote of two-thirds of the members elected to each house of the legislature and is subject to referendum petition.

The provisions of section 14 of Article IV, sections 14, 16, 17, 19, 20, 21, and 22 of Article III, and section 23 of Article II, insofar as they are inconsistent herewith, are hereby superseded. The provisions of section 1 of Article II relating to referendum procedures, insofar as they are inconsistent herewith, are hereby superseded with regard to the salaries governed by this section. [1986 Substitute House Joint Resolution No. 49, p 1529. Approved November 4, 1986.]

Prior amendment of Art. 28 Section 1, see Amendment 20.

AMENDMENT 79

Art. 7 Section 2 - LIMITATION ON LEVIES. Except as hereinafter provided and notwithstanding any other provision of this Constitution, the aggregate of all tax levies upon real and personal property by the state and all taxing districts now existing or hereafter created, shall not in any year exceed one per centum of the true and fair value of such property in money: Provided, however, That nothing herein shall prevent levies at the rates now provided by law by or for any port or public utility district. The term "taxing district" for the purposes of this section shall mean any political subdivision, municipal corporation, district, or other governmental agency authorized by law to levy, or have levied for it, ad valorem taxes on property, other than a port or public utility district. Such aggregate limitation or any specific limitation imposed by law in conformity therewith may be exceeded only

(a) By any taxing district when specifically authorized so to do by a majority of at least three-fifths of the electors thereof voting on the proposition to levy such additional tax submitted not more than twelve months prior to the date on which the proposed levy is to be made and not oftener than twice in such twelve month period, either at a special election or at the regular election of such taxing district, at which election the number of persons voting "yes" on the proposition shall constitute three-fifths of a number equal to forty per centum of the total votes cast in such taxing district at the last preceding general election when the number of electors voting on the proposition does not exceed forty per centum of the total votes cast in such taxing district in the last preceding general election; or by a majority of at least three-fifths of the electors thereof voting on the proposition to levy when the number of electors voting on the proposition exceeds forty percentum of the total votes cast in such taxing district in the last preceding general election: Provided, That notwithstanding any other provision of this Constitution, any proposition pursuant to this subsection to levy additional tax for the support of the common schools may provide such support for a two year period and any proposition to levy an additional tax to support the construction, modernization, or remodelling of school facilities may provide such support for a period not exceeding six years;

(b) By any taxing district otherwise authorized by law to issue general obligation bonds for capital purposes, for the sole purpose of making the required payments of principal and interest on general obligation bonds issued solely for capital purposes, other than the replacement of equipment, when authorized so to do by majority of at least three-fifths of the electors thereof voting on the proposition to issue such bonds and to pay the principal and interest thereon by an annual tax levy in excess of the limitation herein provided during the term of such bonds, submitted not oftener than twice in any calendar year, at an election held in the manner provided by law for bond elections in such taxing district, at which election the total number of persons voting on the proposition shall constitute not less than forty per centum of the total number of votes cast in such taxing district at the last preceding general election: Provided, That any such taxing district shall have the right by vote of its governing body to refund any general obligation bonds of said district issued for capital purposes only, and to provide for the interest thereon and amortization thereof by annual levies in excess of the tax limitation provided for herein, And provided further, That the provisions of this section shall also be subject to the limitations contained in Article VIII, Section 6, of this Constitution;

(c) By the state or any taxing district for the purpose of paying the principal or interest on general obligation bonds outstanding on December 6, 1934; or for the purpose of preventing the impairment of the obligation of a contract when ordered so to do by a court of last resort. [1986 House Joint Resolution No. 55, p 1530. Approved November 4, 1986.]

Prior amendment of Art. 7 Section 2, see Amendments 17, 55, 59, and 64.

Art. 7 Section 2 was later amended by Amendments 90, 95, and 101.

AMENDMENT 80

Art. 4 Section 7 EXCHANGE OF JUDGES - JUDGE PRO TEMPORE. The judge of any superior court may hold a superior court in any county at the request of the judge of the superior court thereof, and upon the request of the governor it shall be his duty to do so. A case in the superior court may be tried by a judge, pro tempore, who must be a member of the bar, agreed upon in writing by the parties litigant, or their attorneys of record, approved by the court and sworn to try the case. However, if a previously elected judge of the superior court retires leaving a pending case in which the judge has made discretionary rulings, the judge is entitled to hear the pending case as a judge pro tempore without any written agreement. [1987 Senate Joint Resolution No. 8207, p 2815. Approved November 3, 1987.]
Art. 4 Section 7 was later amended by Amendment 94.

AMENDMENT 81

Art. 7 Section 1 TAXATION. The power of taxation shall never be suspended, surrendered or contracted away. All taxes shall be uniform upon the same class of property within the territorial limits of the authority levying the tax and shall be levied and collected for public purposes only. The word "property" as used herein shall mean and include everything, whether tangible or intangible, subject to ownership. All real estate shall constitute one class: Provided, That the legislature may tax mines and mineral resources and lands devoted to reforestation by either a yield tax or an ad valorem tax at such rate as it may fix, or by both. Such property as the legislature may by general laws provide shall be exempt from taxation. Property of the United States and of the state, counties, school districts and other municipal corporations, and credits secured by property actually taxed in this state, not exceeding in value the value of such property, shall be exempt from taxation. The legislature shall have power, by appropriate legislation, to exempt personal property to the amount of three thousand ($3,000.00) dollars for each head of a family liable to assessment and taxation under the provisions of the laws of this state of which the individual is the actual bona fide owner. [1988 House Joint Resolution No. 4222, p 1551. Approved November 8, 1988.]
Prior amendment to Art. 7 Section 1, see Amendments 14 and 98.

AMENDMENT 82

Art. 8 Section 10 RESIDENTIAL ENERGY CONSERVATION. Notwithstanding the provisions of section 7 of this Article, any county, city, town, quasi municipal corporation, municipal corporation, or political subdivision of the state which is engaged in the sale or distribution of energy may, as authorized by the legislature, use public moneys or credit derived from operating revenues from the sale of energy to assist the owners of structures or equipment in financing the acquisition and installation of materials and equipment for the conservation or more efficient use of energy in such structures or equipment. Except as provided in section 7 of this Article, an appropriate charge back shall be made for such extension of public moneys or credit and the same shall be a lien against the structure benefited or a security interest in the equipment benefited. Any financing authorized by this article shall only be used for conservation purposes in existing structures and shall not be used for any purpose which results in a conversion from one energy source to another. [1988 House Joint Resolution No. 4223, p 1552. Approved November 8, 1988.]

Prior amendment to Art. 8 Section 10, see Amendment 70.

Art. 8 Section 10 was later amended by Amendments 86 and 91.

AMENDMENT 83

Art. 6 Section 3 WHO DISQUALIFIED. All persons convicted of infamous crime unless restored to their civil rights and all persons while they are judicially declared mentally incompetent are excluded from the elective franchise.

Art. 13 Section 1 EDUCATIONAL, REFORMATORY, AND PENAL INSTITUTIONS. Educational, reformatory, and penal institutions; those for the benefit of youth who are blind or deaf or otherwise disabled; for persons who are mentally ill or developmentally disabled; and such other institutions as the public good may require, shall be fostered and supported by the state, subject to such regulations as may be provided by law. The regents, trustees, or commissioners of all such institutions existing at the time of the adoption of this Constitution, and of such as shall thereafter be established by law, shall be appointed by the governor, by and with the advice and consent of the senate; and upon all nominations made by the governor, the question shall be taken by ayes and noes, and entered upon the journal. [1988 House Joint Resolution No. 4231, p 1553. Approved November 8, 1988.]

AMENDMENT 84

Art. 1 Section 35 VICTIMS OF CRIMES - RIGHTS. Effective law enforcement depends on cooperation from victims of crime. To ensure victims a meaningful role in the criminal justice system and to accord them due dignity and respect, victims of crime are hereby granted the following basic and fundamental rights.

Upon notifying the prosecuting attorney, a victim of a crime charged as a felony shall have the right to be informed of and, subject to the discretion of the individual presiding over the trial or court proceedings, attend trial and all other court proceedings the defendant has the right to attend, and to make a statement at sentencing and at any proceeding where the defendant's release is considered, subject to the same rules of procedure which govern the defendant's rights. In the event the victim is deceased, incompetent, a minor, or otherwise unavailable, the prosecuting attorney may identify a representative to appear to exercise the victim's rights. This provision shall not constitute a basis for error in favor of a defendant in a criminal proceeding nor a basis for providing a victim or the victim's representative with court appointed counsel. [1989 Senate Joint Resolution No. 8200, p 2999. Approved November 7, 1989.]

AMENDMENT 85

Art. 4 Section 31 COMMISSION ON JUDICIAL CONDUCT. (1) There shall be a commission on judicial conduct, existing as an independent agency of the judicial branch, and consisting of a judge selected by and from the court of appeals judges, a judge selected by and from the superior court judges, a judge selected by and from the district court judges, two persons admitted to the practice of law in this state selected by the state bar association, and six persons who are not attorneys appointed by the governor.

(2) Whenever the commission receives a complaint against a judge or justice, or otherwise has reason to believe that a judge or justice should be admonished, reprimanded, censured, suspended, removed, or retired, the commission shall first investigate the complaint or belief and then conduct initial proceedings for the purpose of determining whether probable cause exists for conducting a public hearing or hearings to deal with the complaint or belief. The investigation and initial proceedings shall be confidential. Upon beginning an initial proceeding, the commission shall notify the judge or justice of the existence of and basis for the initial proceeding.

(3) Whenever the commission concludes, based on an initial proceeding, that there is probable cause to believe that a judge or justice has violated a rule of judicial conduct or that the judge or justice suffers from a disability which is permanent or likely to become permanent and which seriously interferes with the performance of judicial duties, the commission shall conduct a public hearing or hearings and shall make public all those records of the initial proceeding that provide the basis for its conclusion. If the commission concludes that there is not probable cause, it shall notify the judge or justice of its conclusion.

(4) Upon the completion of the hearing or hearings, the commission in open session shall either dismiss the case, or shall admonish, reprimand, or censure the judge or justice, or shall censure the judge or justice and recommend to the supreme court the suspension or removal of the judge or justice, or shall recommend to the supreme court the retirement of the judge or justice. The commission may not recommend suspension or removal unless it censures the judge or justice for the violation serving as the basis for the recommendation. The commission may recommend retirement of a judge or justice for a disability which is permanent or likely to become permanent and which seriously interferes with the performance of judicial duties.

(5) Upon the recommendation of the commission, the supreme court may suspend, remove, or retire a judge or justice. The office of a judge or justice retired or removed by the supreme court becomes vacant, and that person is ineligible for judicial office until eligibility is reinstated by the supreme court. The salary of a removed judge or justice shall cease. The supreme court shall specify the effect upon salary when it suspends a judge or justice. The supreme court may not suspend, remove, or retire a judge or justice until the commission, after notice and hearing, recommends that action be taken, and the supreme court conducts a hearing, after notice, to review commission proceedings and findings against the judge or justice.

(6) Within thirty days after the commission admonishes, reprimands, or censures a judge or justice, the judge or justice shall have a right of appeal de novo to the supreme court.

(7) Any matter before the commission or supreme court may be disposed of by a stipulation entered into in a public proceeding. The stipulation shall be signed by the judge or justice and the commission or court. The stipulation may impose any terms and conditions deemed appropriate by the commission or court. A stipulation shall set forth all material facts relating to the proceeding and the conduct of the judge or justice.

(8) Whenever the commission adopts a recommendation that a judge or justice be removed, the judge or justice shall be suspended immediately, with salary, from his or her judicial position until a final determination is made by the supreme court.

(9) The legislature shall provide for commissioners' terms of office and compensation. The commission shall employ one or more investigative officers with appropriate professional training and experience. The investigative officers of the commission shall report directly to the commission. The commission shall also employ such administrative or other staff as are necessary to manage the affairs of the commission.

(10) The commission shall, to the extent that compliance does not conflict with this section, comply with laws of general applicability to state agencies with respect to rule-making procedures, and with respect to public notice of and attendance at commission proceedings other than initial proceedings. The commission shall establish rules of procedure for commission proceedings including due process and confidentiality of proceedings. [1989 Substitute Senate Joint Resolution No. 8202, p 3000. Approved November 7, 1989.]

Prior amendment of Art. 4 Section 31, see Amendments 71 and 77.

Art. 4 Section 31 was later amended by Amendment 97.

AMENDMENT 86

Art. 8 Section 10 ENERGY AND WATER CONSERVATION ASSISTANCE. Notwithstanding the provisions of section 7 of this Article, any county, city, town, quasi municipal corporation, municipal corporation, or political subdivision of the state which is engaged in the sale or distribution of water or energy may, as authorized by the legislature, use public moneys or credit derived from operating revenues from the sale of water or energy to assist the owners of structures or equipment in financing the acquisition and installation of materials and equipment for the conservation or more efficient use of water or energy in such structures or equipment. Except as provided in section 7 of this Article, an appropriate charge back shall be made for such extension of public moneys or credit and the same shall be a lien against the structure benefited or a security interest in the equipment benefited. Any financing for energy conservation authorized by this article shall only be used for conservation purposes in existing structures and shall not be used for any purpose which results in a conversion from one energy source to another. [1989 Senate Joint Resolution No. 8210, p 3003. Approved November 7, 1989.]

Prior amendment of Art. 8 Section 10, see Amendments 70 and 82.

Art. 8 Section 10 was later amended by Amendment 91.

AMENDMENT 87

Art. 4 Section 6 JURISDICTION OF SUPERIOR COURTS. Superior courts and district courts have concurrent jurisdiction in cases in equity. The superior court shall have original jurisdiction in all cases at law which involve the title or possession of real property, or the legality of any tax, impost, assessment, toll, or municipal fine, and in all other cases in which the demand or the value of the property in controversy amounts to three thousand dollars or as otherwise determined by law, or a lesser sum in excess of the jurisdiction granted to justices of the peace and other inferior courts, and in all criminal cases amounting to felony, and in all cases of misdemeanor not otherwise provided for by law; of actions of forcible entry and detainer; of proceedings in insolvency; of actions to prevent or abate a nuisance; of all matters of probate, of divorce, and for annulment of marriage; and for such special cases and proceedings as are not otherwise provided for. The superior court shall also have original jurisdiction in all cases and of all proceedings in which jurisdiction shall not have been by law vested exclusively in some other court; and said court shall have the power of naturalization and to issue papers therefor. They shall have such appellate jurisdiction in cases arising in justices' and other inferior courts in their respective counties as may be prescribed by law. They shall always be open, except on nonjudicial days, and their process shall extend to all parts of the state. Said courts and their judges shall have power to issue writs of mandamus, quo warranto, review, certiorari, prohibition, and writs of habeas corpus, on petition by or on behalf of any person in actual custody in their respective counties. Injunctions and writs of prohibition and of habeas corpus may be issued and served on legal holidays and nonjudicial days. [1993 House Joint Resolution No. 4201, p 3063. Approved November 2, 1993.]

Prior amendment of Art. 4 Section 6, see Amendments 28 and 65.

AMENDMENT 88

Art. 1 Section 11 RELIGIOUS FREEDOM. Absolute freedom of conscience in all matters of religious sentiment, belief and worship, shall be guaranteed to every individual, and no one shall be molested or disturbed in person or property on account of religion; but the liberty of conscience hereby secured shall not be so construed as to excuse acts of licentiousness or justify practices inconsistent with the peace and safety of the state. No public money or property shall be appropriated for or applied to any religious worship, exercise or instruction, or the support of any religious establishment: PROVIDED, HOWEVER, That this article shall not be so construed as to forbid the employment by the state of a chaplain for such of the state custodial, correctional, and mental institutions, or by a county's or public hospital district's hospital, health care facility, or hospice, as in the discretion of the legislature may seem justified. No religious qualification shall be required for any public office or employment, nor shall any person be incompetent as a witness or juror, in consequence of his opinion on matters of religion, nor be questioned in any court of justice touching his religious belief to affect the weight of his testimony. [1993 House Joint Resolution No. 4200, p 3062. Approved November 2, 1993.]

Prior amendment of Art. 1 Section 11, see Amendments 4, 34, and 88.

AMENDMENT 89

Art. 4 Section 3 ELECTION AND TERMS OF SUPREME COURT JUDGES. The judges of the supreme court shall be elected by the qualified electors of the state at large at the general state election at the times and places at which state officers are elected, unless some other time be provided by the legislature. The first election of judges of the supreme court shall be at the election which shall be held upon the adoption of this Constitution and the judges elected thereat shall be classified by lot, so that two shall hold their office for the term of three years, two for the term of five years, and one for the term of seven years. The lot shall be drawn by the judges who shall for that purpose assemble at the seat of government, and they shall cause the result thereof to be certified to the secretary of state, and filed in his office. The supreme court shall select a chief justice from its own membership to serve for a four-year term at the pleasure of a majority of the court as prescribed by supreme court rule. The chief justice shall preside at all sessions of the supreme court. In case of the absence of the chief justice, the majority of the remaining court shall select one of their members to serve as acting chief justice. After the first election the terms of judges elected shall be six years from and after the second Monday in January next succeeding their election. If a vacancy occur in the office of a judge of the supreme court the governor shall only appoint a person to ensure the number of judges as specified by the legislature, to hold the office until the election and qualification of a judge to fill the vacancy, which election shall take place at the next succeeding general election, and the judge so elected shall hold the office for the remainder of the unexpired term. The term of office of the judges of the supreme court, first elected, shall commence as soon as the state shall have been admitted into the Union, and continue for the term herein provided, and until their successors are elected and qualified. The sessions of the supreme court shall be held at the seat of government until otherwise provided by law. [1995 Substitute Senate Joint Resolution No. 8210, p 2905. Approved November 7, 1995.]

AMENDMENT 90

Art. 7 Section 2 LIMITATION ON LEVIES. Except as hereinafter provided and notwithstanding any other provision of this Constitution, the aggregate of all tax levies upon real and personal property by the state and all taxing districts now existing or hereafter created, shall not in any year exceed one percent of the true and fair value of such property in money: Provided, however, That nothing herein shall prevent levies at the rates now provided by law by or for any port or public utility district. The term "taxing district" for the purposes of this section shall mean any political subdivision, municipal corporation, district, or other governmental agency authorized by law to levy, or have levied for it, ad valorem taxes on property, other than a port or public utility district. Such aggregate limitation or any specific limitation imposed by law in conformity therewith may be exceeded only as follows:

(a) By any taxing district when specifically authorized so to do by a majority of at least three-fifths of the voters of the taxing district voting on the proposition to levy such additional tax submitted not more than twelve months prior to the date on which the proposed levy is to be made and not oftener than twice in such twelve month period, either at a special election or at the regular election of such taxing district, at which election the number of voters voting "yes" on the proposition shall constitute three-fifths of a number equal to forty percent of the total number of voters voting in such taxing district at the last preceding general election when the number of voters voting on the proposition does not exceed forty percent of the total number of voters voting in such taxing district in the last preceding general election; or by a majority of at least three-fifths of the voters of the taxing district voting on the proposition to levy when the number of voters voting on the proposition exceeds forty percent of the number of voters voting in such taxing district in the last preceding general election: Provided, That notwithstanding any other provision of this Constitution, any proposition pursuant to this subsection to levy additional tax for the support of the common schools may provide such support for a period of up to four years and any proposition to levy an additional tax to support the construction, modernization, or remodelling of school facilities may provide such support for a period not exceeding six years;

(b) By any taxing district otherwise authorized by law to issue general obligation bonds for capital purposes, for the sole purpose of making the required payments of principal and interest on general obligation bonds issued solely for capital purposes, other than the replacement of equipment, when authorized so to do by majority of at least three-fifths of the voters of the taxing district voting on the proposition to issue such bonds and to pay the principal and interest thereon by annual tax levies in excess of the limitation herein provided during the term of such bonds, submitted not oftener than twice in any calendar year, at an election held in the manner provided by law for bond elections in such taxing district, at which election the total number of voters voting on the proposition shall constitute not less than forty percent of the total number of voters voting in such taxing district at the last preceding general election: Provided, That any such taxing district shall have the right by vote of its governing body to refund any general obligation bonds of said district issued for capital purposes only, and to provide for the interest thereon and amortization thereof by annual levies in excess of the tax limitation provided for herein, And provided further, That the provisions of this section shall also be subject to the limitations contained in Article VIII, Section 6, of this Constitution;

(c) By the state or any taxing district for the purpose of preventing the impairment of the obligation of a contract when ordered so to do by a court of last resort. [1997 House Joint Resolution No. 4208, p 3063. Approved November 4, 1997.]

Prior amendment of Art. 7 Section 2, see Amendments 17, 55, 59, 64, and 79.

Art. 7 Section 2 was later amended by Amendments 95 and 101.

AMENDMENT 91

Art. 8 Section 10 ENERGY, WATER, OR STORMWATER OR SEWER SERVICES CONSERVATION ASSISTANCE. Notwithstanding the provisions of section 7 of this Article, any county, city, town, quasi municipal corporation, municipal corporation, or political subdivision of the state which is engaged in the sale or distribution of water, energy, or stormwater or sewer services may, as authorized by the legislature, use public moneys or credit derived from operating revenues from the sale of water, energy, or stormwater or sewer services to assist the owners of structures or equipment in financing the acquisition and installation of materials and equipment for the conservation or more efficient use of water, energy, or stormwater or sewer services in such structures or equipment. Except as provided in section 7 of this Article, an appropriate charge back shall be made for such extension of public moneys or credit and the same shall be a lien against the structure benefited or a security interest in the equipment benefited. Any financing for energy conservation authorized by this article shall only be used for conservation purposes in existing structures and shall not be used for any purpose which results in a conversion from one energy source to another. [1997 House Joint Resolution No. 4209, p 3065. Approved November 4, 1997.]

Prior amendment of Art. 8 Section 10, see Amendments 70, 82, and 86.

AMENDMENT 92

Art. 8 Section 1 STATE DEBT. (a) The state may contract debt, the principal of which shall be paid and discharged within thirty years from the time of contracting thereof, in the manner set forth herein.

(b) The aggregate debt contracted by the state shall not exceed that amount for which payments of principal and interest in any fiscal year would require the state to expend more than nine percent of the arithmetic mean of its general state revenues for the three immediately preceding fiscal years as certified by the treasurer. The term "fiscal year" means that period of time commencing July 1 of any year and ending on June 30 of the following year.

(c) The term "general state revenues" when used in this section, shall include all state money received in the treasury from each and every source whatsoever except: (1) Fees and revenues derived from the ownership or operation of any undertaking, facility, or project; (2) Moneys received as gifts, grants, donations, aid, or assistance or otherwise from the United States or any department, bureau, or corporation thereof, or any person, firm, or corporation, public or private, when the terms and conditions of such gift, grant, donation, aid, or assistance require the application and disbursement of such moneys otherwise than for the general purposes of the state of Washington; (3) Moneys to be paid into and received from retirement system funds, and performance bonds and deposits; (4) Moneys to be paid into and received from trust funds including but not limited to moneys received from taxes levied for specific purposes and the several permanent and irreducible funds of the state and the moneys derived therefrom but excluding bond redemption funds; (5) Proceeds received from the sale of bonds or other evidences of indebtedness.

(d) In computing the amount required for payment of principal and interest on outstanding debt under this section, debt shall be construed to mean borrowed money represented by bonds, notes, or other evidences of indebtedness which are secured by the full faith and credit of the state or are required to be repaid, directly or indirectly, from general state revenues and which are incurred by the state, any department, authority, public corporation, or quasi public corporation of the state, any state university or college, or any other public agency created by the state but not by counties, cities, towns, school districts, or other municipal corporations, but shall not include obligations for the payment of current expenses of state government, nor shall it include debt hereafter incurred pursuant to section 3 of this article, obligations guaranteed as provided for in subsection (g) of this section, principal of bond anticipation notes or obligations issued to fund or refund the indebtedness of the Washington state building authority.

(e) The state may pledge the full faith, credit, and taxing power of the state to guarantee the voter approved general obligation debt of school districts in the manner authorized by the legislature. Any such guarantee does not remove the debt obligation of the school district and is not state debt.

(f) The state may, without limitation, fund or refund, at or prior to maturity, the whole or any part of any existing debt or of any debt hereafter contracted pursuant to section 1, section 2, or section 3 of this article, including any premium payable with respect thereto and interest thereon, or fund or refund, at or prior to maturity, the whole or any part of any indebtedness incurred or authorized prior to the effective date of this amendment by any entity of the type described in subsection (h) of this section, including any premium payable with respect thereto and any interest thereon. Such funding or refunding shall not be deemed to be contracting debt by the state.

(g) Notwithstanding the limitation contained in subsection (b) of this section, the state may pledge its full faith, credit, and taxing power to guarantee the payment of any obligation payable from revenues received from any of the following sources: (1) Fees collected by the state as license fees for motor vehicles; (2) Excise taxes collected by the state on the sale, distribution or use of motor vehicle fuel; and (3) Interest on the permanent common school fund: Provided, That the legislature shall, at all times, provide sufficient revenues from such sources to pay the principal and interest due on all obligations for which said source of revenue is pledged.

(h) No money shall be paid from funds in custody of the treasurer with respect to any debt contracted after the effective date of this amendment by the Washington state building authority, the capitol committee, or any similar entity existing or operating for similar purposes pursuant to which such entity undertakes to finance or provide a facility for use or occupancy by the state or any agency, department, or instrumentality thereof.

(i) The legislature shall prescribe all matters relating to the contracting, funding or refunding of debt pursuant to this section, including: The purposes for which debt may be contracted; by a favorable vote of three-fifths of the members elected to each house, the amount of debt which may be contracted for any class of such purposes; the kinds of notes, bonds, or other evidences of debt which may be issued by the state; and the manner by which the treasurer shall determine and advise the legislature, any appropriate agency, officer, or instrumentality of the state as to the available debt capacity within the limitation set forth in this section. The legislature may delegate to any state officer, agency, or instrumentality any of its powers relating to the contracting, funding or refunding of debt pursuant to this section except its power to determine the amount and purposes for which debt may be contracted.

(j) The full faith, credit, and taxing power of the state of Washington are pledged to the payment of the debt created on behalf of the state pursuant to this section and the legislature shall provide by appropriation for the payment of the interest upon and installments of principal of all such debt as the same falls due, but in any event, any court of record may compel such payment.

(k) Notwithstanding the limitations contained in subsection (b) of this section, the state may issue certificates of indebtedness in such sum or sums as may be necessary to meet temporary deficiencies of the treasury, to preserve the best interests of the state in the conduct of the various state institutions, departments, bureaus, and agencies during each fiscal year; such certificates may be issued only to provide for appropriations already made by the legislature and such certificates must be retired and the debt discharged other than by refunding within twelve months after the date of incurrence.

(l) Bonds, notes, or other obligations issued and sold by the state of Washington pursuant to and in conformity with this article shall not be invalid for any irregularity or defect in the proceedings of the issuance or sale thereof and shall be incontestable in the hands of a bona fide purchaser or holder thereof. [1999 Senate Joint Resolution No. 8206, p 2387. Approved November 2, 1999.]

Prior amendment of Art. 8 Section 1, see Amendment 60.

Art. 8 Section 1 was later amended by Amendments 103 and 107.

AMENDMENT 93

Art. 29 Section 1 MAY BE INVESTED AS AUTHORIZED BY LAW. Notwithstanding the provisions of sections 5, and 7 of Article VIII and section 9 of Article XII or any other section or article of the Constitution of the state of Washington, the moneys of any public pension or retirement fund, industrial insurance trust fund, or fund held in trust for the benefit of persons with developmental disabilities may be invested as authorized by law. [2000 Senate Joint Resolution No. 8214, p 1919. Approved November 7, 2000.]

Prior amendment of Art. 29 Section 1, see Amendments 49 and 75.

AMENDMENT 94

Art. 4 Section 7 EXCHANGE OF JUDGES - JUDGE PRO TEMPORE. The judge of any superior court may hold a superior court in any county at the request of the judge of the superior court thereof, and upon the request of the governor it shall be his or her duty to do so. A case in the superior court may be tried by a judge pro tempore either with the agreement of the parties if the judge pro tempore is a member of the bar, is agreed upon in writing by the parties litigant or their attorneys of record, and is approved by the court and sworn to try the case; or without the agreement of the parties if the judge pro tempore is a sitting elected judge and is acting as a judge pro tempore pursuant to supreme court rule. The supreme court rule must require assignments of judges pro tempore based on the judges' experience and must provide for the right, exercisable once during a case, to a change of judge pro tempore. Such right shall be in addition to any other right provided by law. However, if a previously elected judge of the superior court retires leaving a pending case in which the judge has made discretionary rulings, the judge is entitled to hear the pending case as a judge pro tempore without any written agreement. [2001 Engrossed Senate Joint Resolution No. 8208, p 2327. Approved November 6, 2001.]

AMENDMENT 95

Art. 7 Section 2 LIMITATION ON LEVIES. Except as hereinafter provided and notwithstanding any other provision of this Constitution, the aggregate of all tax levies upon real and personal property by the state and all taxing districts now existing or hereafter created, shall not in any year exceed one percent of the true and fair value of such property in money: Provided, however, That nothing herein shall prevent levies at the rates now provided by law by or for any port or public utility district. The term "taxing district" for the purposes of this section shall mean any political subdivision, municipal corporation, district, or other governmental agency authorized by law to levy, or have levied for it, ad valorem taxes on property, other than a port or public utility district. Such aggregate limitation or any specific limitation imposed by law in conformity therewith may be exceeded only as follows:

(a) By any taxing district when specifically authorized so to do by a majority of at least three-fifths of the voters of the taxing district voting on the proposition to levy such additional tax submitted not more than twelve months prior to the date on which the proposed levy is to be made and not oftener than twice in such twelve month period, either at a special election or at the regular election of such taxing district, at which election the number of voters voting "yes" on the proposition shall constitute three-fifths of a number equal to forty percent of the total number of voters voting in such taxing district at the last preceding general election when the number of voters voting on the proposition does not exceed forty percent of the total number of voters voting in such taxing district in the last preceding general election; or by a majority of at least three-fifths of the voters of the taxing district voting on the proposition to levy when the number of voters voting on the proposition exceeds forty percent of the number of voters voting in such taxing district in the last preceding general election: Provided, That notwithstanding any other provision of this Constitution, any proposition pursuant to this subsection to levy additional tax for the support of the common schools or fire protection districts may provide such support for a period of up to four years and any proposition to levy an additional tax to support the construction, modernization, or remodelling of school facilities or fire facilities may provide such support for a period not exceeding six years;

(b) By any taxing district otherwise authorized by law to issue general obligation bonds for capital purposes, for the sole purpose of making the required payments of principal and interest on general obligation bonds issued solely for capital purposes, other than the replacement of equipment, when authorized so to do by majority of at least three-fifths of the voters of the taxing district voting on the proposition to issue such bonds and to pay the principal and interest thereon by annual tax levies in excess of the limitation herein provided during the term of such bonds, submitted not oftener than twice in any calendar year, at an election held in the manner provided by law for bond elections in such taxing district, at which election the total number of voters voting on the proposition shall constitute not less than forty percent of the total number of voters voting in such taxing district at the last preceding general election: Provided, That any such taxing district shall have the right by vote of its governing body to refund any general obligation bonds of said district issued for capital purposes only, and to provide for the interest thereon and amortization thereof by annual levies in excess of the tax limitation provided for herein, And provided further, That the provisions of this section shall also be subject to the limitations contained in Article VIII, Section 6, of this Constitution;

(c) By the state or any taxing district for the purpose of preventing the impairment of the obligation of a contract when ordered so to do by a court of last resort. [2002 House Joint Resolution No. 4220, p 2203. Approved November 5, 2002.]

Prior amendment of Art. 7 Section 2, see Amendments 17, 55, 59, 64, 79, and 90.

AMENDMENT 96

Art. 2 Section 15 VACANCIES IN LEGISLATURE AND IN PARTISAN COUNTY ELECTIVE OFFICE. Such vacancies as may occur in either house of the legislature or in any partisan county elective office shall be filled by appointment by the county legislative authority of the county in which the vacancy occurs: Provided, That the person appointed to fill the vacancy must be from the same legislative district, county, or county commissioner or council district and the same political party as the legislator or partisan county elective officer whose office has been vacated, and shall be one of three persons who shall be nominated by the county central committee of that party, and in case a majority of the members of the county legislative authority do not agree upon the appointment within sixty days after the vacancy occurs, the governor shall within thirty days thereafter, and from the list of nominees provided for herein, appoint a person who shall be from the same legislative district, county, or county commissioner or council district and of the same political party as the legislator or partisan county elective officer whose office has been vacated, and the person so appointed shall hold office until his or her successor is elected at the next general election, and has qualified: Provided, That in case of a vacancy occurring after the general election in a year that the office appears on the ballot and before the start of the next term, the term of the successor who is of the same party as the incumbent may commence once he or she has qualified and shall continue through the term for which he or she was elected: Provided, That in case of a vacancy occurring in the office of joint senator, or joint representative, the vacancy shall be filled from a list of three nominees selected by the state central committee, by appointment by the joint action of the boards of county legislative authorities of the counties composing the joint senatorial or joint representative district, the person appointed to fill the vacancy must be from the same legislative district and of the same political party as the legislator whose office has been vacated, and in case a majority of the members of the county legislative authority do not agree upon the appointment within sixty days after the vacancy occurs, the governor shall within thirty days thereafter, and from the list of nominees provided for herein, appoint a person who shall be from the same legislative district and of the same political party as the legislator whose office has been vacated. [2003 House Joint Resolution No. 4206, p 2819. Approved November 4, 2003.]

Prior amendment of Art. 2 Section 15, see Amendments 13, 32, and 52.

AMENDMENT 97

Art. 4 Section 31 COMMISSION ON JUDICIAL CONDUCT. (1) There shall be a commission on judicial conduct, existing as an independent agency of the judicial branch, and consisting of a judge selected by and from the court of appeals judges, a judge selected by and from the superior court judges, a judge selected by and from the limited jurisdiction court judges, two persons admitted to the practice of law in this state selected by the state bar association, and six persons who are not attorneys appointed by the governor.

(2) Whenever the commission receives a complaint against a judge or justice, or otherwise has reason to believe that a judge or justice should be admonished, reprimanded, censured, suspended, removed, or retired, the commission shall first investigate the complaint or belief and then conduct initial proceedings for the purpose of determining whether probable cause exists for conducting a public hearing or hearings to deal with the complaint or belief. The investigation and initial proceedings shall be confidential. Upon beginning an initial proceeding, the commission shall notify the judge or justice of the existence of and basis for the initial proceeding.

(3) Whenever the commission concludes, based on an initial proceeding, that there is probable cause to believe that a judge or justice has violated a rule of judicial conduct or that the judge or justice suffers from a disability which is permanent or likely to become permanent and which seriously interferes with the performance of judicial duties, the commission shall conduct a public hearing or hearings and shall make public all those records of the initial proceeding that provide the basis for its conclusion. If the commission concludes that there is not probable cause, it shall notify the judge or justice of its conclusion.

(4) Upon the completion of the hearing or hearings, the commission in open session shall either dismiss the case, or shall admonish, reprimand, or censure the judge or justice, or shall censure the judge or justice and recommend to the supreme court the suspension or removal of the judge or justice, or shall recommend to the supreme court the retirement of the judge or justice. The commission may not recommend suspension or removal unless it censures the judge or justice for the violation serving as the basis for the recommendation. The commission may recommend retirement of a judge or justice for a disability which is permanent

or likely to become permanent and which seriously interferes with the performance of judicial duties.

(5) Upon the recommendation of the commission, the supreme court may suspend, remove, or retire a judge or justice. The office of a judge or justice retired or removed by the supreme court becomes vacant, and that person is ineligible for judicial office until eligibility is reinstated by the supreme court. The salary of a removed judge or justice shall cease. The supreme court shall specify the effect upon salary when it suspends a judge or justice. The supreme court may not suspend, remove, or retire a judge or justice until the commission, after notice and hearing, recommends that action be taken, and the supreme court conducts a hearing, after notice, to review commission proceedings and findings against the judge or justice.

(6) Within thirty days after the commission admonishes, reprimands, or censures a judge or justice, the judge or justice shall have a right of appeal de novo to the supreme court.

(7) Any matter before the commission or supreme court may be disposed of by a stipulation entered into in a public proceeding. The stipulation shall be signed by the judge or justice and the commission or court. The stipulation may impose any terms and conditions deemed appropriate by the commission or court. A stipulation shall set forth all material facts relating to the proceeding and the conduct of the judge or justice.

(8) Whenever the commission adopts a recommendation that a judge or justice be removed, the judge or justice shall be suspended immediately, with salary, from his or her judicial position until a final determination is made by the supreme court.

(9) The legislature shall provide for commissioners' terms of office and compensation. The commission shall employ one or more investigative officers with appropriate professional training and experience. The investigative officers of the commission shall report directly to the commission. The commission shall also employ such administrative or other staff as are necessary to manage the affairs of the commission.

(10) The commission shall, to the extent that compliance does not conflict with this section, comply with laws of general applicability to state agencies with respect to rule-making procedures, and with respect to public notice of and attendance at commission proceedings other than initial proceedings. The commission shall establish rules of procedure for commission proceedings including due process and confidentiality of proceedings. [2005 Senate Joint Resolution No. 8207, pp 2799, 2800. Approved November 8, 2005.]

Prior amendment of Art. 4 Section 31, see Amendments 85, 77, and 71.

AMENDMENT 98

Art. 7 Section 1 TAXATION. The power of taxation shall never be suspended, surrendered or contracted away. All taxes shall be uniform upon the same class of property within the territorial limits of the authority levying the tax and shall be levied and collected for public purposes only. The word "property" as used herein shall mean and include everything, whether tangible or intangible, subject to ownership. All real estate shall constitute one class: Provided, That the legislature may tax mines and mineral resources and lands devoted to reforestation by either a yield tax or an ad valorem tax at such rate as it may fix, or by both. Such property as the legislature may by general laws provide shall be exempt from taxation. Property of the United States and of the state, counties, school districts and other municipal corporations, and credits secured by property actually taxed in this state, not exceeding in value the value of such property, shall be exempt from taxation. The legislature shall have power, by appropriate legislation, to exempt personal property to the amount of fifteen thousand ($15,000.00) dollars for each head of a family liable to assessment and taxation under the provisions of the laws of this state of which the individual is the actual bona fide owner. [2006 House Joint Resolution No. 4223, p 2117. Approved November 7, 2006.]

Prior amendment of Art. 7 Section 1, see Amendments 14 and 81.

AMENDMENT 99

Article 7 was amended by adding the following section:

Art. 7 Section 12 BUDGET STABILIZATION ACCOUNT. (a) A budget stabilization account shall be established and maintained in the state treasury.

(b) By June 30th of each fiscal year, an amount equal to one percent of the general state revenues for that fiscal year shall be transferred to the budget stabilization account. Nothing in this subsection (b) shall prevent the appropriation of additional amounts to the budget stabilization account.

(c) Each fiscal quarter, the state economic and revenue forecast council appointed and authorized as provided by statute, or successor entity, shall estimate state employment growth for the current and next two fiscal years.

(d) Moneys may be withdrawn and appropriated from the budget stabilization account as follows:

(i) If the governor declares a state of emergency resulting from a catastrophic event that necessitates government action to protect life or public safety, then for that fiscal year moneys may be withdrawn and appropriated from the budget stabilization account, via separate legislation setting forth the nature of the emergency and containing an appropriation limited to the above-authorized purposes as contained in the declaration, by a favorable vote of a majority of the members elected to each house of the legislature.

(ii) If the employment growth forecast for any fiscal year is estimated to be less than one percent, then for that fiscal year moneys may be withdrawn and appropriated from the budget stabilization account by the favorable vote of a majority of the members elected to each house of the legislature.

(iii) Any amount may be withdrawn and appropriated from the budget stabilization account at any time by the favorable vote of at least three-fifths of the members of each house of the legislature.

(e) Amounts in the budget stabilization account may be invested as provided by law and retained in that account. When the balance in the budget stabilization account, including investment earnings, equals more than ten percent of the estimated general state revenues in that fiscal year, the legislature by the favorable vote of a majority of the members elected to each house of the legislature may withdraw and appropriate the balance to the extent that the balance exceeds ten percent of the estimated general state revenues. Appropriations under this subsection (e) may be made solely for deposit to the education construction fund.

(f) As used in this section, "general state revenues" has the meaning set forth in Article VIII, section 1 of the Constitution. Forecasts and estimates shall be made by the state economic and revenue forecast council appointed and authorized as provided by statute, or successor entity.

(g) The legislature shall enact appropriate laws to carry out the purposes of this section.

(h) This section takes effect July 1, 2008. [2007 Engrossed Substitute Senate Joint Resolution No. 8206, pp 3146, 3147. Approved November 6, 2007.]

Art. 7 Section 12 was later amended by Amendment 106.

AMENDMENT 100

Art. 2 Section 29 CONVICT LABOR. The labor of inmates of this state shall not be let out by contract to any person, copartnership, company, or corporation, except as provided by statute, and the legislature shall by law provide for the working of inmates for the benefit of the state, including the working of inmates in state-run inmate labor programs. Inmate labor programs provided by statute that are operated and managed, in total or in part, by any profit or nonprofit entities shall be operated so that the programs do not unfairly compete with Washington businesses as determined by law. [2007 Senate Joint Resolution No. 8212, p 3143. Approved November 6, 2007.]

AMENDMENT 101

Art. 7 Section 2 LIMITATION ON LEVIES. Except as hereinafter provided and notwithstanding any other provision of this Constitution, the aggregate of all tax levies upon real and personal property by the state and all taxing districts now existing or hereafter created, shall not in any year exceed one percent of the true and fair value of such property in money. Nothing herein shall prevent levies at the rates now provided by law by or for any port or public utility district. The term "taxing district" for the purposes of this section shall mean any political subdivision, municipal corporation, district, or other governmental agency authorized by law to levy, or have levied for it, ad valorem taxes on property, other than a port or public utility district. Such aggregate limitation or any specific limitation imposed by law in conformity therewith may be exceeded only as follows:
(a) By any taxing district when specifically authorized so to do by a majority of at least three-fifths of the voters of the taxing district voting on the proposition to levy such additional tax submitted not more than twelve months prior to the date on which the proposed initial levy is to be made and not oftener than twice in such twelve month period, either at a special election or at the regular election of such taxing district, at which election the number of voters voting "yes" on the proposition shall constitute three-fifths of a number equal to forty percent of the total number of voters voting in such taxing district at the last preceding general election when the number of voters voting on the proposition does not exceed forty percent of the total number of voters voting in such taxing district in the last preceding general election; or by a majority of at least three-fifths of the voters of the taxing district voting on the proposition to levy when the number of voters voting on the proposition exceeds forty percent of the number of voters voting in such taxing district in the last preceding general election. Notwithstanding any other provision of this Constitution, any proposition pursuant to this subsection to levy additional tax for the support of the common schools or fire protection districts may provide such support for a period of up to four years and any proposition to levy an additional tax to support the construction, modernization, or remodelling of school facilities or fire facilities may provide such support for a period not exceeding six years. Notwithstanding any other provision of this subsection, a proposition under this subsection to levy an additional tax for a school district shall be authorized by a majority of the voters voting on the proposition, regardless of the number of voters voting on the proposition;
(b) By any taxing district otherwise authorized by law to issue general obligation bonds for capital purposes, for the sole purpose of making the required payments of principal and interest on general obligation bonds issued solely for capital purposes, other than the replacement of equipment, when authorized so to do by majority of at least three-fifths of the

voters of the taxing district voting on the proposition to issue such bonds and to pay the principal and interest thereon by annual tax levies in excess of the limitation herein provided during the term of such bonds, submitted not oftener than twice in any calendar year, at an election held in the manner provided by law for bond elections in such taxing district, at which election the total number of voters voting on the proposition shall constitute not less than forty percent of the total number of voters voting in such taxing district at the last preceding general election. Any such taxing district shall have the right by vote of its governing body to refund any general obligation bonds of said district issued for capital purposes only, and to provide for the interest thereon and amortization thereof by annual levies in excess of the tax limitation provided for herein. The provisions of this section shall also be subject to the limitations contained in Article VIII, Section 6, of this Constitution;

(c) By the state or any taxing district for the purpose of preventing the impairment of the obligation of a contract when ordered so to do by a court of last resort. [2007 Engrossed House Joint Resolution No. 4204, pp 3143-3145. Approved November 6, 2007.]

AMENDMENT 102

Article 16 was amended by adding the following section:
Art. 16 Section 6 INVESTMENT OF HIGHER EDUCATION PERMANENT FUNDS. Notwithstanding the provisions of Article VIII, sections 5 and 7 and Article XII, section 9, or any other section or article of the Constitution of the state of Washington, the moneys of the permanent funds established for any of the institutions of higher education in this state may be invested as authorized by law. Without limitation, this shall include the authority to invest permanent funds held for the benefit of institutions of higher education in stocks or bonds issued by any association, company, or corporation if authorized by law. [2007 Substitute House Joint Resolution No. 4215, p 3145. Approved November 6, 2007.]

AMENDMENT 103

Art. 8 Section 1 STATE DEBT. (a) The state may contract debt, the principal of which shall be paid and discharged within thirty years from the time of contracting thereof, in the manner set forth herein.

(b) The aggregate debt contracted by the state shall not exceed that amount for which payments of principal and interest in any fiscal year would require the state to expend more than nine percent of the arithmetic mean of its general state revenues for the three immediately preceding fiscal years as certified by the treasurer. The term "fiscal year" means that period of time commencing July 1 of any year and ending on June 30 of the following year.

(c) The term "general state revenues" when used in this section, shall include all state money received in the treasury from each and every source whatsoever except: (1) Fees and revenues derived from the ownership or operation of any undertaking, facility, or project; (2) Moneys received as gifts, grants, donations, aid, or assistance or otherwise from the United States or any department, bureau, or corporation thereof, or any person, firm, or corporation, public or private, when the terms and conditions of such gift, grant, donation, aid, or assistance require the application and disbursement of such moneys otherwise than for the general purposes of the state of Washington; (3) Moneys to be paid into and received from retirement system funds, and performance bonds and deposits; (4) Moneys to be paid into and received from trust funds including but not limited to moneys received from taxes levied for specific purposes and the several permanent and irreducible funds of the state and the moneys derived therefrom but excluding bond redemption funds; (5) Proceeds received from the sale of bonds or other evidences of indebtedness.

(d) In computing the amount required for payment of principal and interest on outstanding debt under this section, debt shall be construed to mean borrowed money represented by bonds, notes, or other evidences of indebtedness which are secured by the full faith and credit of the state or are required to be repaid, directly or indirectly, from general state revenues and which are incurred by the state, any department, authority, public corporation, or quasi public corporation of the state, any state university or college, or any other public agency created by the state but not by counties, cities, towns, school districts, or other municipal corporations, but shall not include obligations for the payment of current expenses of state government, nor shall it include debt hereafter incurred pursuant to section 3 of this article, obligations guaranteed as provided for in subsection (g) of this section, principal of bond anticipation notes or obligations issued to fund or refund the indebtedness of the Washington state building authority. In addition, for the purpose of computing the amount required for payment of interest on outstanding debt under subsection (b) of this section and this subsection, "interest" shall be reduced by subtracting the amount scheduled to be received by the state as payments from the federal government in each year in respect of bonds, notes, or other evidences of indebtedness subject to this section.

(e) The state may pledge the full faith, credit, and taxing power of the state to guarantee the voter approved general obligation debt of school districts in the manner authorized by the legislature. Any such guarantee does not remove the debt obligation of the school district and is not state debt.

(f) The state may, without limitation, fund or refund, at or prior to maturity, the whole or any part of any existing debt or of any debt hereafter contracted pursuant to section 1, section 2, or section 3 of this article, including any premium payable with respect thereto and interest thereon, or fund or refund, at or prior to maturity, the whole or any part of any indebtedness incurred or authorized prior to the effective date of this amendment by any entity of the type described in subsection (h) of this section, including any premium payable with respect thereto and any interest thereon. Such funding or refunding shall not be deemed to be contracting debt by the state.

(g) Notwithstanding the limitation contained in subsection (b) of this section, the state may pledge its full faith, credit, and taxing power to guarantee the payment of any obligation payable from revenues received from any of the following sources: (1) Fees collected by the state as license fees for motor vehicles; (2) Excise taxes collected by the state on the sale, distribution or use of motor vehicle fuel; and (3) Interest on the permanent common school fund: Provided, That the legislature shall, at all times, provide sufficient revenues from such sources to pay the principal and interest due on all obligations for which said source of revenue is pledged.

(h) No money shall be paid from funds in custody of the treasurer with respect to any debt contracted after the effective date of this amendment by the Washington state building authority, the capitol committee, or any similar entity existing or operating for similar purposes pursuant to which such entity undertakes to finance or provide a facility for use or occupancy by the state or any agency, department, or instrumentality thereof.

(i) The legislature shall prescribe all matters relating to the contracting, funding or refunding of debt pursuant to this section, including: The purposes for which debt may be contracted; by a favorable vote of three-fifths of the members elected to each house, the amount of debt which may be contracted for any class of such purposes; the kinds of notes, bonds, or other evidences of debt which may be issued by the state; and the manner by which the treasurer shall determine and advise the legislature, any appropriate agency, officer, or instrumentality of the state as to the available debt capacity within the limitation set forth in this section. The legislature may delegate to any state officer, agency, or instrumentality any of its powers relating to the contracting, funding or refunding of debt pursuant to this section except its power to determine the amount and purposes for which debt may be contracted.

(j) The full faith, credit, and taxing power of the state of Washington are pledged to the payment of the debt created on behalf of the state pursuant to this section and the legislature shall provide by appropriation for the payment of the interest upon and installments of principal of all such debt as the same falls due, but in any event, any court of record may compel such payment.

(k) Notwithstanding the limitations contained in subsection (b) of this section, the state may issue certificates of indebtedness in such sum or sums as may be necessary to meet temporary deficiencies of the treasury, to preserve the best interests of the state in the conduct of the various state institutions, departments, bureaus, and agencies during each fiscal year; such certificates may be issued only to provide for appropriations already made by the legislature and such certificates must be retired and the debt discharged other than by refunding within twelve months after the date of incurrence.

(l) Bonds, notes, or other obligations issued and sold by the state of Washington pursuant to and in conformity with this article shall not be invalid for any irregularity or defect in the proceedings of the issuance or sale thereof and shall be incontestable in the hands of a bona fide purchaser or holder thereof. [2010 Senate Joint Resolution No. 8225, p 3129-3132. Approved November 2, 2010.]

Prior amendment of Art. 8 Section 1, see Amendments 60 and 92.

Art. 8 Section 1 was later amended by Amendment 107.

AMENDMENT 104

Art. 1 Section 20 BAIL, WHEN AUTHORIZED. All persons charged with crime shall be bailable by sufficient sureties, except for capital offenses when the proof is evident, or the presumption great. Bail may be denied for offenses punishable by the possibility of life in prison upon a showing by clear and convincing evidence of a propensity for violence that creates a substantial likelihood of danger to the community or any persons, subject to such limitations as shall be determined by the legislature. [2010 Engrossed Substitute House Joint Resolution No. 4220, p 3129. Approved November 2, 2010.]

AMENDMENT 105

Art. 6 Section 1A VOTER QUALIFICATIONS FOR PRESIDENTIAL ELECTIONS. [Repealed by 2011 Senate Joint Resolution No. 8205, p 4281. Approved November 8, 2011.] Prior amendment of Art. 6 Section 1A, see Amendment 46.

AMENDMENT 106

Art. 7 Section 12 BUDGET STABILIZATION ACCOUNT. (a) A budget stabilization account shall be established and maintained in the state treasury.

(b)(1) By June 30th of each fiscal year, an amount equal to one percent of the general state revenues for that fiscal year shall be transferred to the budget stabilization account. Nothing in this subsection (b) shall prevent the appropriation of additional amounts to the budget stabilization account.

(2) By June 30th of the second year of each fiscal biennium, three-quarters of any extraordinary revenue growth shall be transferred to the budget stabilization account. However, no transfer of extraordinary revenue growth under this subsection (b)(2) shall occur in a fiscal biennium following a fiscal biennium in which annual average state employment growth averaged less than one percent per fiscal year. "Extraordinary revenue growth" means the amount by which the growth in general state revenues for that fiscal biennium exceeds by one-third the average biennial percentage growth in general state revenues over the prior five fiscal biennia. In making this determination, the comparability of data shall be maintained by adjusting historical general state revenues to reflect statutory changes to the dedication of state revenues. The transfer under this subsection shall be made only to the extent that it exceeds the total transfers under (1) of this subsection for that fiscal biennium.

(c) Each fiscal quarter, the state economic and revenue forecast council appointed and authorized as provided by statute, or successor entity, shall estimate state employment growth for the current and next two fiscal years.

(d) Moneys may be withdrawn and appropriated from the budget stabilization account as follows:

(i) If the governor declares a state of emergency resulting from a catastrophic event that necessitates government action to protect life or public safety, then for that fiscal year moneys may be withdrawn and appropriated from the budget stabilization account, via separate legislation setting forth the nature of the emergency and containing an appropriation limited to the above-authorized purposes as contained in the declaration, by a favorable vote of a majority of the members elected to each house of the legislature.

(ii) If the employment growth forecast for any fiscal year is estimated to be less than one percent, then for that fiscal year moneys may be withdrawn and appropriated from the budget stabilization account by the favorable vote of a majority of the members elected to each house of the legislature.

(iii) Any amount may be withdrawn and appropriated from the budget stabilization account at any time by the favorable vote of at least three-fifths of the members of each house of the legislature.

(e) Amounts in the budget stabilization account may be invested as provided by law and retained in that account. When the balance in the budget stabilization account, including investment earnings, equals more than ten percent of the estimated general state revenues in that fiscal year, the legislature by the favorable vote of a majority of the members elected to each house of the legislature may withdraw and appropriate the balance to the extent that the balance exceeds ten percent of the estimated general state revenues. Appropriations under this subsection (e) may be made solely for deposit to the education construction fund.

(f) As used in this section, "general state revenues" has the meaning set forth in Article VIII, section 1 of the Constitution. Forecasts and estimates shall be made by the state economic and revenue forecast council appointed and authorized as provided by statute, or successor entity.

(g) The legislature shall enact appropriate laws to carry out the purposes of this section.

(h) This section takes effect July 1, 2008. [2011 Senate Joint Resolution No. 8206, p 4281-4283. Approved November 8, 2011.]

Prior amendment of Art. 7 Section 12, see Amendment 99.

AMENDMENT 107

Art. 8 Section 1 STATE DEBT. (a) The state may contract debt, the principal of which shall be paid and discharged within thirty years from the time of contracting thereof, in the manner set forth herein.

(b) The aggregate debt contracted by the state, as calculated by the treasurer at the time debt is contracted, shall not exceed that amount for which payments of principal and interest in any fiscal year would require the state to expend more than the applicable percentage limit of the arithmetic mean of its general state revenues for the six immediately preceding fiscal years as certified by the treasurer. The term "applicable percentage limit" means eight and one-half percent from July 1, 2014, through June 30, 2016; eight and one-quarter percent from July 1, 2016, through June 30, 2034; eight percent from July 1, 2034, and thereafter. The term "fiscal year" means that period of time commencing July 1 of any year and ending on June 30 of the following year.

(c) The term "general state revenues," when used in this section, shall include all state money received in the treasury from each and every source, including moneys received from ad valorem taxes levied by the state and deposited in the general fund in each fiscal year, but not including: (1) Fees and other revenues derived from the ownership or operation of any undertaking, facility, or project; (2) Moneys received as gifts, grants, donations, aid, or assistance or otherwise from the United States or any department, bureau, or corporation thereof, or any person, firm, or corporation, public or private, when the terms and conditions of such gift, grant, donation, aid, or assistance require the application and disbursement of such moneys otherwise than for the general purposes of the state of Washington; (3) Moneys to be paid into and received from retirement system funds, and performance bonds and deposits; (4) Moneys to be paid into and received from trust funds and the several permanent and irreducible funds of the state and the moneys derived therefrom but excluding bond redemption funds; (5) Moneys received from taxes levied for specific purposes and required to be deposited for those purposes into specified funds or accounts other than the general fund; and (6) Proceeds received from the sale of bonds or other evidences of indebtedness.

(d) In computing the amount required for payment of principal and interest on outstanding debt under this section, debt shall be construed to mean borrowed money represented by bonds, notes, or other evidences of indebtedness which are secured by the full faith and credit of the state or are required to be repaid, directly or indirectly, from general state revenues and which are incurred by the state, any department, authority, public corporation, or quasi public corporation of the state, any state university or college, or any other public agency created by the state but not by counties, cities, towns, school districts, or other municipal corporations, but shall not include obligations for the payment of current expenses of state government, nor shall it include debt hereafter incurred pursuant to section 3 of this article, obligations guaranteed as provided for in subsection (g) of this section, principal of bond anticipation notes or obligations issued to fund or refund the indebtedness of the Washington state building authority. In addition, for the purpose of computing the amount required for payment of interest on outstanding debt under subsection (b) of this section and this subsection, "interest" shall be reduced by subtracting the amount scheduled to be received by the state as payments from the federal government in each year in respect of bonds, notes, or other evidences of indebtedness subject to this section.

(e) The state may pledge the full faith, credit, and taxing power of the state to guarantee the voter approved general obligation debt of school districts in the manner authorized by the legislature. Any such guarantee does not remove the debt obligation of the school district and is not state debt.

(f) The state may, without limitation, fund or refund, at or prior to maturity, the whole or any part of any existing debt or of any debt hereafter contracted pursuant to section 1, section 2, or section 3 of this article, including any premium payable with respect thereto and interest thereon, or fund or refund, at or prior to maturity, the whole or any part of any indebtedness incurred or authorized prior to the effective date of this amendment by any entity of the type described in subsection (h) of this section, including any premium payable with respect thereto and any interest thereon. Such funding or refunding shall not be deemed to be contracting debt by the state.

(g) Notwithstanding the limitation contained in subsection (b) of this section, the state may pledge its full faith, credit, and taxing power to guarantee the payment of any obligation payable from revenues received from any of the following sources: (1) Fees collected by the state as license fees for motor vehicles; (2) Excise taxes collected by the state on the sale, distribution or use of motor vehicle fuel; and (3) Interest on the permanent common school fund: Provided, That the legislature shall, at all times, provide sufficient revenues from such sources to pay the principal and interest due on all obligations for which said source of revenue is pledged.

(h) No money shall be paid from funds in custody of the treasurer with respect to any debt contracted after the effective date of this amendment by the Washington state building authority, the capitol committee, or any similar entity existing or operating for similar purposes pursuant to which such entity undertakes to finance or provide a facility for use or occupancy by the state or any agency, department, or instrumentality thereof.

(i) The legislature shall prescribe all matters relating to the contracting, funding or refunding of debt pursuant to this section, including: The purposes for which debt may be contracted; by a favorable vote of three-fifths of the members elected to each house, the amount of debt which may be contracted for any class of such purposes; the kinds of notes, bonds, or other evidences of debt which may be issued by the state; and the manner by which the treasurer shall determine and advise the legislature, any appropriate agency, officer, or instrumentality of the state as to the available debt capacity within the limitation set forth in this section. The legislature may delegate to any state officer, agency, or instrumentality any of its powers relating to the contracting, funding or refunding of debt pursuant to this section except its power to determine the amount and purposes for which debt may be contracted.

(j) The full faith, credit, and taxing power of the state of Washington are pledged to the payment of the debt created on behalf of the state pursuant to this section and the legislature shall provide by appropriation for the payment of the interest upon and installments of principal of all such debt as the same falls due, but in any event, any court of record may compel such payment.

(k) Notwithstanding the limitations contained in subsection (b) of this section, the state may issue certificates of indebtedness in such sum or sums as may be necessary to meet temporary deficiencies of the treasury, to preserve the best interests of the state in the conduct of the various state institutions, departments, bureaus, and agencies during each fiscal year; such certificates may be issued only to provide for appropriations already made by the legislature and such certificates must be retired and the debt discharged other than by refunding within twelve months after the date of incurrence.

(l) Bonds, notes, or other obligations issued and sold by the state of Washington pursuant to and in conformity with this article shall not be invalid for any irregularity or defect in the proceedings of the issuance or sale thereof and shall be incontestable in the hands of a bona fide purchaser or holder thereof. [2012 Engrossed Senate Joint Resolution No. 8221, p 2429-2432. Approved November 6, 2012.]

Prior amendment of Art. 8 Section 1, see Amendments 60, 92, and 103.

AMENDMENT 108

Art. 2 Section 43 REDISTRICTING. (1) In January of each year ending in one, a commission shall be established to provide for the redistricting of state legislative and congressional districts.

(2) The commission shall be composed of five members to be selected as follows: The legislative leader of the two largest political parties in each house of the legislature shall appoint one voting member to the commission by January 15th of each year ending in one. By January 31st of each year ending in one, the four appointed members, by an affirmative vote of at least three, shall appoint the remaining member. The fifth member of the commission, who shall be nonvoting, shall act as its chairperson. If any appointing authority fails to make the required appointment by the date established by this subsection, within five days after that date the supreme court shall make the required appointment.

(3) No elected official and no person elected to legislative district, county, or state political party office may serve on the commission. A commission member shall not have been an elected official and shall not have been an elected legislative district, county, or state political party officer within two years of his or her appointment to the commission. The provisions of this subsection do not apply to the office of precinct committee person.

(4) The legislature shall enact laws providing for the implementation of this section, to include additional qualifications for commissioners and additional standards to govern the commission. The legislature shall appropriate funds to enable the commission to carry out its duties.

(5) Each district shall contain a population, excluding nonresident military personnel, as nearly equal as practicable to the population of any other district. To the extent reasonable, each district shall contain contiguous territory, shall be compact and convenient, and shall be separated from adjoining districts by natural geographic barriers, artificial barriers, or political subdivision boundaries. The commission's plan shall not provide for a number of legislative districts different than that established by the legislature. The commission's plan shall not be drawn purposely to favor or discriminate against any political party or group.

(6) The commission shall complete redistricting as soon as possible following the federal decennial census, but no later than November 15th of each year ending in one. At least three of the voting members shall approve such a redistricting plan. If three of the voting members of the commission fail to approve a plan within the time limitations provided in this subsection, the supreme court shall adopt a plan by April 30th of the year ending in two in conformance with the standards set forth in subsection (5) of this section.

(7) The legislature may amend the redistricting plan but must do so by a two-thirds vote of the legislators elected or appointed to each house of the legislature. Any amendment must have passed both houses by the end of the thirtieth day of the first session convened after the commission has submitted its plan to the legislature. After that day, the plan, with any legislative amendments, constitutes the state districting law.

(8) The legislature shall enact laws providing for the reconvening of a commission for the purpose of modifying a districting law adopted under this section. Such reconvening requires a

two-thirds vote of the legislators elected or appointed to each house of the legislature. The commission shall conform to the standards prescribed under subsection (5) of this section and any other standards or procedures that the legislature may provide by law. At least three of the voting members shall approve such a modification. Any modification adopted by the commission may be amended by a two-thirds vote of the legislators elected and appointed to each house of the legislature. The state districting law shall include the modifications with amendments, if any.

(9) The legislature shall prescribe by law the terms of commission members and the method of filling vacancies on the commission.

(10) The supreme court has original jurisdiction to hear and decide all cases involving congressional and legislative redistricting.

(11) Legislative and congressional districts may not be changed or established except pursuant to this section. A districting plan and any legislative amendments to the plan are not subject to Article III, section 12 of this Constitution. [2016 Senate Joint Resolution No. 8210. Approved November 8, 2016.]

Prior amendment of Art. 2 Section 43, see Amendment 74.

Made in the USA
Columbia, SC
17 May 2020

97673106R00100